Literary Links

Literary Links

Celebrating the
literary relationship
between Australia
and Britain

ROSLYN RUSSELL

ALLEN & UNWIN
Sydney • London

First published in 1997 by
Allen & Unwin
9 Atchison Street
St Leonards NSW 2065
Australia
Phone: (61 2) 9901 4088
Fax: (61 2) 9906 2218
E-mail   frontdesk@allen-unwin.com.au
URL: http://www.allen-unwin.com.au

National Library of Australia
Cataloguing-in-Publication entry:

Russell, Roslyn.
   Literary links: celebrating the literary relationship
   between Australia and Britain.

   ISBN 1 86448 477 2.
   ISBN 1 86448 502 7 (pbk).

   1. Australian literature—English influences. 2. English
   literature—Australian influences. 3. English literature—
   History and criticism. 4. Australian literature—History
   and criticism. I. National Library of Australia. II. British
   Council (Australia). III. Title.

A820.9

Supported by The British Council as part of the 1997 programme of events, *new*IMAGES: Britain and Australia into the 21st Century.

Set in 10.5/13.5 pt Goudy by Bookhouse Digital Publishing Services, Sydney
Printed by South Wind Productions, Singapore

10 9 8 7 6 5 4 3 2 1

For my parents

PREFACE

This book is the result of a partnership that began early in 1993, when I first met Ian Templeman of the National Library of Australia. We agreed to develop a travelling poster exhibition, based on the style of other successful British Council exhibitions, on the theme of Literary Links between Britain and Australia. The exhibition drew on the Library's comprehensive collection to explore aspects of the historical connection between the two countries in the literary arts. Roslyn Russell was chosen as the writer and curator. The exhibition was designed by Kathy Jakupec.

It was launched on the opening night of the Melbourne Writers' Festival in October 1994. It has been in great demand in the UK and in Australia. Much of the material that Roslyn collected had to be omitted from the poster exhibition. The decision to research further material and to develop the project as a book came as a result of the great enthusiasm shown by Patrick Gallagher of Allen & Unwin.

The book has been published in 1997 for two reasons: 1) to mark the Fiftieth Anniversary of The British Council in Australia, 2) as a newIMAGES project, to create an enduring work to symbolise the evolving relationship between the UK and Australia as we approach the twenty-first century, which charts where the relationship began and indicates the directions in which it is evolving.

In no other field is a shared language and tradition so important, enduring and adaptable as in the field of literature. A shared language in no way inhibits the development of a national cultural identity, nor does a common and critical respect for the literary 'canon' and tradition. This book may help to establish many more Australian books and authors as part of the wider English-language canon. One of the most important *new*IMAGES projects taking place in 1997 is the exchange of new writers, who, it is hoped, will record and jointly publish their perceptions and impressions (six Australians will travel to Britain, six British will travel to Australia). This new writers' exchange will draw attention to the value of writers' visits in each direction. The British team will include Kate Clanchy, Glen Patterson, Simon Armitage, A. L. Kennedy, and Diran Adebayo. The Australian team will include Fotini Epanomitis, Dorothy Porter, Christos Tsiolkas, Sam Watson and Robert Drewe.

The British Council has supported well over 125 visits by writers to Australia since 1960. They usually read and discuss their work at festivals, but also at bookshops, at literary luncheons, on radio and television. They probably command more column inches in the national press than any other type of visiting artist or group, be it an orchestra or a famous theatre company.

The British Council has toured about 100 book and literary poster exhibitions throughout Australia. Together with the visits by writers, the Council can claim to have contributed significantly to the reputation and sales by British writers in Australia. The DTI export figures for the value of British book sales to Australia in 1995 stand at £81.9 million. That is probably an underestimate. Publishers have confirmed that in the year of a successful writer's visit, book sales may be as high as ten thousand copies more than in a normal year. Interviews and reviews continue to appear in the press and on radio and television long after the author has departed.

Visits by authors to countries where I have worked have made a great and long-lasting impact. William Golding went to Greece for the Council shortly before he was awarded the Nobel Prize. Graham Swift came to Australia with Council support in 1996, a week before he was awarded the Booker Prize.

Yannis Ritsos, the famous Greek poet, readily accepted an invitation to celebrate the Worldwide Fiftieth Anniversary of The British Council, in Thessaloniki, in 1984. I had to hire a thousand-seat cinema to accommodate all the guests. In spite of his radical political reputation, he paid warm tribute to the spirit of Lord Byron and to the work of The British Council.

In Roslyn Russell's book, there is no attempt to construct theoretical divisions or positions by use of such terms as 'Commonwealth' or 'Post-Colonial' literature. That may disappoint some readers. They should not misunderstand the purpose of the book. The Council supports controversial academic research as well as providing more straightforward support for the visits of writers. It is not a one-way flow. Where possible, the Council can assist with arrangements for local writers, in countries where it is represented, to meet their counterparts if they are travelling to Britain for the development of collaborative projects or for similar reasons.

Australian writers such as William Yang, Komninos, Mary Morris and others have visited Britain with Council support in recent years. Andrea Stretton visited Britain in 1996 to attend the prestigious British Council Cambridge Literature Seminar, and made a splendid SBS Television programme whilst she was there. She found time to interview and make contact with many other writers.

When I left Prague (where I served as Cultural Attaché) in November 1989, I was appointed to be the new Head of the Council's Literature Department, to take over from the highly-regarded Dr Harriet Harvey-Wood. I never took up the post, because I was required to head up the Eastern and Central Europe Department where work was expanding as a result of the fall of Communism and the serial revolutions.

I have always regretted that I missed that opportunity. This project is a substitute, in some respects.

It is fascinating to read the internal files of The British Council, especially the writers' reports on their visits. Sometime writers publish their impressions of Australia, as Anthony Burgess did in his 'Confessions' and D. J. Enright did in his 'Diaries of a Mendicant Professor'. Others write ambiguous poems or travel-pieces. Sir John Betjeman was ecstatic about his tour of Australia in 1961, as many others have been since then.

I hope that the twelve 'new writers' selected for the *new*IMAGES exchange will feel inspired to write the truth, whatever they may find.

I want to thank—with all my heart—Roslyn Russell for her total commitment to the project; Patrick Gallagher, for agreeing to publish the book; and Ian Templeman, Warren Horton and the staff of the National Library of Australia, for producing the original exhibition and for giving permission to reproduce the illustrations from their priceless collection.

Jim Potts
Director, Australia
The British Council

CONTENTS

ACKNOWLEDGMENTS

A book of this kind relies upon the co-operation and assistance of many people and institutions in providing information and illustrations. I want to express my appreciation to the following for their help, their time and their support in bringing this book to publication. In Australia: Joan Birnie, Dymphna Clark, Barbara Dawson, Robert Darroch, Paul Delprat, Michael Hedger, Sandra Jobson, Barbara Ker Wilson, Jan Nicholas, Elizabeth Ramsey, Francesca Rendle-Short, Ted Richards, Garry Shead, Jo Steele, Michael Thwaites, Kay Walsh, Jill Waterhouse and Michael Wilding. In the United Kingdom: Elspeth Barker, Jonathan Barker, Nina Bawden, Carmen Callil, Jim Crace, Margaret Drabble, Fay Godwin, Richard Holmes, Michael Holroyd, Barry Humphries, Lindsay Kyle, Penelope Lively, Brian Matthews, Alastair Niven, Rose Tremain and Fay Weldon.

I particularly wish to thank the two partners in the original poster exhibition. Jim Potts of The British Council Australia has given this project unflagging support, and The British Council provided the travel grant which enabled me to undertake interviews in the United Kingdom. The National Library of Australia and its Director-General, Warren Horton, have made it feasible by donating free of charge the illustrations used in the original exhibition. My thanks go to Jim Potts and Ian Templeman for their original concept for the exhibition, which is now realised in book form. I am also grateful to the staff of the National Library, particularly in the Main Reading Room and the Pictorial Reading Room, for their patience and unfailingly cheerful service.

I also wish to thank Patrick Gallagher of Allen & Unwin Australia for his support and encouragement, and Karen Ward for her editorial guidance. My husband, Michael Jones, travelled from London to Oxford three times before the weather was fine enough to take the photos reproduced in this book. I thank him for this, and for his informed support throughout the writing process.

The following writers and organisations have given permission for their works to be quoted in this book: Dymphna Clark for works by Manning Clark, Barry Humphries, Richard Holmes, Peters Fraser and Dunlop Group for J. B. Priestley, Francesca Rendle-Short, Paul Slessor and HarperCollins Publishers for 'Beach Burial' from Kenneth Slessor *Selected Poems*, Jo Steele for Barbara Hanrahan, Michael Thwaites, and Michael Wilding, Heather Henderson for Sir Robert Menzies, Oxford University Press, Melbourne for 'Federation' by W. T. Goodge and 'King George V' by Charles W. Hayward, Peter Porter and Oxford University Press for 'Reading *MND* in Form 4B' from *Collected Poems*, Faber and Faber for Sir Keith Hancock, Random House UK for Iris Murdoch. Attempts have been made to contact other copyright holders; any person with information regarding copyright entitlements please contact the publisher.

Roslyn Russell
Canberra
March 1997

INTRODUCTION

In November 1994 The British Council held a cocktail party in its office near Trafalgar Square, at which British and Australian writers, and British Council and Australian High Commission staff, gathered to launch an exhibition. Entitled 'Literary Links between Australia and Britain' and co-sponsored by The British Council and the National Library of Australia, the exhibition of sixteen posters illustrated the literary relationship between Britain and Australia and was launched by the then Australian High Commissioner, Neal Blewett, with the National Library being represented by Ian Templeman. Conviviality and good spirits marked the occasion: one journalist commenting that 'authors like Kathy Lette turned up the volume of the conversation the way extroverts and immigrants tend to do'.[1]

Just over a year later, Fay Weldon handed me my coat and hat as I prepared to go out the front door of her Hampstead home into a snowy early December landscape. As I crossed the doorstep she remarked, 'All British writers in search of inspiration should go to Australia. It gives one a sense of clarity'.[2]

The two strands represented by these events have now come together in this book. The creation of the 'Literary Links' exhibition, of which I was the curator, was the first and most important impetus to its production. The second was my visit to Britain in November–December 1995, sponsored by a British Council travel grant, during which I interviewed a

'Literary Links' exhibition title poster, designed by Kathy Jakupec. The exhibition was launched at the Melbourne Festival in October 1994 by British author Jim Crace, and in London in November that year by the Honourable Neal Blewett, Australian High Commissioner, London. Photograph by Louis Seselja, National Library of Australia. National Library of Australia, The British Council

number of British writers and others concerned with literature in Britain and Australia, and explored the links between them.

This book, though, is, I hope, more than the sum of these two parts. It has always been my belief—shared by James Potts, Director Australia for The British Council, whose support has been crucial in seeing this work come to fruition—that a book could do far more than the exhibition to illustrate the depth and complexity of the literary relationship between the two countries. As I developed the exhibition with National Library designer Kathy Jakupec, it became obvious that the poster format dictated that much material worthy of inclusion had of necessity to be excluded. There were also some issues which could be better explored in book form. The fact that the entire production process took place in Australia also meant that the British end of the story had to be gleaned from sources available in Australian libraries, although The British Council Literature Department helped in locating pictures of British writers. My visit to Britain to speak with British writers on the spot has now given me the material to redress the balance of input between the two countries.

LITERARY LINKS between Australia and Britain

A joint exhibition of the National Library of Australia and The British Council

The 'Literary Links' exhibition was the brainchild of the two men mentioned above—The British Council's Director in Australia, Jim Potts, and the National Library's Assistant Director-General, Cultural and Educational Services, Ian Templeman, who believed that the past and continuing reflection of each country in the literature of the other was a subject worth exploring. They came up with a huge list of British and Australian writers who could feasibly be included in an exhibition to celebrate the literary relationship between the two countries. Australian Heritage Projects, a Canberra-based historical consultancy firm, was engaged to create a poster exhibition based on the ideas generated by Potts and Templeman. It was to comprise sixteen posters—one for the main title and fifteen dealing with separate aspects of the literary relationship between Britain and Australia. It was to be well-illustrated and feature extracts from the work of writers which demonstrated each particular theme. I was given the task of producing the text and selecting the illustrations for the posters.

Looking at the original list, it is interesting to see how closely the final exhibition corresponded, both in terms of inclusion of names and thematic categories, to those that Potts and Templeman identified. Given provisional categories such as 'Visionaries', 'Explorers/Sailors/Scientific Writers', 'Settlers, Colonials', 'Early Commentators', 'Expatriates', 'Tourists and Travellers', 'Miscellaneous Poms—In Oz or On Oz', 'At Oxbridge', 'First Generation Immigrants (born in UK)', 'Republicans', 'Constitutional Monarchists', 'Writers in Residence/British Council Visitors/Festival Guests', it was obvious that an historical emphasis rather than a critical literary approach would inform the finished product. And so it turned out to be. Once the exhibition was completed, all the above categories had been translated into one or another of the themes which are also explored in this book. Some themes were conflated: for example, 'Visionaries' and 'Explorers/Sailors/Scientific Writers' became 'Mythical Australia'. Others were split into more discrete units: 'Travelling Investigators' addressed the subject of visiting commentators; while D. H. Lawrence's 1922 visit earned a poster to itself, entitled 'Prophetic Insight'. Australia's convict past and its reflection in literature, both in Britain and Australia, is illustrated in 'True Patriots All'; while literary works forged in the crucible of the wars to which Australia sent troops to the aid of the 'mother country' are featured in 'Bugles of England'. 'At Oxbridge' became 'Dreaming Spires'. Satirists from both countries earned their own poster— 'Stirrers'. Australian winners of British literary awards were also honoured in 'Prizewinners'.

The Honourable Neal Blewett at the 'Literary Links' launch in London, November 1994.
The British Council

This book aims to take the process further. A new chapter, 'Keeping Australia in Mind', examines the use of Australian characters and settings by modern British writers, and gives examples of their work. Within chapters which correspond to the themes illustrated by the exhibition posters, there is additional material, in the form of editorial commentary, extracts from relevant works and illustrations.

Why write a book about a subject which to some people seems so obvious, even politically incorrect in an Australia which has, until recently, been committed officially to celebrating multiculturalism rather than its British heritage? The phrase most Australians still associate with their country's relationship with Britain is 'cultural cringe': a belief that no intellectual or literary product originating in Australia could be considered equal to those produced in the 'mother country'; and its corollary, that no Australian writer or artist could be said to have 'made it' until he or she had been successful in Britain. But those who fear that celebrating our literary links with Britain means a return to the 'bad old days' of provincials deferring to the metropolis—and being condescended to—could re-examine the matter. There is now ample evidence that those days are behind us, and that Australians win considerable acceptance at home as well as abroad, with no necessity for the latter to precede the former.[3] A part of Australia's maturity as a society, I believe, is an ability to move away from these stereotypes of the past, and to be prepared to acknowledge our debt—literary and otherwise—to what, for many of us, is our cultural heritage.

What many Australians may not be aware of is the extent to which the works of Australian writers—and Australia itself—are appreciated in Britain. The 'Literary Links' exhibition itself has played its part in fostering this appreciation, as it has travelled around Australia and Britain, and to a number of countries overseas. In 1995, Professor Brian Matthews of the Sir Robert Menzies Centre for Australian Studies in London, and Rebecca Hossack, Cultural Attaché at the Australian High Commission, collaborated to stage a series of readings by Australian authors at Australia House. These readings, also called 'Literary Links', were held in the Reading Room, with the exhibition as a backdrop. Up to 500 people, mostly British, came to hear Clive James read from his work—as did Kathy Lette, Peter Porter, Tom Keneally and archaeologist and historian John Mulvaney on other occasions.[4] Other Australian writers have received plaudits in Britain in recent times. A recent article in the *Guardian Weekly* by its theatre critic Michael Billington began: 'We see far too little Australian drama in Britain'. The article reviewed David Williamson's play, *Dead White Males*, describing it as an 'attack on fashionable literary theory and the wilder excesses of the thought police', and concluded that it was 'a deeply Australian play that travels well'.[5] Australian authors are regularly short-listed for high profile literary prizes such as the Booker Prize, most recently Tim Winton for *The Riders* in 1995.

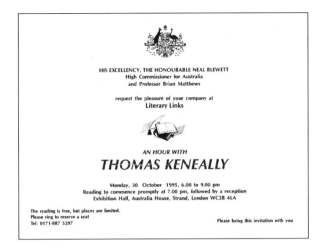

From the British point of view Australia has also become more interesting: as the homeland of key person-alities in British cultural life, such as Peter Porter, Germaine Greer, Clive James, Les Murray and Barry Humphries; and as the origin of literary works of considerable merit. It is also a most receptive country for the works of British writers who, when they come to Australia for literary festivals and book promotion tours, report large and enthusiastic audiences. Australian sales of books by British writers—both past and present—are booming.

Invitation to Tom Keneally's 'Literary Links' reading at Australia House. Australian High Commission, London

Australians still demonstrate considerable allegiance to the British literature of the past, which has achieved spectacular popularity in recent times owing to the spate of televised and filmed versions of classics such as Jane Austen's *Pride and Prejudice*, *Sense and Sensibility* and *Persuasion*, and Charles Dickens' *Martin Chuzzlewit*. Film versions of Shakespeare's plays—Kenneth Branagh's *Much Ado About Nothing*, *Henry V* and *Othello*, Ian McKellen's *Richard III*, and Zeffirelli's *Hamlet*, and the more problem-atic Peter Greenaway adaptation of *The Tempest*, *Prospero's Books*—have delighted and stirred Australian viewers; and the performances of Australian exponents, such as the Bell Shakespeare Company, attract large audiences which include many young people.

Literary societies dedicated to the task of celebrating the life and works of particular British writers are also growing in Australia, both in number of members and writers celebrated. In October 1995 an article in the *Sydney Morning Herald* reported on the 'growing list of literary clubs', with the formation of the Dylan Thomas Society in March 1995, to join others such as the Australia and New Zealand Shakespeare Association, Jane Austen Society of Australia, Brontë Society, Byron Society, Dickens

Society, Kipling Society and the D. H. Lawrence Society.[6] These societies hold meetings and conferences, publish journals—the Jane Austen Society of Australia journal is called *Sensibilities*, and the D. H. Lawrence Society produces *Rananim*—and encourage the production of scholarly works on their chosen writer. Some are purely Australian creations; others, such as the members of the Brontë Society, belong to the worldwide organisation based in Haworth in Yorkshire, although members meet in Sydney once a year.[7] The Kipling Society is also affiliated with the British body; the Melbourne branch, founded in 1938 and being one of a number of branches around the world, including New Zealand, South Africa, British Columbia, Canada and the USA, is now the sole survivor.[8] The Jane Austen Society of Australia has seen spectacular membership growth in recent years; founded in 1989 with 23 members, by June 1996 membership had increased to 350.[9] Susannah Fullerton, President of the Jane Austen Society of Australia, pondered on what the retiring early nineteenth century writer would have thought about being celebrated by having her own literary society in late twentieth century Australia:

> She may have been astonished that her books were being read in a place so far away from where they were written, but surely it would give her pleasure to know that the people in this room have read, re-read and will go on re-reading the books that have added so much enjoyment to their lives.[10]

Australian writers have been tantalised by the fictional possibilities of a famous British writer visiting their country—in reality or in the imagination. Barbara Ker Wilson's *Jane Austen in Australia*, for example, brings Jane Austen to the penal colony at Botany Bay (the persistent name for the settlement in its incarnation as a gaol, despite its actual name of Port Jackson, or Sydney) with her aunt and uncle, James and Jane Leigh Perrott. James has been motivated to make the journey by his fascination with the flora and fauna of New South Wales, after reading descriptions of these by the celebrated Sir Joseph Banks. It is Banks' gift of *Banksia* seeds to Leigh Perrott that sends him—and his niece Jane Austen—to the antipodes, where the society of convict New South Wales is laid open to the visitors. Thus Barbara Ker Wilson, in this single work of creative imagination, creates some of the links between Australia and Britain that will be explored in more detail throughout this book.

In a similar fashion, Margaret Barbalet, in her novel *Steel Beach*, takes D. H. Lawrence's real visit to Australia in 1922 and extends it in an imaginative continuum into the present. This is not the only work based on Lawrence's 1922 visit: there is also a play, by David Allen, *Upside Down at the Bottom of the World*, and a number of poems written on this theme. Writers are not the only ones to have been fascinated by the Lawrence visit: artists Garry Shead and Paul Delprat have contributed paintings on this theme, some of which also appear in this book.

Two factors must be taken into consideration at the outset: that, while every attempt has been made to be as comprehensive as possible, the selection of material is ultimately a personal choice by the author, who recognises that others might have made different selections; and that the major criterion for inclusion in all cases has been the relevance of the work of particular writers to the subject. There are many writers who qualify for inclusion in a book of this kind: the vast numbers of British writers who have visited Australia, the equally vast number of Australian writers who have visited or lived in Britain spring immediately to mind. But it is those who have turned their authorial gaze directly on aspects of the relationship between Australia and Britain who have been selected rather than those whose stay in one or other of the countries has had little impact on their writing. Even using this measure, many writers will have been omitted. This is regrettable, but inevitable.

Australia was, firstly, a subject for British writers to speculate upon. Then it became a prison, and later a place to emigrate. All writing at that time was British—comparing and contrasting the land of their birth with this strange new country. The latter years of the nineteenth century saw Britain as the mecca of all hopes, the proving ground of literary merit, and the source of higher learning. It then became an instrument for the forging of a spirit of Australian nationhood in the rigours of an imperial war. British writers by now had reached an awareness that this new country, while sharing a common language and cultural heritage, was evolving a style of its own, and its society was not simply that of a transplanted Britain.

Some Australian writers also began to chafe under a system that demanded their political allegiance from a vast distance; others felt secure as part of a wider Commonwealth of Nations. From late last century to the present, some Australian writers have felt more comfortable in Britain; while some British writers have come to live in Australia, a number being part of the vast wave of immigration after the Second World War. Some Australian writers have gone to live in Britain, and have added spice through satire and humour: visiting British writers have done the same to Australia. Both Australian and British writers have created plots and characters which bring into focus the perceived differences between the two cultures.

As Jim Potts has said in his preface to this book, I have made 'no attempt to construct theoretical divisions or positions by use of such terms as 'Commonwealth' or 'Post-Colonial' literature'. As he rightly says, this is not the purpose of this book. Indigenous literature, which often takes an understandably negative approach towards the imposition of a European culture upon the Australian natural and cultural environment, has also not been considered for the purposes of this book. However, those interested in these approaches can examine the works of such writers as David Malouf, Xavier Herbert and Mudrooroo, to give three examples among many, and the works of literary critics in this area, for an insight into these perspectives.[11]

At the end of the twentieth century, with distances largely conquered by technology and unified by the enduring ties of a shared cultural heritage and the use of a common language, Australian and British writers and readers participate in an enriching exchange. The differences are acknowledged: the respect they have for one another is undeniable. It is possible that the linguistic, literary and other cultural links that bind the two nations may prove in the long run more enduring than any constitutional bond.

Organisation of chapters

The content of this book has been organised along the following lines. Chapters 1 to 3 deal with the historical background to the story—the early ideas about Australia, and how they were either confirmed or modified once Europeans saw the realities of the Great South Land; the convict settlement in New South Wales which began the European occupation of Australia; and the expansion of the British colonies in Australia as transportation ended and free emigration was encouraged. From Chapter 4 onwards a thematic approach takes over, and the literary relationship between Australia and Britain is examined under a number of different themes. So far as this is possible, these chapters are arranged chronologically, both internally and externally, but there are of course occasions when this ordering is arbitrary. Chapters dealing with more recent aspects of the relationship of course come towards the end of the book, but the storyline of some chapters may begin in the colonial period and extend to the present. This is an inherent feature of the thematic approach which has been followed in this book. The selection of particular writers to illustrate aspects of the literary relationship also follows this pattern; writers have been selected across the historical periods to indicate the chronological range of the topic. This often means that when many writers have been working at the same time in the same thematic area, only a few of them can be selected; and some may be omitted in favour of a single writer working earlier or later in the period. Responsibility for these difficult choices is the writer's alone, and she is aware that others may have made a different selection. Nevertheless, every effort has been made within the limited space available for each chapter to suggest the range of work available, even if only by further reading mentioned in the endnotes to each chapter.

This book makes no attempt at a formal analysis of the works included for their literary qualities; rather they are used as evidence to support the particular themes which have been developed throughout this book. It also does not claim to be a definitive history of the literary relationship between Britain and Australia; the topic is far too vast to be contained within such a narrow compass. But if it recalls forgotten connections, or makes readers aware of important new ones, it will have accomplished its objectives.

1

MYTHICAL AUSTRALIA

On 5 January 1688 a countryman from East Coker in Somerset waded ashore on the northern coast of Western Australia. The names of the geographical features in the area of this landing—Dampier Bay and Buccaneer Archipelago—give us the name of the man and the employment that had brought him there; although there was more to William Dampier than that.[1] Whatever the proximate circumstance that had carried him to that barren coast—possibly a typhoon which swept the privateer, the *Cygnet*, on which he had sailed as an officer with a mutinous crew, southwards—Dampier became the first Englishman to set foot on *Terra Australis Incognita*, the Great South Land, or New Holland as it was also known from the nationality of some of the previous navigators to chart its coastline. Once he arrived back in England on 27 September 1691 at the end of more than twelve years of voyaging, he turned to his diaries of observations to compile *A New Voyage Round the World*, which was published in 1697 and was an immediate success, with two editions appearing that year and another the next. His book, says Neil Rennie, 'made a literary lion of an old sea dog'.[2]

For William Dampier, while undoubtedly a pirate who took part in attacks on Spanish treasure ships in the Philippines, was a skilled natural historian and a clear and convincing writer. His factual and scientifically based prose heralded a new style of travel writing, and one which the

Royal Society recommended as the appropriate mode for the dissemination of useful knowledge.[3] *A New Voyage Round the World* contributed to the production of many accounts of South Sea travel, including those famous imaginary journeys immortalised by Defoe and Swift. Rennie continues:

> Dampier, plundering the Spanish Main and dining with Pepys and Evelyn, revived interest not only in voyages and accounts of voyages generally, but specifically in the South Seas, where Selkirk danced with his goats and Gulliver travelled. Dampier the sailor discovered little of the South Seas, but Dampier the author discovered much. 'To his countrymen he discovered', as one historian says, 'the whole South Seas'.[4]

The reference to Pepys and Evelyn reveals an aspect of Dampier's life—his membership of the society of literati of late seventeenth century Britain—that may appear unexpected for a man who was essentially a piratical racketeer who had, on his own admission, mixed with a pretty rough crowd. His writings gave the former Royal Navy captain turned pirate and son of a Somerset tenant-farmer an entrée to polite society and a place among such literary leading lights as Congreve, Addison, Steele, Gay and Pope.[5] The respectability he derived from the quality of his writing and his scientific observations led the Admiralty to revive his Royal Navy commission and send him out again in HMS *Roebuck* in January 1699 to discover more of the Great South Land. Arriving in Shark Bay in late July, he found no safe harbour and no water, and sailed across to Timor after five weeks with a crew about to succumb to the dreaded scurvy, leaving the Australian coast 'a disappointed man'. His biographer, Christopher Lloyd, says of Dampier's second contact with New Holland that the land he had visited:

> . . . was obviously an area of continental size, so something better might be expected elsewhere; but circumstances prevented him from ever reaching the promised land and his poor report of what he had actually seen was undoubtedly one of the reasons why no fresh enterprise was undertaken to make further discoveries in those parts for another seventy years.[6]

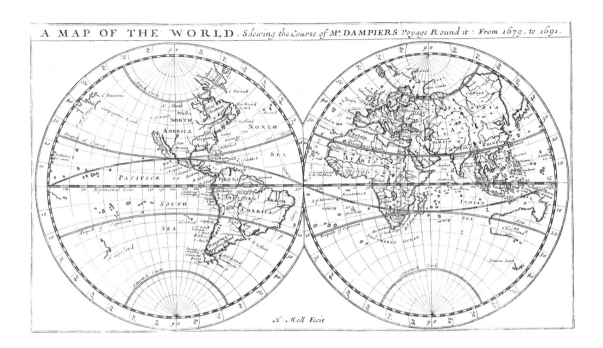

Dampier's visits to New Holland had two literary effects: one was to provide further inspiration for fellow writers to construct imaginary journeys to the antipodes, filled with wonders and reversals of nature and paradoxical occurrences, or making them the site of ideal societies.[7] These works formed part of a mythological tradition stretching back to classical antiquity: Hesiod posited the existence of the Blessed Isles in the antipodes, a notion which would later become the basis for locating a series of imaginary utopias in the Great South Land.[8] The second effect, and one that would be extended further by the next great English journey of exploration in the South Seas, was to bring *Terra Australis Incognita*— the Unknown South Land—into the realm of the known and the actual: fact replacing fiction. Ross Gibson has summed up the duality of the effect of Dampier's writings:

> The *Terra Australis* of longstanding dream was now linked to a world of historical experience. After Dampier the south land became, to British sensibility, a place of daunting fact at the same time as it was paradoxically a site for hopeful fiction. Sobering reality and optimistic fantasy were represented in the same image.[9]

Dampier's epic voyages are shown on this seventeenth-century map, which pictures New Holland (at the extreme right of the map) as joined to New Guinea, and with an unknown region between the Great Australian Bight and Van Diemen's Land (Tasmania). The entire east coast is also missing, not to be included until Cook charted it in 1770. National Library of Australia

So what did Dampier find when he landed on the north-western coast of Australia? His first impressions of New Holland and its people were neither inviting nor flattering. Although his description has been extensively quoted in many other works, it must be included here for its status as the first thing written about Australia by the first Englishman to set foot on its soil and to encounter its indigenous people.

New Holland is a very large tract of Land. It is not yet determined whether it is an Island or a main Continent; but I am certain that it joyns neither to *Asia*, *Africa*, nor *America*. This part of it that we saw is all low even Land, with sandy Banks against the Sea, only the points are rocky, and so are some of the Islands in this Bay.

The Land is of a dry sandy soil, destitute of Water, except you make Wells: yet producing divers sorts of Trees: but the Woods are not thick, nor the Trees very big. Most of the Trees that we saw are Dragon-trees as we supposed; and these too are the largest Trees of any there. They are about the bigness of our large Apple-trees, and about the same heighth: and the rind is blackish, and somewhat rough ... There was pretty long Grass growing under the Trees; but it was very thin. We saw no Trees that bore Fruit or Berries.

We saw no sort of Animal, nor any track of Beast, but once; and that seemed to be the tread of a Beast as big as a great Mastiff-Dog. Here are a few small Land-birds, but none bigger than a Blackbird: and but few Sea-fowls. Neither is the Sea very plentifully stored with Fish, unless you reckon the Manatee and Turtle as such. Of these creatures there is plenty; but they are extraordinarily shy; though the Inhabitants cannot trouble them much, having neither Boats nor Iron.

The Inhabitants of this Country are the miserablest People in the world. The *Hodmadods* of *Monomatapa*, though a nasty People, yet for Wealth are Gentlemen to these; who have no Houses and Skin Garments, Sheep, Poultry, and Fruits of the Earth, Ostrich Eggs, &c. as the *Hodmadods* have: and setting aside their humane shape, they differ but little from Brutes. They are tall, strait bodied and thin, with small long Limbs. They have great Heads, round Foreheads, and great Brows ... They have great Bottle noses, pretty full lips, and wide mouths. The two fore-teeth of their upper Jaw are wanting in all of them, men and women, old and young: whether they draw them out, I know not: Neither have they any Beards. They are long visaged, and of a very unpleasing aspect; having no one graceful feature in their faces. Their hair is black, short and curl'd, like that of the Negroes: and not long and lank like the common *Indians*. The colour of their skins, both of their faces and the rest of their body, is coal black, like that of the Negroes of *Guinea*.

They have no sort of Cloaths; but a piece of the Rind of a Tree ty'd like a Girdle about their Wastes, and a handful of long Grass, or 3 or 4 small green Boughs, full of Leaves, thrust under their Girdle, to cover their nakedness.[10]

The literary legacy of Dampier's voyages includes part of the inspiration for Daniel Defoe's *Robinson Crusoe*. Alexander Selkirk, the original for the character, had shipped with Dampier, who had himself been marooned by the *Cygnet's* crew on Nicobar Island, and Dampier also recounts the story of a Mosquito Indian abandoned for some time on Juan Fernandez Island. Other works which contain identifiable parallels with Dampier's writings include Defoe's *New Voyage Round the World*, and *Captain Singleton*.[11] Jonathan Swift's *Gulliver's Travels* is also cited as based, in part, on Dampier's account of New Holland, with Lilliput located in the region of Lake Torrens, and Houyhnhnm-Land in the Great Australian Bight. Ross Gibson says of Swift's treatment of the new knowledge of Pacific geography that:

> By utilising the image of the south land and all its con-notations, and by drawing on the specious empiricism of geography and cartography, he could strike a balance between experience and imagination. *Gulliver's Travels* is therefore a work of fiction about places of fantasy which are inextricably linked to the real world. Within the New Holland which is portrayed in this work the two worlds of beckoning fantasy and discouraging actuality still co-exist.[12]

Replacing myth with science—Cook's first *Endeavour* voyage, 1768–1771

Eighty years after Dampier had first encountered the inhabitants of New Holland on the inhospitable Western Australian coast, a very different set of travellers left Britain on a voyage of discovery that ranks among the great explorations made by Europeans, and one with enormous implications for science as well as for the fate of the British Empire. Blessed by the Royal Society, instructed by the Admiralty to further investigate the

CAPTAIN COOK

Portrait of Captain James Cook. National Library of Australia

coast of New Holland as well as observe the transit of Venus from Tahiti, furnished with scientific experts by Sir Joseph Banks, the beneficent patron who travelled with them, and commanded by Captain James Cook, one of the greatest navigators the world has ever known—albeit at that time only a humble Lieutenant in the Royal Navy—those who sailed in August 1768 on Her Majesty's bark *Endeavour*, a converted Whitby collier, would determine the future fate of the island continent known to them as New Holland, and from earlier times as *Terra Australis Incognita*. Once the expedition returned to Britain, the country would no longer be *Incognita*, but a possession of the British Crown; while those who charted its eastern coast, described and collected its flora and fauna, and spoke for its future as a British possession in the councils of government, would be given celebrity status among their contemporaries, and the title for Banks of 'the father of Australia' in later generations.

This is not the place to describe the first *Endeavour* voyage: published works abound, from biographies of the leading participants and scholarly editions of their journals, to analyses of the cultural impact of the voyage both on the Pacific region itself and on the metropolitan culture which received the enormous collection of artefacts, botanical and faunal specimens and artworks amassed and created by Banks, Solander, Spöring, Parkinson and Buchan on the journey.[13] As a reviewer of a recent book on exploration has noted, 'the impact of travel has been one of the most rewarding areas of scholarly investigation, noted for synthesizing researches between literature and history, art and anthropology, science and society, all within the context of the economic expansion of nations'.[14] From the contemporary point of view, the items landed at Dover in May 1771 when the expedition returned 'transformed the imagination of Georgian Britain as absolutely as Cook re-drew the map of the Pacific'.[15] As mentioned previously, the chief actors in the enterprise found themselves national celebrities, a fact which explains the shock wave that Cook's violent death in Hawaii later sent through Britain.

Certainly Cook and Banks did not write their journals to command a literary market. Nevertheless accounts of the voyages based on these journals were immensely popular in Britain, with the first appearing two years after the return of the expedition, in 1773. Over a hundred editions of reports from Cook's voyages had appeared before the turn of the century.[16] The most comprehensive work on the Cook voyages, however, is J. C. Beaglehole's three-volume edition of Cook's journals, published between 1955 and 1967, in which, in unvarnished prose, Cook relates his impressions of the new continent which he had been instructed to claim as a British imperial possession.[17] One of the most famous passages from Cook's *Endeavour* journal depicts the inhabitants of *Terra Australis* as people living in harmony with nature, in a passage which was seen by Cook's biographer as his subject's endorsement of the myth of the noble savage.[18]

From what I have said of the Natives of New-Holland they may appear to some to be the most wretched people upon the earth: but in reality they are far more happier than we Europeans; being wholy unacquainted not only with the superfluous but the necessary Conveniences so much sought after in Europe, they are happy in not knowing the use of them. They live in a Tranquillity which is not disturbed by the Inequality of Condition: The Earth and sea of their own accord furnishes them with all things necessary for life; they covet not Magnificent Houses, Household-stuff &c they live in a warm and fine Climate and enjoy a very wholsome Air: so that they have very little need of Clothing and this they seem to be fully sensible of for many to whome we gave Cloth &c to, left it carlessly [*sic*] upon the Sea beach and in the woods as a thing they had no manner of use for. In short they seem'd to set no value upon anything we gave them nor would they ever part with any thing of their own for any one article we could offer them this in my opinion argues that they think themselves provided with all the necessarys of Life and that they have no superfluities …[19]

Several years after Cook's death at the hands of the Hawaiian Islanders, the poet William Cowper contrasted his attitude and behaviour towards the Aboriginal people of Australia with that of the Spanish

From what I have said of the Natives of New Holland they may appear to some to be the most wretched people upon Earth, but in reality they are far more happier than we Europeans; being wholy unacquainted not only with the superfluous but the necessary Conveniencies so much sought after in Europe, they are happy in not knowing the use of them. They live in a Tranquillity which is not disturbed by the Inequality of Condition: The Earth and sea of their own accord furnishes them with all things necessary for life; they covet not Magnificent Houses, Household-stuff &c: they live in a warm and fine Climate and enjoy a very wholsome Air: so that they have very little need of Clothing and this they seem to be fully sencible of for many to whome we gave Cloth &c: to, left it carlessly upon the Sea beach and in the woods as a thing they had no manner of use for; In short they seem'd to set no value upon any thing we gave them nor would they ever part with any thing of their own for any one article we could offer them: this in my opinion argues that they think themselves provided with all the necessarys of Life and that they have no superfluities——
I shall conclude the account of this Country

Colonial artists such as Clement Hodgkinson depicted Aborigines in the idyllic natural settings in which Cook described them as wanting nothing the Europeans could offer. National Library of Australia

explorer Cortez towards the inhabitants of Central America. In a poem of 1781 entitled 'Charity', Cowper idealised the great navigator, picturing Cook as imbued with the Enlightenment ideas of the rights of man, unlike his Spanish counterpart in discovery who had brought conquest and death. Cowper of course was not to know this, but Cook's discovery would lead just as inexorably to destruction and death for the indigenous people of Australia and for their culture as did the savagery of Cortez and the *conquistadores* for the inhabitants of Central America.

> When Cook—lamented, and with tears as just
> As ever mingled with heroic dust,—
> Steer'd Britain's oak into a world unknown,
> And in his country's glory sought his own,
> Wherever he found man, to nature true,
> The rights of man were sacred in his view;
> He soothed with gifts, and greeted with a smile,
> The simple native of the new-found isle;
> He spurn'd the wretch that slighted or withstood
> The tender argument of kindred blood,
> Nor would endure that any should control
> His freeborn brethren of the southern pole.
> But though some nobler minds a law respect,

> That none shall with impunity neglect,
> In baser souls unnumber'd evils meet,
> To thwart its influence, and its end defeat.
> While Cook is loved for savage lives he saved,
> See Cortez odious for a world enslaved![20]

The impact of the other major character aboard the *Endeavour*—Sir Joseph Banks—on the subsequent history of Britain and Australia has also been the subject of much scholarly effort, particularly directed to securing his reputation as a major cultural influence as a well as a prime mover, in his role as adviser to government, in having a British colony established in New South Wales.[21] Harold Carter of the British Museum (Natural History), whose fine 1988 biography of Banks is accepted as the definitive work on his subject, sums up Banks's contribution to the creation of the modern nation of Australia:

> … there is no man of whom it can more truly be said that he was 'the father of Australia'. From before the sailing of the *Endeavour* in 1768 to the anchorage of the 'First Fleet' at Sydney Cove in 1788 the possibility of a white European settlement somewhere on its eastern shore survived on the firm intellectual support of Banks's geographical and biological insights, both instinctive and observed.
>
> From the moment of its inception as a distant plan no man laboured more continuously or constructively to ensure the survival of that remote British outpost through the years of global war, uneasy peace and changing Ministries at home. No man was more steadfast as the ultimate support of successive governors with his advice and help in their lonely struggles facing the challenges of an unstable small society in an enigmatic vast new world. No man did more to ensure that the world map should include Terra Australis as a British settled region with 'sources of wealth of the utmost importance to the future wealth and prosperity of the United Kingdom'.[22]

While Banks made no claims to literary influence, the cultural effect of the collection and classification of the fruits of the *Endeavour*'s voyage

George Stubbs's depiction of a kangaroo, based on a skin collected on the Endeavour *voyage, became a famous image that was even reproduced on souvenir mugs in the later eighteenth century in Britain.* National Library of Australia

which he sponsored and supervised was a shift from the fantastic to the factual. By the time of Banks's death in 1820 taxonomy had replaced tale-telling as the dominant mode of approach to the antipodes, and *Terra Australis Incognita*, in its new incarnation as Botany Bay, had been incorporated within the network of the British imperial enterprise.

Faunal facts and fantasies

Nevertheless, enough remained of magic once the classification and codifying had been done to ensure that the antipodes were still regarded as a region of natural wonders. Once the *Endeavour* expedition had returned to Britain the artist George Stubbs drew a picture of a kangaroo based on the skin of one that Banks had brought home, and this image became immensely popular, appearing in the many published accounts of the voyage, and on souvenir items such as Staffordshire mugs. The 'myths' of the antipodes—the natural freaks that imagination had constructed as living there—were made actual in this strange hopping animal. Then there was the oddest of all—the egg-laying duckbilled milk-producing platypus, whose contemporary name, duck-mole, exactly suggested what appeared to be a combination of two European animals. In this distant land nature really had created opposites—swans that were black instead of white. As Europeans settled in the new land, and live animals were sent back to Britain, their popularity as a symbol of Australia persisted. Opportunities were given to people to see a kangaroo, as John McPhee relates in describing the National Gallery of Australia's example of a popular souvenir mug, made about 1793, depicting Stubbs's kangaroo:

> The first live kangaroo to reach Great Britain was sent in 1792 as a gift to King George III from Governor Phillip. It was placed on public exhibition in Regent's Park, London. Soon several kangaroos were available for public inspection and in 1793 a kangaroo was born in Richmond Park, London, the first to be born outside Australia … In the earliest days of discovery and settlement the kangaroo excited scientific interest. Since then this strong, brave and endearing mammal has captured the Australian imagination. The kangaroo has been a favourite motif for craftsmen of many generations, and has come to represent the nation at all times.[23]

Barron Field, magistrate, poet and close friend of Charles Lamb, far away from England in the infant colony of New South Wales, turned to poetry to express his ideas about the strange animal which he called the 'Spirit of Australia' in his book, *First Fruits of Australian Poetry*. In a comic parody of the panegyric verse popular at that time, he speculated that the kangaroo was a combination of some of the better-known fauna of the northern hemisphere.

Kangaroo, Kangaroo!
Thou Spirit of Australia,
That redeems from utter failure,
From perfect desolation,
And warrants the creation
Of this fifth part of the Earth,
Which should seem an after-birth,
Not conceiv'd in the Beginning,
(For GOD bless'd His work at first,
And saw that it was good),

But emerg'd at the first sinning,
When the ground was therefore curst;—
And hence this barren wood!

Kangaroo, Kangaroo!
Tho' at first sight we should say,
Contradiction be involv'd,
Yet, like discord well resolv'd,
It is quickly harmoniz'd.
Sphynx or mermaid realiz'd.
Or centaur unfabulous,
Would scarce be more prodigious,
Or Labyrinthine Minotaur,
With which great Theseus did war,
Or Pegasus poetical.
Or hippogriff—chimeras all!
But, what Nature would compile,
Nature knows to reconcile;
And Wisdom, ever at her side,
Of all her children's justified.

She had made the squirrel fragile;
She had made the bounding hart;
But a third so strong and agile
Was beyond ev'n Nature's art.
So she joined the former two
In thee, Kangaroo!
To describe thee, it is hard:
Converse of the camélopard,
Which beginneth camel-wise,
But endeth of the panther size,
Thy fore half, it would appear,
Hath belong'd to some 'small deer',
Such as liveth in a tree;
By thy hinder, thou should'st be
A large animal of chace,
Bounding o'er the forest's space—
Join'd by some divine mistake,
None but Nature's hand can make—

Nature, in her wisdom's play,
On Creation's holiday.

For howsoe'er anomalous,
Thou yet art not incongruous,
Repugnant or preposterous.
Better-proportion'd animal,
More graceful or ethereal,
Was never follow'd by the hound,
With fifty steps to thy one bound.
Thou cans't not be amended: no;
Be as thou art; thou art best so.

When sooty swans are once more rare,
And duck-moles the Museum's care,
Be still the glory of this land,
Happiest Work of finest Hand![24]

Richard Whately, who would later argue against continued transportation of convicts to the Australian colonies, in one of the earliest poetic works written about Australia used the country's natural oddities as a metaphor for the general topsy-turvy nature of the place as perceived from the perspective of Britain.

There is a place in distant seas
Full of contrarieties:
There, beasts have mallards' bills and legs,
Have spurs like cocks, like hens lay eggs.
There parrots walk upon the ground,
And grass upon the trees is found;
On other trees, another wonder!
Leaves without upper sides or under.
There pears you'll scarce with hatchet cut;
Stones are outside the cherries put;
Swans are not white, but black as soot.
There neither leaf, nor root, nor fruit
Will any Christian palate suit,
Unless in desperate need you'd fill ye
With root of fern and stalk of lily.

There missiles to far distance sent
Come whizzing back from whence they went;
There quadrupeds go on two feet,
And yet few quadrupeds so fleet;
There birds, although they cannot fly,
In swiftness with your greyhound vie.
With equal wonder you may see
The foxes fly from tree to tree;
And what they value most so wary,
These foxes in their pockets carry.
There the voracious ewe-sheep crams
Her paunch with flesh of tender lambs,
Instead of beef, and bread, and broth,
Men feast on many a roasted moth.
The north winds scorch, but when the breeze is
Full from the south, why then it freezes;
The sun when you to face him turn ye,
From right to left performs his journey.
Now of what place could such strange tales
Be told with truth save New South Wales?[25]

As to the possibility of a better society in the antipodes: the British government, within eighteen years of Cook's claiming of the Australian continent for Britain, took a step that would seem to put such prospects outside the reach of even the most optimistic of fantasists. It would plant its unwanted convicts there, and stamp Botany Bay with a mark of infamy that would for a time extinguish any vision of a utopia in the southern hemisphere.

2

TRUE PATRIOTS ALL

One early winter's night just eighteen months after the foundation of the penal colony at Port Jackson in New South Wales, its civil and military officers gathered in a convict hut to celebrate the King's birthday, 4 June 1789. One of them, Captain Watkin Tench of the Marine garrison, described the entertainment they had come so willingly to see as a respite from the desolation of life in the colony, a performance of George Farquhar's play, *The Recruiting Officer:*[1]

> That every opportunity of escape from the dreariness and dejection of our situation should be eagerly embraced, should not be wondered at. The exhilarating effect of a splendid theatre is well known: and I am not ashamed to confess, that the proper distribution of three or four yards of stained paper, and a dozen farthing candles stuck around the mud walls of a convict-hut, failed not to diffuse general complacency on the countenances of sixty persons, of various descriptions, who were assembled to applaud the representation. Some of the actors acquitted themselves with great spirit, and received the praises of the audience: a prologue and an epilogue, written by one of the performers, were also spoken on the occasion; which, although not worth inserting here, contained some tolerable allusions to the situation of the parties, and the novelty of a stage representation in New South Wales.[2]

Tradition has assigned to the following verse the role of the prologue mentioned by Tench. While it is most unlikely that these were the actual words spoken on this occasion, the verse is a wry summary of the benefits to Britain of the forced expatriation of her least law-abiding citizens to this most distant outpost of empire:

> From distant climes o'er wide-spread seas we come,
> Though not with much éclat or beat of drum,
> True patriots all; for be it understood,
> We left our country for our country's good;
> No private views disgrac'd our generous zeal,
> What urged our travels was our country's weal;
> And none will doubt but that our emigration
> Has prov'd most useful to the English nation.[3]

The entertainment in the convict hut was a light moment at the end of a year-and-a-half of crises, struggle and deprivation. The colony had, since its foundation in late January 1788, endured near starvation as crops failed in the harsh and unfamiliar conditions. The denizens of the small settlement carved out of the bush of Australia had searched eagerly for the sign of a sail that would herald relief: none had come. Convicts and military and civil officers alike were on short rations. No significant progress had been made in gaining the friendship of the country's Aboriginal

The First Fleet arrives at Botany Bay in January 1788, under the command of Captain Arthur Phillip and Captain John Hunter. Illustrated Sydney News, 18 March 1871. National Library of Australia

inhabitants, although large numbers of them had died of smallpox, possibly as a result of this first prolonged contact with Europeans.

A bright future for the convict colony in New South Wales could not have been predicted. And the situation became worse: one of the colony's only two warships, the flagship of the First Fleet, the *Sirius*, was wrecked at Norfolk Island less than a year after the theatrical performance, and a day before the next King's birthday celebration an elderly convict, Thomas Owen, collapsed and died of starvation.[4] Relief came when the *Lady Juliana*, the first ship of the Second Fleet, entered Sydney Harbour on 3 June 1790. Over the next few weeks more ships arrived with their cargoes of near-expiring human beings, an indictment of the venal contractors who undertook to transport the convicts.[5] The ships also brought the first detachment of the New South Wales Corps, a military unit sent to replace the Marines, and one whose name would later become synonymous with the insurrection against Governor Bligh known as the Rum Rebellion.[6]

The arrival of one of these ships was described with a somewhat uncharacteristic dramatic flourish by David Collins, Judge-Advocate of the colony, in his comprehensive work, *An Account of the English Colony in New South Wales*:

> Early in the morning of the 23rd, one of the men at the Lookout discerned a sail to the northward, but, the weather coming on thick, soon lost sight of it. The bad weather continuing, it was not seen again until the 25th, when word was brought up to the settlement, that a large ship, apparently under jury-masts, was seen in the offing; and on the following day the *Surprise* transport ... anchored in the cove from England, having on board one captain, one lieutenant, one surgeon's mate, one serjeant, one corporal, one drummer, and twenty-three privates of the New South Wales corps; together with two hundred and eighteen male convicts ...
>
> We had the mortification to learn, that the prisoners in this ship were very unhealthy, upwards of one hundred being now in the sick list on board. They had been very sickly also during the passage, and had buried forty-two of these unfortunate people. A portable hospital had fortunately been received by the *Justinian*, and there now appeared but too great a probability that we should soon have patients enough to fill it; for the signal was flying at the south head for the other transports, and we were led to expect them in as unhealthy a state as that which had just arrived ...
>
> We were not mistaken in our expectations of the state in which they

might arrive. By noon the following day, two hundred sick had been landed from the different transports. The west side afforded a scene truly distressing and miserable; upwards of thirty tents were pitched in front of the hospital and the adjacent huts, were filled with people, many of whom were labouring under the complicated diseases of scurvy and the dysentery, and others in the last stage of either of those terrible disorders, or yielding to the attacks of an infectious fever.

The appearance of those who did not require medical assistance was lean and emaciated. Several of these miserable people died in the boats as they were rowing on shore, or on the wharf as they were lifting out of the boats; both the living and the dead exhibiting more horrid spectacles than had ever been witnessed in this country. All this was to be attributed to confinement, and that of the worst species, confinement in a small space and in irons, not put on singly, but many of them chained together. On board the *Scarborough* a plan had been formed to take the ship, which would certainly have been attempted, but for a discovery which was fortunately made by one of the convicts (Samuel Burt) who had too much principle left to enter into it. This necessarily, *on board that ship*, occasioned much future circumspection; but Captain Marshall's humanity considerably lessened the severity which the insurgents might naturally have expected. On board the other ships, the masters, who had the entire direction of the prisoners, never suffered them to be at large on deck, and but a few at a time were permitted there. This consequently gave birth to many diseases. It was said, that on board the *Neptune* several had died in irons; and what added to the horror of such a circumstance was, that their deaths were concealed, for the purpose of sharing their allowance of provisions, until chance, and the offensiveness of a corpse, directed the surgeon, or some one who had authority in the ship, to the spot where it lay.[7]

Despite this dismal scene, one thing was clear: contrary to the fears of some of its inhabitants the colony had not been forgotten; supplies had been sent earlier from England, but the *Guardian*, transporting them, had been wrecked. The store ship *Justinian* had brought additions to the stores safely to the settlement. The colony would face deprivation again, but its sense of isolation would never be so complete. Contact had been re-established with Britain, and soon the convict colony was replicating itself around the Australian continent: Hobart, established on the island of Van Diemen's Land (Tasmania) in August 1802, was followed by Port Dalrymple (now Launceston) in November 1804.

Convicts toil at clearing the land, with the growing settlement of Sydney behind them, in John Carmichael's 1829 engraving, 'Sydney from Woolloomooloo Hill'.
National Library of Australia

The convict system itself became more complex, as successive governors sought to deal with problems which had not been considered when the First Fleet set out from Portsmouth in 1787. A 'ticket-of-leave' system was instituted by Governor Phillip in 1801, so that convicts whose sentences had expired or who had displayed exemplary conduct could work on their own account and eventually be reintegrated in civil society, at least in the Australian colonies—they were not wanted back in Britain. For those whose repentance was not evident, a worse fate lay in store. More settlements were founded as places of 'secondary punishment', where repeat offenders or recalcitrant prisoners were sent. Their names form a litany of misery reflected in the literature of the convict period: among the earliest, Port Macquarie, New South Wales, settled March 1821, and Macquarie Harbour, Van Diemen's Land, settled in August 1822. The first settlement in what is now Queensland was made at Redcliffe in September 1824, and was later moved to the present site of Brisbane, then known as Moreton Bay.[8] In May 1825, Norfolk Island, where an earlier settlement had been abandoned, was reoccupied, to become a byword for the worst brutalities of the convict system. Just over five years later Port Arthur, on the Tasman Peninsula of Van Diemen's Land (now Tasmania), was established, for the same purpose. The Swan River colony (now Perth, Western Australia) was founded with free settlers in June 1829, but was later

obliged to accept convicts, and was the last place to which they were sent. Over 160 000 convicts had been sent from Britain to the Australian colonies between 1788 and 1868, when the system of transportation finally came to an end.

Literature which deals with the convict period of Australia's history will be considered here in three groups. The first, 'Officers and convicts', comprises accounts by the participants in the enterprise of nation building hand-in-hand with the administration of the criminal justice system. Narratives of the colony's early days by military officers David Collins, Watkin Tench, John Hunter, William Bradley, Surgeon John White, Ralph Clark and others, were published in Britain. Accounts by convicts in various forms—chapbooks, letters, ballads, and novels—also found a ready readership back home in Britain and are included in this group.

The second group, 'Convicts and literature in Britain', deals with the influence of the convict system in Australia—termed for literary purposes 'Botany Bay'[9]—on literature back in England. The penal colony in New

Augustus Earle pictures a government gaol gang in 1830 emerging from Sydney's Hyde Park Barracks for a day's work. At least two of them have chains around their ankles, a convict overseer dangles a large bunch of keys, while a soldier directs operations. National Library of Australia

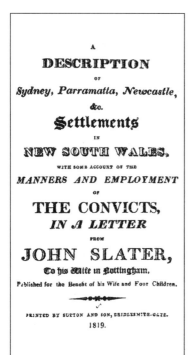

A

DESCRIPTION

OF

Sydney, Parramatta, Newcastle,

&c.

Settlements

IN

NEW SOUTH WALES,

WITH SOME ACCOUNT OF THE

MANNERS AND EMPLOYMENT

OF

THE CONVICTS,

IN A LETTER

FROM

JOHN SLATER,

To his Wife in Nottingham,

Published for the Benefit of his Wife and Four Children.

PRINTED BY SUTTON AND SON, BRIDLESMITH-GATE.

1819.

This letter from John Slater, transported in 1817, to his wife, was published to raise money to allow his family to emigrate to join him in New South Wales. It is one of many such publications which circulated in Britain at that time, and two copies of it survive in the National Library of Australia. National Library of Australia

South Wales was the physical location for hopes and aspirations centring around a belief in the redemptive power of suffering; and, on a more material level, a place where unpromising human material could transform adversity into prosperity. The most famous example of this is Charles Dickens' mention, in his novel *Great Expectations*, of New South Wales as the source of the wealth of his convict character Abel Magwitch.

The final group, 'Storytellers of the convict system', features works of literature dealing with the convict period from the perspective of non-participants, a process which began before transportation had ended, and has continued to the present. Both British and Australian writers have explored the convict experience in Australia in literary works.

Officers and convicts

Examples of the writings of military officers Watkin Tench and David Collins have already been quoted here; Tench's narrative in particular provides many more skilful observations of life in early New South Wales. It was not long before the literate members of the convict population were also committing their experiences to print, in mass-produced chapbooks which circulated in Britain, in the popular *Newgate Calendar*, and in works such as Henry Savery's novel *Quintus Servinton*, the first novel by a convict published in Australia, but designed to be sold in Britain.[10] Many convict writers expressed contrition for the crimes that brought them to the antipodes, and vowed to lead lives of virtue hereafter, thus reinforcing the popular notion that penitents could be purged of their crimes by suffering.

The effects of such improving sentiments, it was believed, should not be confined just to recipients of letters from distant New South Wales. The clergyman benefactor of Margaret Catchpole, transported for stealing a horse to help her criminal lover, published her letters from Sydney to himself and his wife.[11] Catchpole was troubled by the vice and brutality of the penal settlement of which she became a part in January 1802, and her compassion for the victims of its worst features is obvious in this extract from her letters:

I grieve to say, my dear lady, that this is one of the wickedest places in the world. I never heard of one, excepting those of Sodom and Gomorrah, which could come up to it in evil practices. People are so bold, so shameless, and so sinful, that even crime is as familiar as fashion in England. Religion is the last thing thought of, even by the Government, which sends out criminals that most want it. The Rev. Mr Johnson, who is almost the only clergyman in the whole country, comes frequently to the Foundling Asylum; but he tells my mistress that the town of Sydney is like a place of demons. Government is at great expense in the police establishment, to keep our poor bodies in subjection; but I am sure, if our souls were but a little more thought of, Government would have many thousand times better subjects ...

All the things you gave me arrived in safety with me, and are of great service to me. Oh! how I wish that many poor creatures, whom I see around me, had some of the blessings which I have! There are some who have been here for years, who have their poor heads shaved, and are sent up the Coal River [Newcastle]. They have to carry coals from daylight until dark. They are badly fed; and though very bad men, who actually sell their rations of bread for three days for a little rum, yet they ought not to be left without instruction, as they totally are, until they perish.

Norfolk Island is a terrible place to be sent to. Those only who are incorrigible are sent to this place, with a steel collar round their necks, to work in gangs.

I have no Government work to do; nor has the officer of Government anything to do with me. When there is a general muster of the convicts, then only I shall have to appear, and give account of myself. Some days I am permitted to go and see a friend at a distance, if I have any, either at Paramatta [*sic*], twenty miles, Gabley [Toongabbie?], thirty, or Hawkesbury, forty miles from Sydney; but then I shall have to get a passport, or I should be taken up,

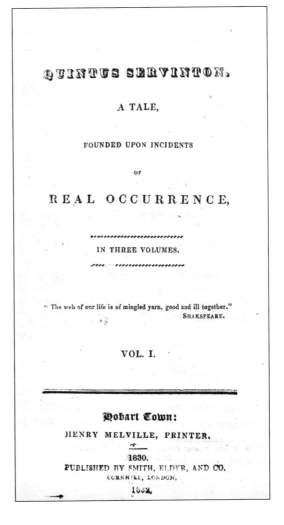

QUINTUS SERVINTON,

A TALE,

FOUNDED UPON INCIDENTS

OF

REAL OCCURRENCE,

IN THREE VOLUMES.

" The web of our life is of mingled yarn, good and ill together."
SHAKSPEARE.

VOL. I.

Hobart Town:
HENRY MELVILLE, PRINTER.
1830.
PUBLISHED BY SMITH, ELDER, AND CO.
CORNHILL, LONDON,
1832.

Title page of Quintus Servinton, *the first novel to be published in Australia by a convict,* Henry Savery. It was *then circulated widely in Britain.* National Library of Australia

This watercolour by Augustus Earle shows the 'female factory' at Parramatta, several miles from Sydney. Women who were not assigned as servants to military and civil officials, or those who had proven troublesome, worked here to produce goods such as textiles for the colony. National Library of Australia

and put into prison as a runaway. A very little will get a person into prison here; but it requires a great deal of interest to get him out again.[12]

Margaret Catchpole acquiesces in her punishment, and hopes to atone for her crime by a reformed life. Francis McNamara—known as 'Frank the Poet'—struck a far more defiant note against the system in 'The Convict's Tour of Hell'. In this poem Frank the Poet, a former highwayman, dies and is ferried by Charon free of charge across the River Styx to Hell. When he arrives there he discovers that the Devil doesn't want him, but prefers to play host to those who have been tormentors of convicts, such as the notorious Captain Patrick Logan of Moreton Bay:[13]

I knocked at the gate, then louder still,
When out rushed the Devil, with, 'What's your will?'
'Oh!' said I, 'I've come here to dwell
And share my fate with you in hell.'
Cried Satan, 'That can't be I'm sure,
For I detest and hate the poor.
None shall in my kingdom stand

Except the wealthy and the grand.
So Frank! I think you've gone astray,
FOR CONVICTS NEVER COME THIS WAY,
But soar to heaven in droves and legions,
A place so called in the upper regions!'
'Oh well! as I am in no hurry,
Have you got here one Capt. Murray?'
'Oh yes, he is within this place,
Would you like to see his face?'
'No, heaven forefend that I should view him,
For on board the *Phoenix* hulk I knew him.
But who is that in yonder blaze
On fire and brimstone seems to graze?'
'He's Captain Logan, of Moreton Bay,
And Williams—killed the other day,
Was overseer at Grose's farm,
And did you convicts no small harm.
Cooke, who discovered New South Wales,
And he who first invented gaols,
Are both tied to a fiery stake
That stands in yonder boiling lake.
Hark! hear you not that dreadful yelling?
It comes from Dr Wardell's dwelling;
And yonder see those fiery chairs?
They're fitted up for Beaks and Mayors,
And men of all judicial orders,
Traps, bankers, lawyers and recorders.'[14]

The horrors of penal servitude in the Australian colonies were often delineated in convict autobiographies. *The Adventures of Martin Cash*, for example, forms an important link between autobiography and the product of a novelist's imagination. Cash's description of a device used to punish a convict named Campbell was later used by Marcus Clarke as a source for the punishment aspects of penal servitude in *For the Term of His Natural Life*. Here is Cash's account of Campbell's fatal punishment:

About this time a new instrument of torture had just been invented, in the shape of an iron frame about six feet long and two-and-a-half wide, with

Captain Patrick Logan, explorer, and much-hated Commandant of the Moreton Bay settlement, whose murder by Aborigines was the cause of great rejoicing among his convict charges. John Oxley Library, Brisbane

round iron bars placed transversely, about twelve inches apart. The prisoner being placed in a horizontal position upon this frame, with his head projecting over the end, and without any support, was then firmly lashed with cords, and in this awful agony he was left in darkness for twelve hours. Campbell was subjected to this punishment and solitary confinement so often and for such a length of time, that at last he was found dead on the stretcher when the gaoler visited his cell. From the time Campbell was first sentenced until his murder, a period of six months, he had not been altogether twelve days out of solitary confinement. As there was no person to investigate the matter the sacrifice of Campbell passed like sunshine.[15]

Convicts and literature in Britain

The convict experience in Australia was soon reflected in literary works in Britain. Two works from this period, one from the early days of transportation to Botany Bay, and the other from close to the end of the convict system, develop two distinct themes associated with penal servitude in the literature of the time. Robert Southey in his *Botany Bay Eclogues* of 1794, and Charles Dickens in his 1861 novel, *Great Expectations*, saw transportation as a means of redemption or of self-improvement, at least by the acquisition of wealth, if not enhanced social standing.

Southey's *Botany Bay Eclogues* takes a number of individuals—including one woman, the prostitute Elinor—a soldier, sailor and farmer, and others, and contrasts their present condition in Botany Bay with their lives back in England. For some, there is much repining over families lost and fondly remembered landscapes; for others there is the terror of this strange country; some express contrition, others optimism. Elinor the prostitute recognises that her fate here is no worse than that which awaited her in her home country—miserable death after disgrace—and resolves to seek spiritual redemption through suffering in exile:

Welcome, ye savage lands, ye barbarous climes,
Where angry England sends her outcast sons,
I hail your joyless shores! My weary bark,
Long tempest-tost on Life's inclement sea,
Here hails her haven! welcomes the drear scene,
The marshy plain, the brier-entangled wood,
And all the perils of a world unknown,—

London Calls...

Australia in the 1890s witnessed a blossoming of literature and art, with writers and artists developing a new and vital interpretation of their country as the colonies prepared for a federal union. Nevertheless, even as they were articulating a national identity, Australian writers believed it was obligatory to travel to Britain to gain acceptance and recognition. London was for Australians the great cultural metropolis, the centre of the English-language publishing world. Britain was for many Australians, then and for years to come, their spiritual and intellectual home. Australian writers' work also reached a wider market in Britain, and this translated into bigger sales both there and in Australia. The pilgrimage to Britain was undertaken by a number of Australian writers, including Henry Lawson, Miles Franklin, Louise Mack, Dorothea Mackellar, Louis Becke, Vance Palmer, Louis Esson and Ethel Turner.

Henry Lawson took his own advice to the aspiring Australian writer to 'go steerage, stow away, swim, and seek London', before his genius turned to gall, or beer' in Australia. Lawson, his wife, Bertha, and their two children left for England in April 1900, remaining there until May 1902. Lawson claimed later that the visit had been 'wonderfully successful from a literary point of view', it had been his 'high tide'. His work was featured in British journals, and three prose collections, *The Country I Come From* (1901), *Joe Wilson and His Mates* (1901) and *Children of the Bush* (1902), were published in Britain. At a personal level the reverse was the case. Lawson began drinking again, and Bertha was confined for a time in Bethlem Hospital. Their relationship was irretrievably damaged. Lawson, despite his literary success, admitted that his health had completely broken down, and he 'must come home for a year or two', but would return, 'for London calls, and one must hear'. He never did.

Bust of Henry Lawson at Footscray, Melbourne by Clive Stevenson, 1896. National Library of Australia

In Lawson's 'Joe Wilson in England', Joe Wilson is looking after some business for a wool firm and living in Harpenden, where Lawson lived for part of his time in England. He affirms his admiration for the English and contrasts their social mores with those of the Australian bush.

Their unconventionality consist of carelessness in dress, manners and talk, and dropping in at all hours without notice? It wouldn't do in England. It would interfere with other people's comfort and privacy, and liberty ... And people are invited to each other's homes by letter, and accept by letter, because England is more crowded than the bush, and there are more people to converse. It's done for the comfort and convenience of all parties ... I'd like to see the two peoples understand each other.

Henry Lawson, 'Joe Wilson in England', *A Fantasy of Man: Henry Lawson Complete Works, 1901–1922*, Sydney, Lansdowne Press, 1984.

Henry Lawson's poem 'Jack Cornstalk' describes the impact of the visiting Australian's size and demeanour on citizens of London.

*I met Jack Cornstalk in London to-day,
He saw me and stared from over the way.
Oh! the colours faced Londoners stared with surprise
As his hair and his height, as compared with his size;
For his trousers were short and his collar was low,
And—there's not room to say-ee in London, you know!*

Henry Lawson, 'Jack Cornstalk', *Children of the Bush*, London, Methuen, 1902.

Australian writers living in London continued to draw on their Australian experiences. In her famous poem 'My Country' Dorothea Mackellar, speaking of her love for 'a sunburnt country', evoked the 'green and shaded lanes' of the English landscape as compared to the 'wide brown land' of Australia.

Illustration for title page of Dorothea Mackellar's *My Country* in Australia, plus J.J. Hilder, reproduced by the Art of J.J. Hilder, Sydney, Angus & Robertson, 1918.
National Library of Australia

Louise Mack continued to feel the enchantment of England even when she was living there. In her novel *An Australian Girl in London*, her heroine, Sylvia Leighton, contrasts living in England with life in Australia.

Every afternoon, away in far Australia, there comes over us all a half-past-two-in-the-afternoon feeling, an intolerable ennui, a sense of emptiness and discontent, a longing for something large and full that cannot be estimated ... It is our remoteness that palls us. We are so far, far off. Our sense too warm with English blood, and London calls, calls, and we are here, a whole world away. That is the meaning of the half-past-two-in-the-afternoon feeling. It is a sudden sense of our great distance from the full intellectual life of the old world, from music and art.

I had it often. I lost it when I came to London. At half-past two in the afternoon now there rolls over me a great, gorgeous sense of intense happiness.

Louise Mack, *An Australian Girl in London*, London, T. Fisher Unwin, 1902.

Louise Mack in London. Photograph from Lone Hand, 1 December 1912. National Library of Australia

Miss Franklin of 1906. She was thirty-six and in England.

Unable to attract the interest of Australian publishers, Miles Franklin sent her manuscript of *My Brilliant Career* to London with Henry Lawson. She later travelled to Britain herself in 1915, after describing the lure of London for a 30th-generation Australian in the final chapters of *My Career Goes Bung*.

And there is always England. England with her ancient historic beauties—traditions ... Her castles and cathedrals, her tried towers, her brooks are as clear to my records and closed eyes as the scents and features of 'Possum Gully'... Home London much better than I do Sydney. Through song and story it has permeated every fibre of my mind since I could first write a pictured page, while I have spent scarcely a month in but one corner of Sydney. London—THE BIG SMOKE—London, where our dreams come true.

England acclaimed my first homegrown effort. England may welcome my second and third. I will arise and go to Mother England.

Miles Franklin, *My Career Goes Bung*, Melbourne, Georgian House, 1946.

'Literary Links' poster, 'London Calls', tells the story of Australian writers who went to Britain around the turn of the century to win recognition, essential for their acceptance in their native land. National Library of Australia and The British Council

Captain William Dampier by Edmund Dyer (copy of painting by James Murray). National Library of Australia

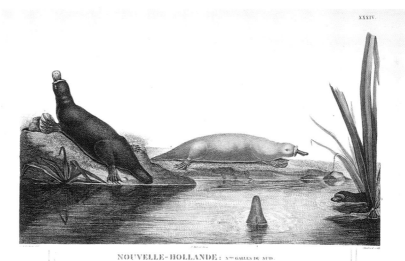

XXXIV.

NOUVELLE-HOLLANDE : N°™ GALLES DU SUD.

C. A. Lesueur's drawing of the 'paradoxical' platy-pus, from Peron and Freycinet's Voyage de découvertes aux Terrés Australes (1807–16). The term 'duck-mole' was also used to describe this animal, with its duck-like bill and soft dark fur. National Library of Australia

JANE AUSTEN
IN AUSTRALIA

A Novel

BARBARA KER WILSON

Barbara Ker Wilson's novel, Jane Austen in Australia, *takes the celebrated early-nineteenth century novelist on a fictional journey to the colony of New South Wales.* Design and illustration by Kate Barry, picture courtesy of Barbara Ker Wilson

John Hamilton Mortimer's group portrait of Cook, Banks, Lord Sandwich and two others, around 1771. National Library of Australia

For Elinor has nothing new to fear
From fickle fortune! All her rankling shafts
Barbed with disgrace, and venomed with disease,
Have pierced my bosom, and the dart of death
Has lost its terrors to a wretch like me ...

What though the garb of infamy I wear,
Though day by day along the echoing beach
I cull the wave-worn shells; yet day by day
I earn in honesty my frugal food,
And lay me down at night to calm repose,
No more condemned the mercenary tool
Of brutal lust, while heaves the indignant heart
With Virtue's stifled sigh, to fold my arms
Round the rank felon, and for daily bread
To hug contagion to my poisoned breast;
On these wild shores Repentance' saviour hand
Shall probe my secret soul; shall cleanse its wounds,
And fit the faithful penitent for heaven.[16]

An early illustration, by F. A. Fraser, of the encounter between a young boy, Pip, and the escaped convict Magwitch in the churchyard in Charles Dickens' 1861 novel, Great Expectations. When the terrified Pip brings Magwitch some food, he has no idea that this action will determine his future. Chapman and Hall edn, London, circa 1870. National Library of Australia

Charles Dickens in *Great Expectations* saw New South Wales not as a place of ennobling suffering, but an opportunity for a convicted felon to better himself and to triumph over the social system which had blighted his life. A convict, Abel Magwitch, aided by a small and terrified boy, Pip, encountered in a churchyard during an escape attempt from a prison hulk, vows to take his revenge on society by making his small helper into a 'gentleman'. With this goal in mind he avoids further punishment in the penal colony, and once he has gained his ticket-of-leave sets about amassing a fortune, which he arranges with the lawyer Jaggers to spend on Pip's education and all the appurtenances of the life of a 'London gentleman'. His arrival in England to view the product of his strange

enterprise is by no means welcome, however, to the recipient of his bounty, who is appalled at the source of his prosperous condition. Dickens in no way characterises Magwitch as a spiritually redeemed character: he has merely become rich, but the convict taint is upon him still. In this extract Magwitch tells the horrified Pip that the knowledge that his money was being used to create a gentleman had sustained him in the society from which he had come:

> 'And then, dear boy, it was a recompense to me, look'ee here, to know in secret that I was making a gentleman. The blood horses of them colonists might fling up the dust over me as I was walking; what do I say? I says to myself, "I'm making a better gentleman nor ever *you'll* be!" When one of 'em says to another, "He was a convict, a few years ago, and is an ignorant common fellow now, for all he's lucky," what do I say? I says to myself, If I ain't a gentleman, nor yet ain't got no learning, I'm the owner of such. All on you owns stock and land; which on you owns a brought-up London gentleman! This way I kep myself a-going. And this way I held steady afore my mind that I would for certain come one day and see my boy, and make myself known to him, on his own ground.'
>
> He laid his hand upon my shoulder. I shuddered at the thought that for anything I knew, his hand might be stained with blood.[17]

Storytellers of the convict system

As the system of convict transportation diminished, the result of anti-transportation movements by the increasing number of free settlers in the Australian colonies—the oldest colony, New South Wales, saw the end of transportation in 1852 over sixty years after it had been the rationale for its foundation—literature came to the aid of an Australian society which was becoming increasingly concerned to put the most positive gloss on its convict pioneers, and to condemn the system which had perpetrated the horrors associated with the names of Port Arthur, Norfolk Island and Moreton Bay. Caroline Leakey's 1859 novel, *The Broad Arrow*, was published before transportation ended, and prefigures in theme and content the pre-eminent novel of the convict era, Marcus Clarke's *For the Term of His Natural Life*.[18]

The process began in earnest with the publication in 1874 of this novel by an English emigrant. Clarke's hero, Rufus Dawes, has been wrongly convicted and subjected to persistent brutality made even more terrible by his essential nobility and self-sacrificial acts. *For the Term of His Natural Life* had enormous impact; for many people this somewhat melodramatic work summed up the convict system as a whole, a situation which its adaptation into a popular film in the 1920s did nothing to diminish. In this extract the novel's heroine, Sylvia, discovers Dawes, who had saved her life when she was a child, in the same position of torture as Martin Cash described as causing Campbell's death. This discovery is made even more dreadful by the fact that it is her husband, Port Arthur Commandant Maurice Frere, who has ordered Dawes's punishment. Dawes had also saved Maurice Frere's life, and the Commandant consequently hated the convict, and lived in dread that his wife would recover her memory of her childhood rescuer. Here Sylvia visits the prison and demands to see Dawes to allay her fears that he is being victimised, and finds them, all too horribly, confirmed:

One sultry afternoon, when the Commandant had gone on a visit of inspection, Troke, lounging at the door of the New Prison, beheld, with surprise, the figure of the Commandant's lady.

'What is it, ma'am?' he asked, scarcely able to believe his eyes.

'I want to see the prisoner Dawes.'

Troke's jaw fell.

'See Dawes?' he repeated.

'Yes. Where is he?'

Troke was preparing a lie. The imperious voice, and the clear steady gaze, confused him.

'He's here.'

'Let me see him.'

'He's—he's under punishment, ma'am.'

'What do you mean? Are they flogging him?'

'No; but he's dangerous, ma'am. The Commandant—'

'Do you mean to open the door or not, Mr Troke?'

Troke grew more confused. It was evident that he was most unwilling to open the door.

'The Commandant gave strict orders—'

'Do you wish me to *complain* to the Commandant?' cried Sylvia with a touch of her old spirit, and jumping hastily at the conclusion that the gaolers were, perhaps, torturing the convict for their own entertainment. 'Open the door at once!—at once!'

Thus commanded, Troke, with a hasty growl of its 'being no affair of his, and he hoped Mrs. Frere would tell the captain how it happened,' flung open the door of a cell on the right hand of the doorway. It was so dark that, at first, Sylvia could distinguish nothing but the outline of a framework, with something stretched upon it that resembled a human body. Her first thought was that the man was dead, but this was not so—he groaned. Her eyes, accustoming themselves to the gloom, began to see what the 'punishment' was. Upon the floor was placed an iron frame about six feet long, and two and half feet wide, with round iron bars, placed transversely, about twelve inches apart. The man she came to seek was bound in a horizontal position upon this frame, with his neck projecting over the end of it. If he allowed his head to hang, the blood rushed to his brain and suffocated him, while the effort to keep it raised strained every muscle to agony pitch. His face was purple, and he foamed at the mouth. Sylvia uttered a cry. 'This is no punishment; it's murder! Who ordered this?'

'The Commandant,' said Troke, sullenly.

'I don't believe it. Loose him!'

'I daren't, ma'am,' said Troke.

'Loose him, I say! Hailey!—you sir, there!' The noise had brought several warders to the spot. 'Do you hear me? Do you know who I am? Loose him, I say!' In her eagerness and compassion, she was on her knees by the side of the infernal machine, plucking at the ropes with her delicate fingers. 'Wretches, you have cut his flesh! He is dying! Help! You have killed him!'

The prisoner, in fact, seeing this angel of mercy stooping over him, and hearing close to him the tones of a voice that for seven years he had heard but in his dreams, had fainted. Troke and Hailey, alarmed by her vehemence, dragged the stretcher out into the light, and hastily cut the lashings. Dawes rolled off like a log, and his head fell against Mrs. Frere. Troke roughly pulled him aside, and called for water. Sylvia, trembling with sympathy and pale with passion, turned upon the crew. 'How long has he been like this?'

'An hour,' said Troke.

'A lie!' said a stern voice at the door. 'He has been there nine hours!'[19]

Clarke's epic story was followed by literary works such as Price Warung's (William Astley) short stories of the system, and in the next century by Eleanor Dark's *The Timeless Land* trilogy and Thomas Keneally's *Bring Larks and Heroes*.[20] The most recent work in this category is by a British writer, Jane Rogers, whose 1995 novel, *Promised Lands*, is based on the experiences of Lieutenant William Dawes in the early colony. Her

C. A. *Lesueur, an artist with a visiting French expedition in 1802, pictured the growing settlement of Sydney from Dawes Point, named after William Dawes, the principal character in Jane Rogers' novel,* Promised Lands. National Library of Australia

novel has Dawes participating in the rigours of the early settlement as he attempts to construct buildings with inefficient and surly convict labour and inadequate tools, and observes the relations between the naval Governor, Arthur Phillip, the convicts and the Aboriginal people. She also treats subjects which have created concern in Australia in relation to the treatment of the country's indigenous people at the time of this first extended contact with Europeans.

Rogers' hero Dawes suspects that a convict, Barnes, permitted by him to sleep in the hospital storeroom, has caused the disastrous epidemic of smallpox which wiped out large numbers of Aboriginal people in the Sydney area by giving to them—possibly as an act of revenge for their killing of his homosexual protector—glass vials containing sample variolus matter designed for inoculation. This passage relates the moment when Dawes, hearing from Watkin Tench the news that the vials are missing, makes the connection between them, the convict Barnes, and the smallpox epidemic:

> 'The samples have gone.'
> It took him a while to make sense of Watkin's words.
> 'White says they have mislaid the samples. They were in the hospital stores, he is pretty sure, but when he looked last night he couldn't find them.'

'Someone has taken them?'

'Perhaps.'

'And given them to the natives?'

'I don't know. It's only guesswork. They may have been put somewhere else; he is not certain.'

'The samples are missing, and the natives have the smallpox.'

'Yes.' Watkin stood stiffly, and brushed his coat. 'It's cold. Shall we return?' William followed close behind his dark shape.

'But who *would*? Who would do such a thing?'

'Not the doctors, obviously—'

'Well who else had access to the hospital stores?' As he asked the question, William realized he already knew the answer. Convict guards. Like Barnes.[21]

Rogers' use of historical characters such as William Dawes and Watkin Tench thus brings us full circle from Tench's description of the King's birthday celebration in 1789 which began this chapter. The convict system in Australia has, since its inception, provided material for a wide range of literary expression both in Britain and Australia, a rich lode which has been far from exhausted.

3
'A NEW BRITANNIA'

In 1789 Erasmus Darwin wrote a prophetic poem, 'Visit of HOPE to Sydney Cove near Botany Bay' for the opening page of *The Voyage of Governor Phillip to Botany Bay*, published that year. It was accompanied by a representation of a medallion illustrating the poem's theme, crafted by master potter, Josiah Wedgwood, from pipeclay used by Aborigines which had been sent by Phillip from the new colony.

Where Sydney Cove her lucid bosom swells,
Courts her young navies, and the storm repels;
High on a rock amid the troubled air
HOPE stood sublime, and wav'd her golden hair;
Calm'd with her rosy smile the tossing deep,
And with sweet accents charm'd the winds to sleep;
To each wild plain she stretch'd her snowy hand,
High-waving wood, and sea-encircled strand.
'Hear me,' she cried, 'ye rising Realms! record
'Time's opening scenes, and Truth's unerring word.—
'There shall broad streets their stately walls extend,
'The circus widen, and the crescent bend;
'There, ray'd from cities o'er the cultur'd land,
'Shall bright canals, and solid roads expand.—
'There the proud arch, Colossus-like, bestride

'Yon glittering streams, and bound the chafing tide;
'Embellish'd villas crown the landscape-scene,
'Farms wave with gold, and orchards blush between.—
'There shall tall spires, and dome-capt towers ascend,
'And piers and quays their massy structures blend;
'While with each breeze approaching vessels glide,
'And northern treasures dance on every tide!'—
Then ceas'd the nymph—tumultuous echoes roar,
And JOY's loud voice was heard from shore to shore—
Her graceful steps descending press'd the plain,
And PEACE, and ART, and LABOUR, join'd her train.[1]

Erasmus Darwin's poem, decorated with a representation of a medallion created by Josiah Wedgwood from clay from New South Wales, predicts a bright future for the new colony.

National Library of Australia

VISIT OF HOPE
To SYDNEY-COVE,
NEAR BOTANY-BAY.

WHERE Sydney Cove her lucid bosom swells,
Courts her young navies, and the storm repels;
High on a rock amid the troubled air
HOPE stood sublime, and wav'd her golden hair;
Calm'd with her rosy smile the tossing deep,
And with sweet accents charm'd the winds to sleep;
To each wild plain she stretch'd her snowy hand,
High-waving wood, and sea-encircled strand.
"Hear me," she cried, "ye rising Realms! record
" Time's opening scenes, and Truth's unerring word.–
" *There* shall broad streets their stately walls extend,
" The circus widen, and the crescent bend;
" *There*, ray'd from cities o'er the cultur'd land,
" Shall bright canals, and solid roads expand.—
" *There* the proud arch, Colossus-like, bestride
" Yon glittering streams, and bound the chafing tide;
" Embellish'd villas crown the landscape-scene,
" Farms wave with gold, and orchards blush between.–
" *There* shall tall spires, and dome-capt towers ascend,
" And piers and quays their massy structures blend;
" While with each breeze approaching vessels glide,
"And northern treasures dance on every tide!"—
Then ceas'd the nymph– tumultuous echoes roar,
And Joy's loud voice was heard from shore to shore—
Her graceful steps descending press'd the plain,
And PEACE, and ART, and LABOUR, join'd her train.

Darwin's poem, lyrically evoking transplanted Georgian town planning, agrarian abundance, and bustling mercantile activity, sounded a note of optimism amid the inauspicious beginnings of the convict colony, and indicated that hopes for a better society in the antipodes had not died in Britain. Darwin looked beyond the sordid present into a time of future social harmony, economic prosperity —and respectability. 'Botany Bay', with its tainted associations of convictism, was to be transmuted into 'Sydney Cove'—a different place altogether.[2]

By the end of the third decade of British settlement in Australia, there were signs that Darwin's prophecy was about to be fulfilled. It was appropriate that a 'currency lad'—a young man born in the colony to a surgeon and a convict woman, and a member of an exploring party which pushed out the boundaries of the settlement by crossing the Blue Mountains in 1813 and sighting the fertile western plains—led the movement to elevate the colony from its position as a repository for convicts into a society of the free-born. Two literary works by this young man, William Charles Wentworth, signalled to the British public that the colony was ready to receive large numbers of free settlers to tip the balance against the convict influence. The first of these, *A Statistical, Historical, and Political Description of the Colony of New South Wales and its dependent Settlements in Van Diemen's Land ...*, was published in 1819, becoming a source book for those interested in emigrating to Australia.[3] Several years later, after entering Peterhouse to 'keep a few terms' at Cambridge, Wentworth wrote a poem for the Chancellor's gold medal on the set topic of 'Australasia', coming second out of twenty-seven entrants.[4] Ken Inglis has remarked that the 'winning poem offered a very remote view of the colonies', while Wentworth's 'established in the first line that the author was born there and was homesick'.[5] 'Australasia', dedicated to Governor Macquarie, prophesied a magnificent destiny for Britain's possession in the southern hemisphere, one which could be the salvation of Britishness in some dark future for the 'mother country':

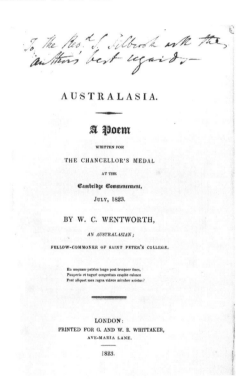

Title page of W. C. Wentworth's 'Australasia', with the author's handwriting at the top. National Library of Australia

> And, oh Britannia! shouldst thou cease to ride
> Despotic Empress of old Ocean's tide;—
> Should thy tam'd Lion—spent his former might,—
> No longer roar the terror of the fight;—
> Should e'er arrive that dark disastrous hour,
> When bow'd by luxury, thou yield'st to pow'r;—
> When thou, no longer freest of the free
> To some proud victor bend'st the vanquish'd knee;—
> May all thy glories in another sphere
> Relume, and shine more brightly still than here;
> May this, thy last-born infant,—then arise,
> To glad thy heart, and greet thy parent eyes;
> And Australasia float, with flag unfurl'd,
> A new Britannia in another world.[6]

Artists also contributed to an altered perception of the convict colony in New South Wales. In 1823, the same year as Wentworth's 'Australasia' was published, Londoners could visit Burford's in the Strand to view a mechanical panorama of the town of Sydney created by Major James Taylor in watercolour, published in aquatint by Robert Havell. The

Major James Taylor created this popular image of Sydney, which could be seen as part of a panorama at Burford's in the Strand in 1823.
National Library of Australia

panorama showed New South Wales 'in Arcadian terms, as a place where, contrary to historical record, all was harmonious'.[7] Bernard Smith has analysed the messages conveyed to the British audience by this popular work in *European Vision and the South Pacific*:

> Taylor contrives to appeal to the variety of interests which the Colony had aroused in England since its establishment. The officers of the 48th Regiment who walk in the grounds of the Military Hospital, and the Hospital itself with its convalescents in their long gowns, help to signify the rise of the civilized arts in the distant Colony, and are sharply contrasted with native groups beside their primitive dwellings. The natives themselves afford a further contrast between cultivated society and wild nature, since those in or near the precincts of the Hospital are clothed sufficiently not to give offence whereas those beside their own dwellings in the open fields still go stark naked. Similar contrasts are pointed by the cultivated European flowers in the hospital garden and the native

flowers beyond, and between the cleared pastures of the foreground and the monotonous brush of the Cumberland Plain looking towards the Blue Mountains in the distance.[8]

These works of literature and art heralded a wave of propaganda to induce emigration to the Australian colonies. In the mid-nineteenth century the names of Samuel Sidney, Alexander Harris and Caroline Chisholm were linked with that of the pre-eminent British novelist of the day—Charles Dickens. Emigration was seen as an answer to the plight of the urban and rural poor, always a concern of Dickens, and emigrants' guides such as Sidney's *Australian Hand-book* soon came to his notice. The *Hand-book* had published the works of Alexander Harris, who had spent sixteen years in the Australian colonies, and whose works, *Settlers and Convicts*, and later *The Emigrant Family*, reinforced the notion that by thrift and hard work a man could prosper in the antipodes. Sidney's *Handbook* had also published details of Mrs Caroline Chisholm's Family Colonization Loan Society, and letters to her from successful emigrants to the Australian colonies.[9]

Mrs Chisholm, unlike Samuel Sidney, who drew on his brother's Australian knowledge but had never been there himself, and the rather shadowy figure of Alexander Harris,[10] was a public figure, 'one of the most famous women in England'.[11] Robert Lowe, a supporter of Caroline Chisholm's family colonisation scheme, was one of a number of poets, both colonial and British, who inscribed tributes to her charitable work. They included Walter Savage Landor, Henry Kendall, and an anonymous poet in *Punch* magazine who penned 'A Carol on Caroline Chisholm' in 1853.[12] Lowe's tribute to Caroline Chisholm was written while she was still in the colony:

> The guardian angel of her helpless sex,
> Whom no fatigue could daunt, no crosses vex,
> With manly reason and with judgement sure,
> Crowned with the blessings of the grateful poor;
> For them, with unrepining love, she bore
> The boarded cottage and the earthen floor,
> The sultry day in tedious labour spent,
> The endless strain of whining discontent,
> Bore noonday's burning sun and midnight's chill,

*Caroline Chisholm,
by A. C. Hayter.
National Library of
Australia*

The scanty meal, the journey lengthening still;
Lavished her scanty store on their distress,
And sought no other guerdon than success.
Say, ye who hold the balance and the sword—
Into your lap the wealth of nations poured—
What have ye done with all your hireling brood
Compared with her, the generous and the good?
Much ye receive, and little ye dispense;
Your alms are paltry, and your debts immense;
Your toil's reluctant, freely hers is given:
You toil for earth, she labours still for heaven.[13]

On her return to Britain in 1845 from Sydney, where she had set up shelters for single women bounty emigrants to save them from prostitution and degradation, Mrs Chisholm's work to organise family migration to Australia also attracted Dickens' attention. He publicised it in his journal, *Household Words*, and became an enthusiastic proponent of her family colonisation scheme. Dickens admired Mrs Chisholm, but was unimpressed by her skills as a domestic manager after a visit to her Islington house, and could not resist the satirical impulse, possibly using her as one of the sources for the character of Mrs Jellyby, the tireless philanthropist in *Bleak House* who neglected her family responsibilities to organise a colonisation scheme in Africa.[14]

Mrs Jellyby, a minor character in *Bleak House*, was not the only possible literary outcome of Dickens' involvement with Caroline Chisholm, Samuel Sidney and other proponents of emigration schemes. Australia and emigration thereto provided him with a solution to an almost insoluble literary problem— what to do with the feckless but ever-optimistic Wilkins Micawber in *David Copperfield*, whose path in life, if continued, could lead only to degradation for himself and his numerous family. Coral Lansbury outlined Dickens' problem—and its solution:

Charles Dickens. Town and Country Journal, *25 June 1870*

> Dickens had Wilkins Micawber on his hands—undoubtedly the most unemployable character in literature. Dickens knew, as did his readers, that it was inconceivable that Micawber would ever find prosperity in the England of the Murdstones and Mr Dombey. Caroline Chisholm, with all the kindness and intelligence of Betsy Trotwood, convinced Dickens that there was a country where Micawber might well flourish.[15]

Dickens accordingly sent Micawber and his family to Port Middlebay—in reality, Melbourne—where against the odds he flourished, becoming a magistrate. The good-hearted Peggotty family also migrated, and the sad complement of 'fallen women' in their party—'little Em'ly' and Martha— found redemption in the bush of Australia.[16]

The Australian colonies repaid Dickens' positive attention to them by an enthusiastic reception of his books and their distinctive characters. The *Pickwick Papers* was published in a pirated edition in Tasmania in 1838, and sold 30 000 copies in the Australian colonies.[17] Coral Lansbury has described a Christmas party on Kangaroo Island in South Australia with a Pickwickian theme.[18] When Dickens died in 1870 Australia mourned his loss as that of a national hero. Newspapers and journals marked his passing with obituaries, including this tribute in verse from *Melbourne Punch*:

Toll the bell, soft and slow!

For he that lov'd us well is gather'd to his rest;

The head, that toil'd so long our mother-land to know,

Lies pillow'd on her breast.

…

The cunning hand is cold

That drew with wondrous skill the characters that live

In ev'ry heart—the good, the bad, the true, the bold,

The fondly amative.

…

Toll the bell—Peace to thee:

We owe thee hours of mirth and purifying tears.

Lov'd, cherish'd in a nation's heart thou e'er shalt be,

Through all the coming years.[19]

The transforming power of gold

While the waves of emigration to Australia and the successes some made of their lives there were slowly eroding the taint of Botany Bay, it took the discovery of gold in the early 1850s to transform British perceptions of Australia. The pattern of emigration shifted from families and disadvantaged single women to single males—gold seekers. Ken Inglis has described the effects of this change:

> Gold doubled the population of Australia in less than ten years. Half a million people sailed out from the United Kingdom between 1852 and 1861—more in some years than went to the United States, for at last Victoria and New South Wales really did have an advantage as places of emigration. More than half—a higher proportion than ever before—were people paying their own fares. In the golden colony of Victoria, to which most of the newcomers rushed, seven in every ten were unassisted. Gold drew a higher proportion of men with education, professional experience and good connexions.[20]

A decade after the gold rushes had begun, the Victorian government displayed a golden pyramid at the International Exhibition in London in

1862. 'A great centre of attraction', the golden pyramid was, according to William Hardman, 'one of the most interesting things in the Exhibition'[21] and was much commented upon. The *Illustrated London News*, for example, poetically described the 'Australian pillar of gold' as having 'just been set a-glittering by the midday sun'.[22] Victoria, whose government had 'gone to great expense to forward an enormous collection', nevertheless found itself subsumed within the general denominator of 'Australia'. The golden pyramid was a physical expression of the 'boosterism' of the Australian colonies, particularly gold-enriched Victoria. What the gilded pyramid—or obelisk—actually represented was 'the actual amount of gold found in the colony since 1851, about 800 tons, or £103 million sterling'. As if this wasn't enough to make a splash on the London scene, in addition Victoria's 'manufactures and industry are well represented, and a more extensive and varied collection has never before been sent from any British colony to Europe'.[23]

Gold was sensational, but wool—from the rich pastures of what explorer Thomas Mitchell had called 'Australia Felix'—was a steady and reliable source of prosperity, and one which attracted those with capital to invest in the Australian colonies. Its contribution to the colony's wealth was also displayed for the benefit of the crowds who visited the Exhibition in London: they saw in the Victorian exhibit 'a pair of trophies, one in the front and the other in the rear of their court, built up entirely of bales and samples of Port Phillip wool'. The extent of the wealth they represented was impressive; from its first settlement the colony had 'furnished upwards of 300 million bales of wool to markets of Europe, worth more than £20 million sterling'.[24] The *Record of the International Exhibition* commented that 'Notwithstanding the counter-attractions of the goldfields, the crop of wool has

Arch made from wool bales in the Victorian exhibit in the London International Exhibition of 1862. While gold had glamour, wool was a steady source of prosperity for the Australian colonies. Record of the International Exhibition 1862

not declined, but sheep farming is pursued as steadily and profitably as ever'.[25] From its original incarnation as 'Botany Bay', Australia was becoming the Land of the Golden Fleece.

A new life in a new land

What happened to those who took up the challenge of emigration to Australia last century? Their experiences were varied, but many accounts of British settler life in the Australian colonies have common elements. Diaries, letters, descriptions of the colony for intending emigrants tell of hardships endured, of homesickness, unfamiliar social patterns, the servant problem, and relations with the Aborigines, often reflecting a belief in racial and cultural superiority, and the notion that the land was empty for their taking—*terra nullius*—leading to the decimation of Aboriginal people and their dispossession of their land. Most became accustomed to the new land, appreciating the benefits of the move from Britain; but others were never reconciled to life in the Australian colonies and returned home. By the closing decades of the century some of the British migrants who stayed had become major contributors to the literary culture of the Australian colonies. Homesick Britishers would certainly have provided a large share of the market for the vast amount of British literature shipped out to Australia—one-third of the books published in Britain in the 1880s were sold in the Australian colonies.[26]

Getting there

Those travelling to the Australian colonies required considerable hardihood: the voyage out had its own perils and discomforts, before the then unfamiliar shores were reached. Perils of the sea, disagreeable companions, rodents and disease could be the companions of those setting out to make a new life in the antipodes. Mary McConnel,[27] who left 1840s Scotland for the colony at Moreton Bay (now Brisbane), related one of the trials of the passage:

> We had a disagreeable experience of rats abounding day and night. My husband knew my antipathy to these rodents, and brought two terriers with us—one from Skye, the other English. One we always had in our cabin, the

other was invariably out on loan! When at meals I always sat with my heels under me, the only protection I could have at these times. At 10 p.m., Mrs Hobbs, the doctor's mother, used to have supper in the Cuddy, which was usually bread and cheese and porter. I sometimes sat and chatted with her while she was having it. One night a large rat came on the table, and went straight for the cheese, when there was quite a tussle, but the old lady came off victorious. I did not go anymore ... [28]

Mary McConnel had her first sight of Moreton Bay on 1 May 1849, and was desolated by the sight: 'What a dreary waste of water the bay looked ... It seemed really to me as if we had come to the end of the known world, and no other had dawned upon us'.[29]

David and Mary McConnel, who arrived in Australia in 1849, and were early settlers in the area which is now the Brisbane suburb of Bulimba. National Library of Australia

Settling in

George Fletcher Moore emigrated to Western Australia in 1830 and lived there for ten years. His letters were later published and give a vivid picture of settler life in a new colony. They describe the problems of farming, contacts with the Aborigines, the servant problem, and give advice to intending immigrants. After a year in the colony he wrote an optimistic song, which he sang at the first ball given by Governor Stirling in Perth in September 1831:

From the old Western world, we have come to explore
The wilds of this Western Australian shore;
In search of a country, we've ventured to roam,
And now that we've found it, let's make it our home.
    And what though the colony's new, Sirs,
    And inhabitants yet may be few, Sirs,

We see them *encreasing* here too, Sirs,
So *Western Australia* for me.

With care and experience, I'm sure 'twill be found
Two crops in the year we may get from the ground;
There's good wood and good water, good flesh and good fish,
Good soil and good clime, and what more could you wish.
  Then let everyone earnestly strive, Sirs,
  Do his best, be alert and alive, Sirs,
  We'll soon see our colony thrive, Sirs,
  So *Western Australia* for me.

No lions or tigers we dread here to meet,
Our innocent *quadrupeds* hop on *two feet*;
No tithes and no taxes we now have to pay,
And our *geese* are all *swans*, as some witty folks say.
  Then we live without trouble or stealth, Sirs,
  Our currency's all sterling wealth, Sirs,
  So here's to our Governor's health, Sirs,
  And *Western Australia* for me.[30]

Early settlers in the Australian colonies did what they could to reproduce in the bush the comforts of a British home. Ada Cambridge, a clergyman's wife and later to become one of Australia's best known colonial novelists, described the hospitality she experienced in the home of a Victorian settler:

I used to be much struck with the contrast of his cherished 'imported' furniture with its homely setting—the cheval glass and the mahogany wardrobe on the perhaps bare, dark-grey hardwood floor—incongruities of that sort, which somehow always seemed in taste. Never have I known greater luxury of toilet appointments than in some of those hut-like dwellings. In the humblest of them the bed stood always ready for the casual guest, a clean brush and comb on the dressing-table, and the easy house-slippers under it. And then the paper-covered canvas walls used to belly out and in with the wind that puffed behind them; oppossums used to get in under the roof and run over the canvas ceilings, which sagged under their weight, showing the impression of their little feet and the round of their bodies where they sat down.[31]

Distance

The distance between them dominated the relationships of those who emigrated and those they left behind. For much of the nineteenth century letters were the only way in which those relationships could be maintained. Graeme Davison has described the problems besetting these correspondents on both sides of the world:

> We seldom consider how deeply the consciousness of early colonial Australians was marked by the time-gap in communication between themselves and the Mother Country. At a personal level, it meant that every letter home was written in the knowledge that, by the time it was received, three months later, the circumstances that prompted it may have entirely changed, and even that

George Baxter's painting, News from Australia, *shows the delight that a letter from the Australian colonies could bring to those back in England.* National Library of Australia

the recipient or the sender may no longer be alive. Understandably, people sometimes did not write immediately with ominous news, but awaited the outcome, good or bad, rather than leave their loved ones at the other end of the world suspended in uncertainty ... Australian immigrants and their families frequently remind themselves of the agonising time-gap that separated them. As they report on how they are, they try to anticipate how their news will find the recipients many months hence. More versed in speech than writing, and used to the easy familiarity of daily contact, they struggle to make their feelings felt across the great gulf of time and space.[32]

Charles Lamb in London provided a poignant example of this problem. He strove vainly to bridge the distance between himself and his friend Barron Field in Sydney, and wondered about the nature of society there in a letter, later published in *The Essays of Elia* as 'Distant Correspondents':

My dear F.—When I think how welcome the sight of a letter from the world where you were born must be to you in that strange one to which you have been transplanted, I feel some compunctious visitings at my long silence. But, indeed, it is no easy effort to set about a correspondence at a distance. The weary world of waters between us oppresses the imagination. It is difficult to conceive how a scrawl of mine should ever stretch across it. It is a sort of presumption to expect that one's thoughts should live so far ... I cannot imagine to myself whereabouts you are. When I try to fix it, Peter Wilkins's island comes across me. Sometimes you seem to be in the *Hades of Thieves*. I see Diogenes prying among you with his perpetual fruitless lantern. What must you be willing by this time to give for the sight of an honest man! You must almost have forgotten how *we* look. And tell me what your Sydneyites do? are they thieving all day long? Merciful Heaven! what property can stand against such a depredation! ... Is there much difference to see, too, between the son of a thief and the grandson? or where does the taint stop? Do you bleach in three or four generations? ... I am insensibly chatting to you as familiarly as when we used to exchange good-morrows out of our old contiguous windows, in pump-famed Hare Court in the Temple. Why did you ever leave that quiet corner?—Why did I?—with its complement of four poor elms, from whose smoke-dyed barks, the theme of jesting ruralists, I picked my first ladybirds! My heart is as dry as that spring sometimes proves in a thirsty August, when I revert to the space that is between us; a length of passage enough to render obsolete the phrases of our English letters before they reach you.[33]

Rachel Henning came first to Australia in 1853, returned to England three years later, then settled permanently in Australia in 1861. Her letters to her family, written between 1853 and 1882, were published in the *Bulletin* in 1951 and 1952, and illustrated by Norman Lindsay. Dale Spender has described Rachel Henning as 'one of the most significant contributors to the Australian literary tradition', a 'pioneer in every sense of the word' who 'gave a new dimension to story-telling when she took the art of letter writing to new heights', and the book based on her letters is one of the most illuminating and readable accounts of colonial life available.[34]

Social differences

Emigrants to the Australian colonies could not expect to find the niceties of social distinction preserved in what was a frontier environment, and for some of them this was a disturbing feature of colonial life, and one which they hoped to see improved in time. Mary McConnel was horrified at the treatment she and her husband received while staying at an inn at Wivenhoe in Queensland:

> We had a private room, if one could call such a room private, the partition of which, separating it from the public room, was of woodern [sic] boards six feet high! It was the same in our bedroom ... We were very tired, and glad to return to rest. Through the space between the partition and the shingled roof every sound was heard, and, as the night wore on, the talk of the bullock-drivers became unbearable. My husband went to the landlord to ask if he could not quiet them. It was no use; their money was as good as other people's, they said, so we had to endure it ... [35]

Well-to-do settlers in Australia often complained about the problems of servants—getting them, keeping them, and dealing with a different social atmosphere in which deference by servants towards their employers was by no means guaranteed. Rachel Henning's description is typical of the complaints found in many accounts of life in the Australian colonies:

You have no idea what a plague the servants are here. If a few married ladies meet, it is quite ridiculous to hear the chorus of lamentation that they strike up. One has had a new American stove knocked to pieces; another every scrap of crockery broken; another her gowns pawned; another, bills run up in her name in every shop in the town. All the buckets have been let fall down all the wells and the name of the 'followers' is legion. I suppose it is an evil that will mend itself as more servants come out here ... [36]

Aborigines

Dealings with Aboriginal people were an important subject in settler accounts of life in Australia. William Thornley, in *An Emigrant in Van Diemen's Land*, gave a hair-raising account of an attack by Aborigines which saw his farm burned and nearly resulted in his death.[37] Mary McConnel and Rachel Henning, both at the time in Queensland, describe contacts with Aboriginal people, and reveal the contemporary attitudes which led to the dispossession of the indigenous people so graphically described in the works of historians such as Henry Reynolds.[38]

British settlers distinguished between two types of Aboriginal people—servants and 'wild blacks'. The first provided a source of amusement and required saint-like patience to deal with their odd ways; the second were feared and pushed with considerable violence away from the settled areas. Mary McConnel described some of the first group encountering a church service: 'When they saw people going in and singing, etc, they said, "Goorai! budgery corobery!" and when the sermon began one or two of the men gesticulated like the minister, upsetting him a good deal ...'[39] She also revealed the prevailing attitude of white settlers towards Aboriginal ownership of the land, in her description of an Aboriginal woman, 'Long Kitty', at Cressbrook station: 'She would look proudly over the country and say, stretching out her arms, "All this 'yarmen' (land) belonging to me." It did seem hard to have it all taken from them, but it had to be. They cultivated nothing: they were of no use on it.'[40]

Rachel Henning described the way in which Aboriginal men working for her brother helped to retrieve belongings stolen by tribal Aborigines at Exmoor station, near Bowen in Queensland:

We had the wild blacks on the run last week. They came down from the hills and robbed the shepherd's hut at the Two Mile station, carrying off everything he possessed; even his comb. Biddulph and the two station blacks Alick and Billy gave chase, and tracked the tribe to their camp among the hills, where they found the whole of the stolen property. They burnt the camp, and brought away all their weapons, as a lesson to them to keep off the run in future; but Biddulph would not allow the boys to shoot them as they were very anxious to do. They brought away some curiously carved boomerangs, and some most formidable-looking clubs made of a very heavy sort of wood, and with rough teeth carved on the top of them.[41]

On another occasion Henning reported a visit from the Mounted Police who were 'in pursuit of two runaway blacks', but 'on their way back they are going to stop and clear our station of wild blacks'.[42] In these few simple words is encapsulated the policy of 'dispersal' of tribal Aboriginal people as practised in colonial Queensland, using the feared Mounted Native Police whose ferocity against their own kind was legendary.

Henning's Aboriginal servants, Alick and Biddy, and their domestic spats, were the comic turn of her letters, and their treatment by the other servants at least preserved one of the social distinctions, when she reported their meal arrangements: 'The blacks are not allowed to dine with the white aristocracy. They "takes their meals in the wash'ouse", or, in other words, on a bench outside the kitchen door.'[43]

The literary scene

In 1866 George Barton, historian and literary critic, and brother of Edmund Barton, who became the first prime minister of the Commonwealth of Australia in 1901, began his survey of literature in New South Wales with these words:

To trace the growth of letters in this community, from the earliest period of our history to the present time, and to shew in what manner that growth has been influenced by the productions of the 'Mother Country' are the objects sought to be accomplished in these pages. With us, Literature requires to be considered in two aspects: first, as a native or indigenous product; and secondly, as a foreign or imported one. Too young to possess a 'national literature' of our own, the consideration of foreign influence becomes an all-important one.[44]

The difficulties of nurturing a 'national literature' were indeed great: Barton described the comparative success of local and imported periodical literature and books, with the balance heavily in favour of the latter. English periodicals, for example, were in great demand: the local community was 'prejudiced against local productions—or, if not prejudiced, at least unwilling to support them'.[45] There were other obstacles to the publishing of local literature in Sydney: 'The first is, that the expense is nearly twice as great; and the second, that no work published in the Colonies has any chance of finding a sale in London'.[46] Barton's complaints were to be echoed for many years by Australian writers, who were obliged either to go to London to find a publisher or, alternatively, to achieve success there before being accepted as a success back in Australia. Nevertheless, Barton believed that his survey of literature in New South Wales would demonstrate that the fledgling Australian literary scene showed some promise:

Moore's Australian Book Mart, Sydney, 1870, one of the stores which were selling one-third of British book production to Australian colonists by the 1880s.
Illustrated Sydney News, *11 May 1870*

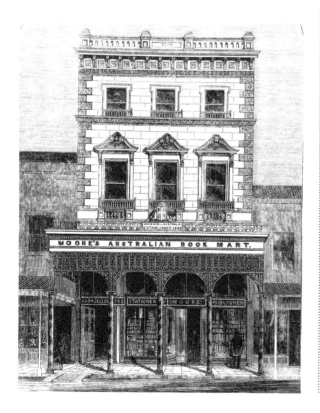

Looking at this catalogue of our performances, it will probably be considered that more has been done among us in the way of literature than might have been expected. We have not suffered ourselves to be discouraged by the difficulties in our path, and we have not neglected the few advantages we possess. In every department of letters we have produced something of more or less value—something to show that original intellects have been at work ... we may say that the rough groundwork of a 'national literature' has been laid. One or two volumes display the unmistakeable hand of genius. The splendid scenery of our native land has not remained unsung; something distinctively Australian has resulted from its worship. In prose Fiction, more than one creditable effort has been made. The History of the Colony—in a great measure, of all Australia—has been exhaustively written. Our narratives of Exploration have been read with interest in circles far beyond our own firesides.[47]

The export of Australian literature to Britain became a common phenomenon. The success of writers such as Rolf Boldrewood and Marcus Clarke in Britain is well attested, and non-fiction titles were also popular, for example, the 'narratives of exploration' mentioned by Barton had commanded a wide audience in Britain. Many writers' work was serialised in magazines in Australia before its publication in Britain in book form. Ada Cambridge was one such writer who, with two other Australian women writers, Rosa Praed and Tasma (Jessie Couvreur) was published extensively in Britain. Cambridge, Praed and Tasma worked in the tradition of what Susan Sheridan has called 'the domestic romance in an Australian setting' which 'may be thought of as a colonial survival of the Jane Austen novel, a tale of courtship and marriage, concerned

with the relationships between moral character and social status in a period of gradual social transition'.[48] Many short stories by Australian writers found their way into anthologies which encouraged links between British and Australian readers. Fiona Giles, working in the British Library, found many such stories when researching works by nineteenth century Australian women writers published in anthologies with titles such as *Coo-ee: Tales of Australian Life by Australian Ladies* of 1891, and *By Creek and Gully: Stories and Sketches … by Australian Writers in England* of 1899.[49]

By the closing decades of the century, when Australians were debating, then preparing for the political union of the Australian colonies, the writers among them were still obliged to seek the imprimatur of London endorsement before they could be fully accepted in their native land. Australia, despite the surge of nationalist writing in the 1890s fostered by the new journal, the *Bulletin*, was still 'a new Britannia'—acceptance by the old Britannia was, for many, a necessary precondition of their writer's status. The call of London was for them at least as compelling as the call of the Australian bush.

Ada Cambridge, who came to Victoria in 1870 with her clergyman husband, George Cross. A prolific novelist, she also wrote poetry and two autobiographical works, Thirty Years in Australia *and* The Retrospect. *National Library of Australia*

4

BUGLES OF ENGLAND

In February 1885 the news reached Australia, via the electric telegraph, that a hero of the British Empire, General Charles Gordon, had been slain by the insurgent forces of the Mahdi at Khartoum in the Sudan. This incident inspired the formation of the first of the 'expeditionary forces' that Australia would send to Britain's wars, a tradition that endured until the mid-twentieth century. British and Australian writers began to talk about Australians and war, and the theme has persisted in the literature of both countries ever since.

Speculation as to whether Britain would accept an offer by William Bede Dalley, the acting premier of the colony of New South Wales, of a military contingent to help fight the Mahdi and avenge Gordon's death even took travelling historian James Anthony Froude's mind off the savage mosquito bites he had sustained while staying at Sydney's exclusive Australian Club: 'The club reading-room after breakfast was full of gentlemen in eager and anxious conversation on the auxiliary force. Was it right to have made the offer, and would the offer be accepted?'[1] Opinion was not unanimous: Froude reported some people saying that 'this Egyptian war was a war of England's own seeking, and for them to mix themselves up with it would be at once gratuitous and useless, and an unjustifiable burden upon the colonial resources'.[2]

The waiting time was anxious; Froude now experienced for himself the effects of distance from Britain that always made Australians feel isolated from the scene of decision-making, even with improved communications. His historian's mind perceived the irony of the situation: 'The answer from Lord Derby had been delayed. Something was said to be wrong with the telegraph on the Persian frontier. Strange to think that communication between London and an island at the Antipodes should be carried on through ancient Parthia and across the rivers of Ecbatana and Babylon'.[3] But the problem was overcome: 'the wires were replaced quickly, and brought a warm and grateful assent'. Froude, an imperial federationist, watched with interest the reaction to the news and, while he reported the contrary view, believed that his assumptions as to the essential 'Englishness' of the Australian colonists were proving to be well-founded:

Visiting English historian J. A. Froude saw for himself the enthusiasm of the people of New South Wales about sending a contingent to the Sudan in February 1885. National Library of Australia

To be allowed to share in the perils and glories of the battlefield, as part of a British army, was regarded at once as a distinction of which Australia might be proud and as a guarantee of their future position as British subjects. The help which they were now giving might be slight, but Australia in a few years would number ten millions of men, and this small body was an earnest of what they might do hereafter. If ever England herself was threatened, or if there was another mutiny in India, they would risk life, fortune—all they had—as willingly as they were sending their present contingent. It was a practical demonstration in favour of Imperial unity.

Volunteers crowded to enrol their names. Patriotic citizens gave money on a scale which showed that little need be feared for the taxpayer. Archbishop Moran, the Catholic Primate, gave a hundred pounds, as an example and instruction to the Irish; others, the wealthy ones, gave a thousand. The rush of feeling was curious and interesting to witness. The only question with me was if it would last … If the force went and was cut to pieces, if it was kept in garrison and not exposed in the field, if it suffered from sickness or from any one of the innumerable misadventures to which troops on active service are liable, the sense of glory might turn to discontent, the tide would change, and worse might follow than if the enterprise had never been ventured. The opposition was not silenced; I listened for a quarter of an hour to an orator haranguing a crowd in a public park. He spoke well, and I was glad that I had not to answer him. 'What was this war in the Soudan?' he said; 'who were these poor Arabs, and why were we killing them? By our own confession they were brave men who were fighting for the liberty of their country. Why had we invaded them? Did we want to take their country from them? If it was necessary for our own safety there would be some excuse, but we had ostentatiously declared that after conquering them we intended to withdraw. Neither we nor anyone could tell what we wanted' …

The crowd listened, and here and there, especially when the speaker dwelt on the right of all people to manage their own affairs, there were mur-

The Bulletin *satirised the 'jingoes' who were eager for war in 1885.* National Library of Australia

How About "Dilly" Dalley, Now?

murs of approval; but the immense majority were indifferent or hostile. The man, in fact, was speaking beside the mark. The New South Wales colonists cared nothing about the Sudan. They were making a demonstration in favour of national identity ... There was a desire, too, to show those who had scorned the colonists, and regarded them as a useless burden on the Imperial resources, that they were as English as the English at home. We might refuse them a share in our successes. We could not and should not refuse them a share in our trials. 'You do not want us', they seemed to say, 'but we are part of you, bone of your bone; we refuse to be dissociated from you'.[4]

Froude's fear that the New South Wales contingent would be used in a secondary role in the Sudan was prophetic: the contingent returned to public indifference, and disappointment that they had done nothing more dashing than build a railway. The patriotic fervour that greeted the acceptance of Dalley's offer had given way to ridicule of the 'jingoes', particularly by the new force in Australian literary and cultural life, the nationalistic magazine, the *Bulletin*. Its satirising of 'a little boy at Manly' who had volunteered his penny to help to avenge General Gordon was an effective counter to the sabre-rattlers.[5]

War in South Africa

In 1899 Britain called upon her Australian colonies for troops to fight the Boers in South Africa. The Australian colonial governments, fearful of another Sudan-type anticlimax, initially held back. Nevertheless, once troops were committed, imperial patriotism once more became a dominant theme, although some eminent citizens, such as G. Arnold Wood of the University of Sydney, made no secret of their opposition, and the *Bulletin* once again declared itself against the involvement of Australian troops on the eve of the federation of the colonies. This war, too, despite some high points such as the relief of Mafeking, was not one to be much celebrated in literature, despite the fact that Andrew Barton (Banjo) Paterson was a war correspondent. It is remembered by many in Australia, in fact, because a minor literary figure, Harry 'The Breaker' Morant, was executed with another Australian soldier for shooting Boer prisoners and a German missionary. He penned a poem, 'Butchered to Make a Dutchman's Holiday' in his cell while awaiting execution, giving his comrades this advice:

> But we bequeath a parting tip
>> For sound advice of such men,
> Who come across in transport ship
>> To polish off the Dutchmen!
>
> If you encounter any Boers
>> You really must not loot 'em!
> And if you wish to leave these shores,
>> For pity's sake, DON'T SHOOT 'EM![6]

Much of the literature inspired by the Boer War took the form of imperialist doggerel, but one of the more disturbing works written about the war in Australia was a parody of Rudyard Kipling's 'The White Man's Burden', by J. K. McDougall, which pictured the troops fighting in South Africa as the tools of plutocrats:

> Ye are the White Man's engines;
> Ye fight and force for him;
> Fill up his cup of vengeance,
> Yea, fill it to the brim.
> Paid bullies of the robbers,
> Your murders are not sin;
> Kill for the trusts and jobbers—
> Sock ye the bay'nets in.[7]

Joseph Furphy, author of the celebrated Australian novel, *Such is Life*, also turned a satiric eye on Australian soldiers as dupes of money power and imperialism:

> O be sure the Good Time Coming shall achieve its glorious birth
> When the patriot owns his blunder, and the boodler owns the earth![8]

Australians and the First World War

Memories of less-than-glorious military actions are short, and new nations bent on proving themselves are prone to extravagant gestures. When war broke out in August 1914, Australia's prime minister to be, Andrew Fisher, pledged to support the mother country to the utmost limits. Patriotic fervour for the empire's cause ran high, and men rushed the recruiting stations to enlist in the Australian Imperial Force (AIF). Corporal J. D. Burns penned 'For England' before he enlisted in the First AIF. He served at Gallipoli, and was killed in action in September 1915. His poem expressing the idealism of the young Australian recruits to the cause of empire, resembling that of their Sudan contingent forebears thirty years before, became a popular patriotic work in Australia and England:

> The bugles of England were blowing o'er the sea,
> As they had called a thousand years, calling now to me:
> They woke me from dreaming in the dawning of the day,
> The bugles of England—and how could I stay?
>
> . . .
>
> O, England, I heard the cry of those who died for thee,
> Sounding like an organ-voice across the winter sea;
> They lived and died for England, and gladly went their way,
> England, O England—how could *I* stay?[9]

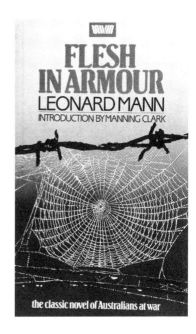

Leonard Mann's novel Flesh in Armour *tells the story of Australian soldiers on the Western Front, and on leave in England. Allen & Unwin Australia*

Australian writers and artists in the fighting forces, like their British counterparts, were affected profoundly by the experience. The First World War produced many novels by Australians describing the soldier's life. These include Martin Boyd, *When Blackbirds Sing*, Ion L. Idriess, *The Desert Column*, Frank Dalby Davison, *The Wells of Beersheba*, and H. R. Williams, *The Gallant Company*.[10] Leonard Mann's *Flesh in Armour* paints a vivid picture of Australian soldiers in London, in the trenches of the western front, and in hospital in Britain.[11] Frederic Manning served in a British regiment on the Somme and Ancre fronts in 1916, and in his novel *Her Privates We* he drew on this experience to convey the sights and sounds of trench warfare. He described the period of waiting before an attack on an enemy position.

> The boy on the firestep watched his front intently. The expectation that he would see something move, or a sudden flash there, became almost desire. But nothing moved. The world grew more and more still; the dark became thinner; soon they would stand to. He could see the remains of the building now, almost clearly. There was nothing there, nothing, the world was empty, hushed,

awaiting dawn. And then, as he watched it less keenly, something from the skies smote that heap of rubble, the shadowy landscape in front of him blurred and danced, and a solid pillar of blackness rose into the air even before he heard the explosion, spreading out thicker at the top like an evil fungus; spread, and dissolved again, and the heap of rubble was no longer there.[12]

Australians gained a new image in Britain: as gallant soldiers, but no respecters of authority. In some works by British authors—both autobiographical and fictional—they were assigned a darker reputation. Robert Graves, in his autobiography, *Goodbye to All That*, relates atrocity stories which describe Australian soldiers committing violent acts against German prisoners. Graves, declaring that the only thing to be said of Australians 'was that they were only two generations removed from the days of Ralph Rashleigh and Marcus Clarke', and that they may have achieved their brutal reputation from 'the overseas habit of bragging and leg-pulling', then provided a 'first-hand account' of an Australian soldier's action:

An Australian: 'Well, the biggest lark I had was at Morlancourt when we took it the first time. There were a lot of Jerries in a cellar and I said to 'em: "Come out, you Camarades." So out they came, a dozen of 'em, with their hands up. "Turn out your pockets," I told 'em. They turned 'em out. Watches and gold and stuff, all dinkum. Then I said: "Now back to your cellar, you sons of bitches." For I couldn't be bothered with 'em. When they were all down I threw half a dozen Mills bombs in after 'em. I'd got the stuff all right, and we weren't taking prisoners that day.'[13]

Works of fiction, such as Anthony Price's 1974 novel, *Other Paths to Glory*, perpetuate the negative aspects of the reputation of Australia's First World War soldiers while expressing admiration for their fighting qualities. Price's old British soldier recalling an incident during the battle of the Somme in 1916 almost parallels Graves' account of the behaviour of Australian soldiers:

... 'Arr—the Aussies—Anzacs we called 'em then—they were the boys! Steal the shine off your buttons, they would. Good lads, though—Jerry was scared of them, I reckon. Don't blame him.'

'It was the Australians who relieved your battalion on Hameau Ridge, wasn't it?'

'That's right. Came through Bully Wood at the double when I was helping with the wounded—cor, and they were fightin' mad then! "No prisoners" they were shoutin'—"No prisoners". They'd had some trouble with prisoners, that's what one of 'em told me … And there was this Jerry prisoner too, just a kid, and this Aussie comes up and says "Stand up", and Jerry stands up— and I *knew* what he was goin' to do an' I says "You can't do that" an' he says "You just watch me, mate" and he poops him.'

'Poops him?'

'Kills him—shoots him. "That's settled the bugger", he says, and off he goes as cool as you like. I remember that just like it happened yesterday— "That's settled the bugger", he says. Cor!'

If Sanitary Corporal Hayhoe had felt any disapproval at Australian behaviour in 1916, the passage of time had erased it, reducing it to history. There was even a faint suggestion of admiration, a tacit acknowledgement that maybe the killer had been acting with instinctive logic better suited to conditions in Bully Wood at the time.[14]

Women and the war

Australian women writers responded in different ways to the war. Novelist and journalist Mary Marlowe became a nurse at Quex House in Kent, the home—and museum— of noted collector Major Powell-Cotton, which had been converted into a military hospital; and Mary Edgeworth David was an army driver in London and Edinburgh.[15] Louise Mack was in Belgium at the outbreak of war and wrote of her experiences in *A Woman's Experiences in the Great War*, and Miles Franklin served as a nurse in Serbia with the Scottish Women's Hospital at Ostrovo.[16] Novelists Mary Grant Bruce and Ethel Turner, who wrote for young people, quickly produced novels featuring characters—Jim and Wally in the case of Mary Grant Bruce's *Billabong* series, and 'the Cub' in the novels of Ethel Turner—replete with manly virtues who left Australia to go to war, and deriding the 'slackers' who would not 'do their bit' for the empire's cause.[17]

Louise Mack wrote of her experiences in wartime Belgium in A Woman's Experiences in the Great War, *published in 1915.* National Library of Australia

Vance Palmer evoked the desolation of the landscape after a battle in his poem 'The Farmer Remembers the Somme'. National Library of Australia

Memories of war

By war's end, disillusionment with the patriotic fervour that had motivated so many to enlist had set in. Two unsuccessful conscription campaigns in 1916 and 1917 had divided the Australian community. Some writers could not shake off the grim memories of war. Martin Boyd concluded his novel *When Blackbirds Sing* with his hero, Dominic, throwing his medals, including his Military Cross, into the pond on his farm. These medals had, he believed, been 'given him for his share in inflicting that suffering, that agony multiplied and multiplied beyond the possibility of calculation'.[18] Vance Palmer's poem, 'The Farmer Remembers the Somme', pictures a returned soldier farmer haunted by visions of the wartime past amid the scenes of his daily life:

I have returned to these:
The farm, and the kindly Bush, and the young calves lowing;
But all that my mind sees
Is a quaking bog in a mist—stark, snapped trees,
And the dark Somme flowing.[19]

From the time of the landing at Gallipoli and throughout the war and beyond, the name of C. E. W. Bean became synonymous with the Anzac legend. First his journalistic accounts, then his official histories of the campaigns, defined the First World War for Australians. He was the inspiration behind the creation of the Australian War Memorial, and the relics he and his team collected at Gallipoli in 1919—a journey recollected in his 1948 book, *Gallipoli Mission*—were the genesis of its magnificent collections of the artefacts of war.

The Second World War

Works of literature dealing with the Second World War are just as numerous and diverse as those associated with the earlier world conflict. As well as novels, memoirs and poems dealing with the traditional battlefront of the infantryman, there are works about the air force, the navy—and the prisoner of war camp.[20] Australian soldiers captured after the failure of the campaign in Greece and Crete in 1941 were interned in German prisoner of war camps. Barney Roberts in his memoir, *A Kind of Cattle*, and Don Watt, in *Stoker*, tell of their experiences in German prison camps, with the latter imprisoned in the horrific conditions of Auschwitz.[21] The fall of the British fortress in the Far East, the Singapore naval base, in February 1942 meant the internment of the Australian Eighth Division, along with other units of the British Army, in the prison camps of the Japanese. Russell Braddon caused a sensation with his 1952 novel, *The Naked Island*, about his four years as a prisoner of war in Changi and on the Burma–Thailand railroad. The text of the book was complemented by British artist Ronald Searle's drawings made in Changi.[22] Randolph Stow's novel, *The Merry-Go-Round in the Sea*, and David Malouf's *The Great World* both draw on the experiences of Australians as prisoners of the Japanese.[23]

Seeing Britain's war at first hand

As in the previous war, many Australian servicemen, such as the 27 000 who had enlisted in the Empire Air Training Scheme and served in the Royal Air Force, spent time training and on leave in Britain.[24] Civilians also shared wartime experiences with the British people. Manning Clark at Oxford became aware of war approaching as he prepared his Master of Arts thesis on the nineteenth-century French historian, Alexis de Tocqueville. What was happening around him was too pressing to be excluded, the present and the recent past obtruding into his scholarly endeavours, as he explained in the preface to his thesis:

> October 1938 was an unpropitious moment to begin historical research: The lights of the 'low, dishonest decade' were flickering fitfully; only the Cliveden set and the pacifists were striving to keep them alight. Some students comforted themselves with the reflection that Boethius had written his 'Consolations of Philosophy' while the barbarians were sacking Rome, while Henri Pirenne had written his 'History of Europe' without books or notes as a Belgian prisoner of war in Germany. In retrospect the hopes with which we calmed our troubled minds seem not only pretentious but pathetic. We clung desperately to the illusion that our activities were important, though no one

knew why. Even on Friday September 1st, 1939, none of the regular readers at the Bodleian were absent. At lunch time the attendant merely asked us to bring our gas masks in the afternoon: research as usual appeared to be the motto of the students. If the past was our escape from the present, at least there was a tacit assumption that this painful reproach should not be mentioned in our presence. And what better introduction to dream-land could the student have than the musty tomes and the sheltered rooms of the Bodleian Library?[25]

Australian Prime Minister Robert Menzies on 3 September 1939 broadcasts to the nation the news of the outbreak of the Second World War.
National Library of Australia

Australia's prime minister Robert Menzies broadcast to his fellow Australians on 3 September 1939 the news that they were at war as a consequence of Britain declaring war on Germany after the Nazi invasion of Poland. Menzies then travelled to London in 1941 to consult with Winston Churchill and the British War Cabinet about Australia's role in the conflict, and witnessed the effects of the Blitz, which he experienced at first hand, describing in his diary, later published as *Dark and Hurrying Days*, an air raid on London on 16 April 1941:

Tonight the enemy is passing overhead. You can hear him. The search lights are operating—and the crack of the guns in the park opposite is deafening ...

Later. I was wrong. They were not passing. 460 of them were attacking London, and a dozen large bombs fell within 100 yards of the Dorchester. It was a terrible experience. Invited up to the second floor for a drink with two elderly ladies ... we had scarcely sat down when a great explosion and blast shattered the windows of the room, blew the curtains in, split the door, and filled the room with acrid fumes. Twice the whole building seemed to bounce with the force of the concussion. Twice I visited the ground floor, and found it full of white-faced people ...

The sky beyond the Palace was red with fire and smoke, the sky was flashing like lightning. It is a horrible sound to hear the whistle of a descending stick of bombs, any one of them capable of destroying a couple of five-storey houses, and to wonder for a split second if it is going to land on your windows!

Just before dawn, at about 5 a.m., Tritton, Landau and I went for a walk to see the damage. There were buildings down and great craters within 100 yards of the hotel on the side away from the park. In Brook Street buildings were blazing. A great plume of red smoke rose from Selfridge's. Gas mains blazed in Piccadilly. The houses fronting the Green Park were red and roaring. There were craters and fallen masonry in the streets, and the fear of an unexploded bomb lurking around every corner. Wherever we walked, we crunched over acres of broken glass. This is the 'new order'. How can it go on for years?[26]

Poets at war

War's grim realities, not patriotic effusions, are paramount in the creative writing of Australians about this last worldwide conflict in which their country was involved in conjunction with British forces. For Australian poet Michael Thwaites, a lieutenant in the Royal Volunteer Naval Reserve, the gallantry of Captain Fogarty Fegen, commander of the merchant cruiser H.M.S. *Jervis Bay*, pitted against the Nazi battleship *Admiral Scheer*, ranked with other heroic and decisive moments of history and legend. The *Jervis Bay*, with its 'few old six-inch guns' and its 'meagre fourteen knots', was no match for the *Admiral Scheer*, armed with eleven-inch guns in triple turrets, the 'pride of the German builders' craft'. Thwaites, in his poem, 'The *Jervis Bay*', pictures the moment when Fegen, in defence of the convoy his ship was escorting, turns at bay and faces the enemy—and certain death:

Rarely it comes, and unforeseen,
In the life of a man, a community, a nation,
The moment that knits up struggling diversity
In one, the changing transverse lights
Focussed to a pin-point's burning intensity
Rarely and unforeseen.

But in a minute is the timeless and absolute
Fulfilment of centuries and civilisations,
When the temporal skin lays bare the eternal bone,

And this mortal puts on immortality.
In that stark flash the unregarding universe
Is a hushed agony. The suns and planets
Stay: the dewdrop dares not tremble:
The dead leaf in the electric air
Waits: and the waterfall still as a photograph
Hangs in that intolerable minute.
And the dead and the living, all are there
With those that shall be, all Creation
Pausing poised in the ticking of Eternity,
Held at one white point of crisis.
But what does he know, he at the focus,
The man or the nation? Joy and terror knows,
But chiefly a blessèd sweet release,
The complex equation at a stroke resolved
To simple terms, a single choice,
Rarely and unforeseen.

So Fegen stood, and Time dissolved,
And Cradock with his ships steamed out
From Coronel, and in the pass
Of Roncesvalles a horn was sounding,
And Oates went stumbling out alone
Into that Antarctic night,
And Socrates the hemlock drank
And paid his debts and laid him down,
And through the fifty-three, *Revenge*
Ran on, as in Thermopylæ
The cool-eyed Spartans looked about,
Childe Roland, trembling, took and blew,
The *Jervis Bay* went hard-a-port.

'Hard-a-port' and 'Hard-a-port, sir.' The white spray flying,
She heeled and turned and steadied her course for where the foe was lying,
And not a man but knew the fate that he had turned to meet
And yet was stirred to fight till death and never know retreat.[27]

Kenneth Slessor, Australian poet and war correspondent, pondered the pathos of war in 'Beach Burial', a poem written in the aftermath of the

battle of El Alamein. It is arguably one of the greatest literary works produced by an Australian on the theme of war:

Softly and humbly to the Gulf of Arabs
The convoys of dead sailors come;
At night they sway and wander in the waters far under,
But morning rolls them in the foam.

Between the sob and clubbing of the gunfire
Someone, it seems, has time for this,
To pluck them from the shallows and bury them in burrows
And tread the sand upon their nakedness;

And each cross, the driven stake of tidewood,
Bears the last signature of men,
Written with such perplexity, with such bewildered pity,
The words choke as they begin—

'*Unknown seaman*'—the ghostly pencil
Wavers and fades, the purple drips,
The breath of the wet season has washed their inscriptions
As blue as drowned men's lips,

Dead seamen, gone in search of the same landfall,
Whether as enemies they fought,
Or fought with us, or neither; the sand joins them together,
Enlisted on the other front.[28]

At the end of the Second World War in August 1945—a mere sixty
years since imperialistic fervour had inspired the Sudan contingent, and
thirty years since the landing at Gallipoli—the mood had changed completely. The war, while it evoked deeds of great heroism, was seen largely
as a grim necessity, with the sons of the Anzacs of Gallipoli and the western front succeeding their fathers alongside their British peers in a war of
defence. Both British and Australians owed an enormous debt to another
world power, the United States of America. The call of empire would, in
the post-war period in Australia, be replaced by a perceived necessity to
support a 'great and powerful friend'.

5

TRAVELLING INVESTIGATORS

In 1852 Ellen Clacy, a young English lady with a sardonic eye and a gift for translating her impressions into words, arrived in an Australian city. Stranded by the non-arrival of a mail steamer, Clacy and her companions were forced to seek accommodation in a private dwelling. She had to sleep in the same bed as the mistress of the house, and soon became aware of some of the features of colonial life: 'Dogs (Melbourne is full of them) kept up an incessant barking; revolvers were cracking in all directions until daybreak, giving one a pleasant idea of the state of society'. Daytime revealed other hazards for those venturesome enough to leave the house: '… in the colonies, at this season of the year, one may go out prepared for fine weather, with blue sky above, and dry under foot, but in less than an hour, should a colonial shower come on, be unable to cross some of the streets without a plank being placed from the middle of the road to the pathway, or the alternative of walking in water up to the knees'.[1] The weather is still the same, but just over a hundred years later another British visitor, Jan Morris in 1962, could claim that Melbourne's Collins Street was the only one in Australia with a true metropolitan flavour: 'It is … recognizably one of the great streets, and a morning walk along it is a conversation with the continent'.[2]

From Clacy's visit to Morris's and beyond, British writers have come to see what this place in the antipodes is like, and to pass on their impressions to the British public. Be they novelists or journalists, social scientists or historians, the views of these travelling investigators have been quoted extensively in Britain and in Australia, and have both confirmed and countered prejudices held by the citizens of one country about the other. Some of the investigators have encountered social and physical situations unknown to most Australians, including contact with Aboriginal people in remote areas. Their impressions, frequently backed by research into local history, society and geography, have offered informed insights into the life of the country. There are some things on which all have concurred—the beauty of Sydney Harbour being one. Most have agreed that the system of class relations in Britain had not reproduced itself in Australia, but opinions have differed as to the type of society which has evolved here. Their analyses of Australian society, particularly of its materialism, have prompted various predictions of the country's future.

Many have made the journey, but an account which tried to include them all would result in a mere list of names and titles. Instead we will follow the tracks of a small collection of these travelling investigators, whose visits to Australia span the years from the early 1850s to the 1990s. We have already met one of them, a young woman on her way to visit the Victorian goldfields. The others include elderly and not-so-elderly gentlemen of varying degrees of fame and celebrity, and several keen-eyed and sharp-tongued social analysts and journalists. Novelists Ellen Clacy and Anthony Trollope, historian J. A. Froude, social investigators Sidney and Beatrice Webb, composer and broadcaster Thomas Wood, balletomane and writer Arnold Haskell, travel writer Jan Morris and journalist Bruce Chatwin here represent the multitudes of their compatriots who came to Australia to see what manner of place it was.

Some of these visitors were either handicapped or were assisted in attaining this goal—depending on theirs or the reader's point of view—by the fact that they were already well-known names in the places they visited. This had advantages: they had access to those responsible for pulling the levers of power and forming policies for the new country. It also had disadvantages: it took an extremely determined visitor to overturn the agenda of his or her eager hosts. Some were in consequence more successful at investigating a broad spectrum of Australian society than others. Nineteenth-century visitors in particular were inclined to reflect the prevailing attitude of the Australian colonists to the indigenous people of the country in terms which make disquieting reading today. Nevertheless, most of these investigators were sufficiently eager to see what they came to see, and were able to escape their well-meaning guides to discover the things that they really wanted to find out. Very few of them were evasive about the outcome of their investigations, and their frankness has in some cases caused resentment in the country they examined.

Expectations

What did these travelling investigators expect to find when they came to Australia? Their preparations for the journey varied, and their preconceptions were also diverse. Celebrated British novelist Anthony Trollope's son Frederic already lived there, and Trollope had researched Australian conditions by the time he visited Australia in 1871. Historian James Anthony Froude, with his imperial federationist views, looked to find another Britain in the antipodes in 1885. Both Trollope and Froude saw the Australian colonies as prime locations for British migrants, and had no hesitation in recommending that the less privileged sections of British society should consider a move to the antipodes. They were less inclined to suggest such a course of action for those of more elevated status. Sidney and Beatrice Webb, Fabian social investigators, were uncharacteristically ill-prepared for their Australian experience in 1898, and they arrived—particularly Beatrice—with sensibilities jangled by their travels in the United States and New Zealand.[3] Composer Thomas Wood, about to leave England for two years in Australia in the early 1930s, was given an advance report by an admiral who had served on the Australian Naval Station and had encountered Australians at Gallipoli:

Anthony Trollope, who visited Australia, where his son was living, in 1871 and 1872, and wrote an extensive account of his travels and investigations.
National Library of Australia

'A great country in many ways, my dear doctor, and a great people—in many ways. You'll probably like both. I did, although of course things may have changed by now … But the place is full of contradictions—incongruities—just like the people. You'll see for yourself when you go. They take no interest in any country except Australia—and they call England Home. They tear one another to bits; but they sulk if a stranger

Dr Thomas Wood, composer and broadcaster, with Australian soldier 'cobbers' in London in 1941. National Library of Australia

criticizes anything—thin skins there, so be careful. They ought to be the freest nation on earth, and yet they go and tie themselves hand and foot with rules and regulations. And money! That sets the standard of taste, or it used to. I don't suppose things have changed much in this respect, whatever they've done in others. The furniture will make you cry; and so will half the politicians … But the one thing you must not do is to judge Australia, real Australia, by the rank and file of its politicians.'

He leaned forward and knocked out his pipe.

'But there's something which balances all this.'

'What's that?' I said.

'Friendship. They'll do anything for you if you meet them half-way. They can't do enough for you if they take to you. They are the most hospitable people I've ever come across in the whole of my life. And you'll find good cobbers wherever you go.'

'What's a cobber?'

He told me.[4]

Arnold Haskell came to Australia in the mid-1930s 'by complete accident'. From being 'completely, even aggressively uninterested in that particular continent', he became one of its most fervent converts. His 1940 book, *Waltzing Matilda*, tells 'the story of how a man fell in love with a continent'.[5] That this was as totally unexpected as Haskell claimed is manifest in his description of what he had thought Australia was all about: 'Sheep and cricket, tin roofs everywhere, more sheep, more cricket, sand and rabbits; hospitality, hearty but uncouth, and, of course, the famous cockney accent that raised smug laughs from the superior when heard in the Movietone News; how I laughed myself'.[6] Unable to find a book in which to read what he wanted to know about his new love, Haskell determined to visit again and write one himself; the book he wrote 'tells of how I became disabused and then enchanted, and of how I returned for a further period of six months, covering 14 000 miles in an attempt to study the continent and provide a background for my enchantment'.[7]

Other visitors explored broader themes, using Australia as a case study. Bruce Chatwin's 1984 visit was inspired by reading T. G. Strehlow's *Songs of Central Australia*, and his goal was to study the condition of nomadism as it manifested itself among Aboriginal people, rather than to assess the nature of the wider society, although on his travels through Central Australia he encountered an interesting range of idealists, pragmatists and misfits among the non-Aboriginal population.[8]

Australian society

The nature of the society which had evolved in Australia was one of the most interesting aspects of the country for its British visitors. The people, particularly last century, were predominantly of British stock—what had been the influence of this new country upon them?

Ellen Clacy portrayed the rawest possible manifestations of frontier life in Australia in her book, *A Lady's Visit to the Gold Diggings of Australia 1852–53*. Her descriptive and narrative gifts and the information she supplied about gold mining made her account an 'instantaneous success' in England.[9] Her audience back in Britain was left in no doubt as to the fate of gentility on the Australian goldfields after reading her descriptions of a goldfields store, and night-time at the diggings:

> The stores at the diggings are large tents generally square or oblong, and everything required by a digger can be obtained for money, from sugar-candy to potted anchovies; from East India pickles to Bass's pale ale; from ankle jack boots to a pair of stays; from a baby's cap to a cradle; and every

Sandhurst (Bendigo) in 1855, not long after Ellen Clacy's visit, in an engraving by goldfields artist S. T. Gill.
National Library of Australia

apparatus for mining, from a pick to a needle. But the confusion—the din—the medley—what a scene for a shop walker! Here lies a pair of herrings dripping into a bag of sugar, or a box of raisins; there a gay-looking bundle of ribbons beneath two tumblers, and a half-finished bottle of ale. Cheese and butter, bread and yellow soap, pork and currants, saddles and frocks, wide-awakes and blue serge shirts, green veils and shovels, baby linen and tallow candles, all are heaped indiscriminately together; added to which there are children bawling, men swearing, store-keeper sulky, and last, not *least*, women's tongues going nineteen to the dozen …

But night here at the diggings is the characteristic time: murder here—murder there—revolvers cracking—blunderbusses bombing—rifles going off—balls whistling—one man groaning with a broken leg—another shouting because he couldn't find his way to his hole, and a third equally vociferous because he has tumbled into one—this man swearing—another praying—a party of bacchanals chanting various ditties to different time and tune, or rather minus both. Here is one man grumbling because he has brought his wife with him, another ditto because he has left his behind, or sold her for an ounce of gold or a bottle of rum. Donny-brook Fair is not to be compared to an evening at Bendigo.[10]

English-style gentility nevertheless was often found in the Australian colonies: in late nineteenth-century Adelaide, J. A. Froude was struck by the familiarity of social arrangements when he visited the Collector of Customs and his family in 1885:

> I found an agreeable and intelligent gentleman in an airy room with cool mats instead of carpets, opening into a verandah, where his ladies were engaged over the national five o'clock tea. We were 12,000 miles from England; yet we were in England still; and England at its best, so far as I could gather from the conversation.[11]

Froude found the same thing when he travelled on to Melbourne: 'it was English life over again: nothing strange, nothing exotic or original, save perhaps in greater animation of spirits'.[12] He began, however, to register disappointment at the style of social life in the colonies when he was invited by Lady Loch, wife of the governor, 'to the park to hear the band play, and to see the rank, beauty and fashion of Victoria'. These did not come up to standard, in Froude's eyes: 'horses, riders, phaetons, curricles, tandems, were of a scratch description, and the scene was gipsy-like and scrambling, like what one sees at an English country racecourse.'[13]

Froude's faith in Victorian society was restored by a visit to the Melbourne Club, where he met the 'principal men', whose social and financial standing had been secured by the operation of social Darwinism in the goldfields society described by Ellen Clacy forty years before:

> They are the survivors of the generation of adventurers who went out thither forty years ago, on the first discovery of the gold fields—those who succeeded and made their fortunes while others failed. They are thus a picked class, the seeming *fittest*, who had the greatest force, the greatest keenness, the greatest perseverance ... There is not in Melbourne, there is not anywhere in Australia, the slightest symptom of a separate provincial originality either formed or forming. In thought and manners, as in speech and pronunciation, they are pure English and nothing else. There is more provincialism far in Exeter or York than in Melbourne or Sydney.[14]

How can one account for Froude's not noticing things that other commentators—before and since—have dwelt upon at length: among them the Australian informality of manners and egalitarian spirit, and above all, the much-derided Australian accent? The answer lies in his book: he and his son were given free passes on the railways of both Victoria and New South Wales; they only visited those two colonies, 'where energy and enterprise had accomplished the most', and while there were fêted by the upper echelons of colonial society, and stayed at places like the Melbourne Club and the exclusive Australian Club in Sydney.[15] Nevertheless, Froude's interest in constructing Australians as simply transplanted Britons could not survive the reality altogether; he rebuked Australians for not showing an interest in 'deeper spiritual problems', in what Keith Dunstan has called his 'most quotable and most damning phrase': 'It is hard to quarrel with men who only wish to be innocently happy'.[16]

Just over a decade later, when Beatrice and Sidney Webb visited Australia, they were not at all inclined to see Australian society as an antipodean version of Englishness. The Webbs, during their 1898 visit, decided that Australians suffered the defects of youth, displaying 'vulgarity and a rather gross materialism', and were 'inclined to self-indulgence and disinclined for regular work'.[17] In fact, 'vulgar' is the most persistent adjective in the Webbs' account of Australians. Beatrice Webb's most severe strictures were reserved for Australian women, whom she roundly condemned. They were 'in an unpleasant stage of development', and the 'low tone of all classes of colonial society in all that concerns private life is to my mind mainly the result of the lack of education, strenuousness and refinement of the women'.[18] Even when women took an interest in matters other than trivia, Beatrice was unforgiving and harsh. When she addressed a meeting of the Victorian socialists, she found in the front seats 'a dozen or so hard-featured graceless women, the Council of the Women's Suffrage Society'.[19] Even Australia's upper-class women failed to impress the caustic Fabian. A visit to one of the women of the a'Beckett family organised by Professor Harrison Moore in an attempt to convince her that she was 'too hasty in her generalisations' did not deflect Beatrice's criticisms:

> All I gathered from her was that the well-to-do young woman has £50 a year to dress on and in order to be always dressed up in smart light-coloured blouses, in a dirty town, has to put in a good deal of dress-making. The rather purposeless refinement of the a'Becketts—one of the only aristocratic families in Australia—did not modify my impression of the typical Australian well-to-do woman.[20]

The impression of an egalitarian, almost a levelling society, committed to materialist goals persisted well into the twentieth century. In the early 1930s Thomas Wood said that 'Australian society is built up on the principle that a man is as "good as the next"'. Wood went further: 'As observers have pointed out, he tends to think himself twice as good as the next', and:

> Australian attention has been concentrated for so long on getting a job of work done, making money in the process, and having a good time afterwards, that the habit still persists of looking upon anything which has no immediate connexion with these three prime interests as a triviality not worth serious attention.[21]

Other commentators besides Froude identified a spiritual hunger amidst the material wealth of the country: Jan Morris in the 1960s discerned that Australia 'cried out for something beyond the bank balance and the bungalow'; it was 'a place of endless echoing mystery and intuition, what the aborigines would call a dreamtime country, where history has no meaning unless you take a grip on it, and nothingness will beat you in the end unless you saddle up for a gesture'.[22]

Changing perspectives on indigenous Australians

Those travelling investigators who came to Australia in the latter part of the nineteenth century, and even those who came before the Second World War, tended to subscribe to the prevailing attitude among non-Aboriginal Australians that the indigenous people of the country were on their way to extinction. Some, such as Trollope, acknowledged what had been done to the Aboriginal people as a result of white settlement, but regarded British occupation as a strategic necessity. After a visit to a missionary establishment at Rama Yuck, in Gippsland, Trollope outlined the existing situation:

> It has been only natural, only human, that efforts should be made by the invading race to ameliorate the condition of these people, and—to use the word most common to our mouths—to civilise them. We have taken away their land, have destroyed their food, have made them subject to our laws which are antagonistic to their habits and traditions, have endeavoured to make them subject to our tastes, which they hate, have massacred them when they defended themselves and their possessions after their own fashion, and have taught them by hard warfare to acknowledge us to be their masters. We have done the job with perhaps as little cruelty as was com-

Cook's murder in the
Sandwich Islands
(Hawaii) in 1779, seen
in this painting by George
Carter, Death of
Captain Cook, *became*
a dramatic subject for
artists attracted to the
romance of his voyages
of discovery. National
Library of Australia

Letters and other commu-
nications from the old
country stirred feelings of
homesickness and nostal-
gia among British settlers
in Australia. Edward
Hopley, A primrose from
England *(lithograph by*
J. R. Dicksee), 1856.
National Library of
Australia

Above: *The penitentiary at Port Arthur, Tasmania, once a notorious place of secondary punishment for persistent convict offenders, and the setting for part of Marcus Clarke's* For the Term of His Natural Life. *It is now a historic site.* Photograph by Roslyn Russell

Left: *Hyde Park convict barracks, designed by the convict architect Francis Greenway and opened in May 1819 during Lachlan Macquarie's term as governor.* Photograph by Roslyn Russell

Ambroise-Louis Garneray's painting, Portsmouth Harbour with prison hulks of c1814 shows a line of prison ships similar to those in which convicts were kept before being transported to the Australian colonies. National Library of Australia

patible with such a job. No one I think will say that the English should have abstained from taking possession of Australia because such possession could not be secured without injury to the blacks. Had the English abstained, the Dutch or the French would have come, and certainly would not have come with lighter hands.[23]

Trollope described the remnant of the tribes that survived the settlement process as having 'melted away'; the fragments remaining 'growing still smaller and smaller', with missionaries toiling among them to preserve them.[24] Arnold Haskell before the Second World War believed that the representation of Aboriginal people in travel guides about Australia was an example of 'the eternally negative point of view' of the country that these books fostered. Presentation of Australia, he believed, should focus on 'recounting the lives, thoughts, and works of the many eminent painters rather than the pathetic state of the rapidly dwindling aboriginal', setting a dominant Eurocentric culture in opposition to the indigenous one, which would not be valued properly until several decades after Haskell's visit, either in Australia or overseas.[25]

Since Trollope and Haskell wrote, attitudes towards the culture and the status of indigenous Australians had changed. Anthropologists such as Sir William Baldwin Spencer and Frank Gillen, T. G. Strehlow, A. P. Elkin, and Ronald and Catherine Berndt had investigated Aboriginal culture and described its complexity. A new respect for this race which had adapted itself so successfully to Australia's harsh environment was emerging, and capturing the interest of British writers, among others. Bruce Chatwin went to Central Australia in 1984 to study the traditional relationship of nomadic Aboriginal people to their country.[26] Chatwin's 'novel of ideas', *The Songlines*, explores the 'songlines' or 'Dreaming-tracks', invisible pathways which cross the country, and act as a source of personal identity and as indicators of territorial boundaries for Aboriginal people. Chatwin had long been fascinated by the human desire to wander and, having 'a presentiment that the "travelling phase" of my life might be passing' (he died of AIDS in 1989) decided that he 'should set down on paper a résumé of the ideas, quotations and encounters which had amused and obsessed me; and one which I hoped would shed light on what is, for me, the question of questions: the nature of human restlessness'.[27] The schema Chatwin used to explore this phenomenon was dualistic: a journey through Central Australia to find out more about the songlines was interspersed with a collection of fragments he had penned over the years in a series of special black oilskin notebooks, including quotations, brief descriptions of encounters in isolated regions of the world, and notes of reading.

Chatwin joined Arkady Volchok, who was working with Aboriginal people to determine sacred sites in the landscape, under threat from a projected railway line. Under Arkady's guidance and sponsorship Chatwin met Aboriginal people, and in conversation with them and with Arkady (who supplied the necessary interpretation) unravelled how the songlines worked. Concurrent with this search, and the exegesis of the spiritual significance of these 'Dreaming-tracks', Chatwin encountered the people of Central Australia and captured them in words which do not gloss over the negative aspects of territorian existence, for both Aboriginal and European. His description of Marian, who accompanied a group of Aboriginal women to determine the sacred significance of women's places threatened by the railway, gives an indication of both her character and the harshness of the social and physical environment:

> Since leaving Alice Springs, she'd driven 300 miles; treated a boy for scorpion bite; dosed a baby for dysentery; drawn an elder's abscessed tooth; sewn up a woman who'd been beaten by her husband; sewn up the husband, who'd been beaten by the brother-in-law …
>
> So what was it, I wondered, about these Australian women? Why were they so strong and satisfied, and so many of the men so drained?[28]

The songlines, Chatwin discovered, were fundamental to an Aboriginal's understanding of the creation of the world, and his place in that world. Arkady explained 'how each totemic ancestor, while travelling through the country, was thought to have scattered a trail of words and musical notes along the line of his footprints, and how these "Dreaming-tracks" lay over the land as "ways" of communication between the most far-flung tribes'. Chatwin then saw that 'the whole of Australia could be read as a musical score'.[29] This had important implications when trying to identify specific sacred sites, Arkady said:

> It was one thing to persuade a surveyor that a heap of boulders were the eggs of the Rainbow Snake, or a lump of reddish sandstone was the liver of a speared kangaroo. It was something else to convince him that a feature-less stretch of gravel was the musical equivalent of Beethoven's Opus III.
>
> By singing the world into existence, he said, the Ancestors had been poets in the original sense of *poesis*, meaning 'creation'. No Aboriginal could

conceive that the created world was in any way imperfect. His religious life had a single aim: to keep the land the way it was and should be. The man who went 'Walkabout' was making a ritual journey. He trod in the footsteps of his Ancestor. He sang the Ancestor's stanzas without changing a word or note—and so recreated the Creation.

'Sometimes,' said Arkady, 'I'll be driving my "old men" through the desert, and we'll come to a ridge of sandhills, and suddenly they'll all start singing. "What are you mob singing?" I'll ask, and they'll say, "Singing up the country, boss. Makes the country come up quicker."'[30]

Chatwin and Arkady talked to Flynn, an ex-Benedictine Aboriginal priest, who had left his Church after becoming involved with the land rights campaign, about the songlines. He explained how:

Before the whites came ... no one in Australia was landless, since everyone inherited, as his or her private property, a stretch of the Ancestor's song and the stretch of country over which the song passed. A man's verses were his title deeds to territory. He could lend them to others. He could borrow other verses in return. The one thing he couldn't do was to sell or get rid of them ...[31]

Chatwin learned about 'ritual knowledge' and the role of a 'ritual manager',[32] about Aboriginal beliefs about 'spirit-conception', when a baby in the womb acquires his Ancestor, and his tjuringa.[33] He explained the role of the tjuringa, a plaque of stone or mulga wood with enormous significance: 'It is the actual body of the Ancestor ... It is a man's *alter ego*; his soul; his obol to Charon; his title-deed to country; his passport and his ticket "back in"'. Loss or destruction of a tjuringa was literally 'the end of the world' for an Aboriginal person.[34]

Chatwin concludes *The Songlines* with a description of three dying men, who had come to the place where their tjuringas were stored, the place for 'going back', to become their Ancestors on their deaths: 'They were all right. They knew where they were going, smiling at death in the shade of a ghost-gum'.[35]

Australian cities

Most of the investigators mentioned here dwelt at length on the cities of Australia, and their comments were far too numerous to include more than a mere sample, taken from across a wide range of time. We have already read comments on Melbourne by Clacy, Froude and Morris: their fellow investigators have supplied similar statements for other Australian cities.

Anthony Trollope found Perth in the 1870s 'a very pretty town', and Hobart 'as pleasant a town of the size as any I know'.[36] Mount Wellington, he said, was 'just enough of a mountain to give excitement to ladies and gentlemen in middle life'.[37] Thomas Wood said that Hobart 'has the air of an English country town which has shed its old houses and wandered down to the sea for a rest'.[38] The Webbs in 1898 preferred Adelaide as the 'pleasantest' Australian city, with 'far more amenity than is possible to restlessly pretentious Melbourne, crude chaotic Sydney, or shadily genteel Brisbane'.[39]

Most visitors to Australia commented on the beauty of Sydney Harbour. Anthony Trollope felt that he could not do it justice with mere words: 'I despair of being able to convey to any reader my own idea of the

The waterfront at Hobart, with Mount Wellington in the background, in the nineteenth century. Tasmania was popular with British travellers, who regarded it as the most similar to England of all the Australian colonies. National Library of Australia

beauty of Sydney Harbour. I have seen nothing equal to it in the way of land-locked sea-scenery—nothing second to it.'[40] For Beatrice and Sidney Webb, its 'exquisite harbour' was one of Sydney's few redeeming features.[41] Thomas Wood defied 'any one to hug his sorrows while he is sailing in Sydney Harbour'.[42]

The city of Sydney itself was a different matter. J. A. Froude in 1885 believed that the climate was responsible for the traits that were already developing in the Sydneysiders he met:

> Four generations have passed since Sydney became a city, and the colonists there have contracted from the climate something of the character of a Southern race. Few collections of human beings on this planet have so much to enjoy, and so little to suffer; and they seem to feel it, and in the midst of business to take their ease and enjoy themselves ...[43]

Thomas Wood called 1930s Sydney 'an exotic: a lovely and petulant spendthrift, going its own wilful headstrong vivid way'.[44] Jan Morris's first impressions of Sydney in 1962 were unflattering, and raised the hackles of Sydneysiders: 'The origins of Sydney are unsavoury, her history is

Sydney Botanic Gardens, drawn by J. A. Froude, who said of the gardens that 'I think I have never in my life gazed on a scene so entirely beautiful'. Ships of the naval squadron can be seen between the trees. National Library of Australia

disagreeable to read, her temper is coarse, her organization seems to be slipshod, her suburbs are hideous, and her politics often crooked, her buildings are mostly plain, her voices rasp on the ear'.[45] Worse was to come; this comment brought the wrath of Sydney's socialites down on Morris's head:[46]

> ... this place feels cruelly aloof. Perhaps it is the origins of Sydney that invoke this sensation—for despite the sophistries of her society ladies, she was founded by the scum of England, only six generations ago. Perhaps it is the expressions on the faces of those ladies themselves, so steely, scornful and accusatory, as though they are expecting you (which Heaven forbid) to offer them an improper suggestion.[47]

Thirty years later Jan Morris wrote a book devoted simply to Sydney, as part of a survey of late imperial cities. In 1992, despite her feelings that there was a certain insubstantiality about the place, she conceded Sydney to be, 'by general consent, one of the great cities of the world'.[48]

Australia's newest city was also inspected by travelling investigators. Arnold Haskell visited Canberra just before the Second World War. To believe that this was the national capital of Australia required an act of faith on his part that he found impossible to achieve:

> Driving from the railway station it takes a considerable time to discover the capital. I doubt if I ever did. I discovered gardens and flowering shrubs of exceptional beauty, everchanging views of hills and distant mountains, also a site for a capital city. I did have one glimpse of the city itself, at night from a dominating hill when it suddenly came into view as a milky way of light. Imagination filled in the rest.
>
> Canberra is still a city of the imagination, taking splendid life only from the faith of its inhabitants. I should, I think, have stayed a while and studied it. I should have been moved by its gigantic plan and tried to see it through the eyes of those that lived there, many of them with pioneering enthusiasm. I could not.
>
> I saw only an immense exhibition ground many years before the opening of the exhibition itself, and for a variety of reasons I doubted whether the exhibition would ever come into being.[49]

Jan Morris visited Canberra twenty years later, after the Menzies government had committed itself to bringing the plan for Canberra to fruition. While admitting that Canberra in 1962 was still 'a bit of a mess', the enthusiasm of the city's planners, the National Capital Development Commission, was 'infectious' as they displayed their charts and plans to the visitor:

These pictures of pre-Second World War Canberra confirm Arnold Haskell's description of Australia's national capital in Waltzing Matilda.
Top: Civic Centre and northern suburbs, late 1920s.
Below: Northern suburbs from Mount Ainslie, c1935.
Photos by Ted Richards, Manuka Photo Centre, ACT

... as they explain it all to you, so you will begin to envisage the pattern of it cohering outside your window, and feel that this huge sprawling colourless entity will one day possess a queer excitement of its own, the peculiar extra-sensory excitement that is the meaning of Australia. Already Canberra buzzes with noble intentions, making her the very antithesis of Sydney up the road and indeed is impressive in her accomplishments, too ... I really do doubt if you can find, anywhere below the equator, a livelier assembly of talents than is resident among the half-cock splendours of Canberra.[50]

The range of statements on Australia presented here, the diversity of backgrounds of those making them, and the different historical periods in which they were made, mean that reaching a conclusion about them is well nigh impossible. Suffice to say that the comments made by these travelling investigators, in many cases, reveal as much about themselves as they do about Australia.

6

LONDON CALLS

Henry Lawson was fed up: with not earning enough from his poems and short stories to support himself and his family; with hearing of the deaths of other Australian writers—Henry Kendall, Adam Lindsay Gordon, Barcroft Boake—from despair or suicide; with the scant recognition Australian literature gained in the land of its production. In 1892 his emotions burst forth in verse:

Southern men of letters, vainly seeking recognition here—
Southern men of letters, driven to the Northern hemisphere!
It is time your wrongs were known; it is time you claimed redress—
Time that you were independent of the mighty Northern press.
Sing a song of Southern writers, sing a song of Southern fame
Of the dawn of arts and letters and your native country's shame.

In the land where sport is sacred, where the laborer is a god,
You must pander to the people, make a hero of a clod!
What avail the sacrifices of the battles you begin
For the literary honour of the land we're living in?
Print a masterpiece in Melbourne, and it will be lost, I ween,
For your weakest stuff is clever in a London magazine.[1]

Lawson had identified a central problem for Australian writers. Australia in the 1890s had experienced a blossoming of literature and art, with writers and artists developing a new and vital interpretation of their country as the colonies prepared for a federal union. Nevertheless, even as they were articulating a national identity, and seeking a role for their writing independent of the culture of Britain and Europe, writers such as Lawson believed it was obligatory to be published in Britain so that Australian audiences would grant the 'niggard recognition' he mentioned in his 1892 poem.[2] Better still, Lawson advised aspiring writers in the *Bulletin* in 1899, to travel to Britain, or elsewhere, to gain acceptance and recognition—or take more drastic measures to end their misery in Australia:

> My advice to any young Australian writer whose talents have been recognised, would be to go steerage, stow away, swim and seek London, Yankeeland, or Timbuctoo—rather than stay in Australia till his genius has turned to gall, or beer. Or failing this—and still interested in human nature and literature—to study elementary anatomy, especially as applies to the cranium—and shoot himself carefully with the aid of a looking glass.[3]

Portrait of Henry Lawson by Norman Carter. National Library of Australia

Lawson sought financial support from Lord Beauchamp, the new governor of New South Wales, and collector David Scott Mitchell, telling them that he could 'win fame and fortune in London' if he could 'raise the necessary'.[4] They both obliged. Lawson left for London, with his wife Bertha and his two children, in late April 1900. Just before he left, he arranged to have the manuscript of a novel by 'Miles Franklin' sent to him in London, as he had promised the writer that he would 'Take it home' to try to organise its publication in Britain.[5]

London was for Australians the great cultural metropolis, the centre of the English-language publishing world. Britain was, for many Australians then and for years to come, their spiritual and intellectual home. Australian writers' work also reached a wider market in Britain, and this translated into bigger sales both there and in Australia. The pilgrimage to Britain was undertaken by a number of Australian writers from the 1890s up to and throughout the First World War. As well as Lawson, they included Miles Franklin (via the USA), Louise Mack and Barbara Baynton.

Living in London

Henry Lawson and his family remained in Britain until May 1902. Lawson claimed later that the visit had been 'wonderfully successful from a literary point of view'.[6] His work was featured in British journals, and three prose collections, *The Country I Come From*, *Joe Wilson and His Mates* and *Children of the Bush*, were published in Britain. At a personal level the reverse was the case: Lawson began drinking heavily again, and Bertha was confined for a time in Bethlem Hospital as her mental state deteriorated. Their relationship was irretrievably damaged. Lawson, despite his literary success, admitted that his health had 'completely broken down', and he 'must come home for a year or so'. But Lawson had by no means abandoned the idea of a London base: 'I know London as well as I know the Bush, and propose to write of London for the Australian papers and of Australia for the London papers'.[7] Despite this optimistic plan, Lawson's fortunes had begun the downward spiral that would see him become a pathetic wreck cadging drink money from his friends disembarking from ferries at Circular Quay, buttonholing his publisher for the price of a beer, and spending time in Darlinghurst Gaol on vagrancy charges, until his death in 1922.[8]

However, Lawson's time in London produced insights into London—and English—life, and a number of comparisons between these and life in Australia. In 'Joe Wilson in England', Joe Wilson is 'looking after some business for a wool firm' and living in Harpenden, a village in Hertfordshire where Lawson lived for part of his time in England. He affirms his admiration for the English, and contrasts their social mores with those of the Australian bush and is critical of claims that Australians are unconventional and warmhearted by contrast with English conservatism:

> Does unconventionality consist of carelessness in dress, manner and talk, and dropping in at all hours without notice? It wouldn't do in England. It would interfere with other people's comfort and privacy, and liberty. Here you write to make an appointment with a businessman because he's got no time

for people who drop in, without warning, about nothing in particular. And people are invited to each other's homes by letter, and accept by letter, because England is more crowded than the Bush, and there are more people to entertain. It's done for the comfort and convenience of all parties … The reserve and conventionality is mostly out of consideration for the feelings, rest, and comfort of others. The conventionalities are really to save time and trouble in a crowded country. But I've got to hate the word 'unconventionality' as much as I hated the word 'conventionality'. I'd like to see the two peoples understand each other. Seems to me the English, though they know little of Australia, get to understand us sooner than we do them; they are trained and educated to learn, and they take the trouble to do it. No intelligent man can travel in Europe and America without getting in the end to admire and respect the English.[9]

Their manner was not the only thing distinguishing Australians from the English. Lawson's 1901 poem, 'Jack Cornstalk', describes the impact of a visiting Australian's size and demeanour on the citizens of London:

I met Jack Cornstalk in London to-day,
He saw me and coo-eed from over the way.
Oh! the solemn-faced Londoners stared with surprise
At his hair and his height as compared with his size;
For his trousers were short and his collar was low,
And—there's not room to coo-ee in London, you know![10]

Once Lawson had arrived back in Australia, he bestowed advice on other Australian writers thinking of making the journey to London, perhaps revealing his feelings about life there more truly than some of his other writing on England:

Take a cheap flat and live as cheaply as you can in North London or somewhere, or a cottage in a quiet little farming village up the Thames—avoid a middle-class village, for the narrowness and paltriness of people, whose whole soul is in 'keeping up appearance', would drive you mad. And few Australians can stand 'apartments' or a London landlady for any length of time. Don't bother about letters of introduction—I took a parcel home, kindly sent by friends, and never used one.

    There is room and magazines for good work in England and Scotland, and the editors want the work—not letters of introduction. In good work,

simple domestic yarns and true sketches of the better side of human nature,
of man, woman and child nature, go best now …

    Work hard and do good work, and keep to yourself.[11]

Louise Mack was in London at much the same time as Henry Lawson. Her 1902 novel, *An Australian Girl in London*, uses the device of a series of letters from her heroine Sylvia Leighton to contrast life in London with life in Australia. Sylvia at first finds the vastness and indifference of London intimidating as an Australian trying to make her way there:

At first we Australians are all surprised to find London so small. That is because our eyes are accustomed to great distances, and because we judge by what we see. We think we are looking at all London. Months and months after we begin to realise that it is impossible ever to look at London.

    Only in fragments can this great city be taken into the eye. We can but see one piece at a time. Our first impression is that all is so much smaller than we expected. But by-and-by comes the hour when we go out to do battle with London. Then comes home to us its immensity …

    You arrive at your destination in wonder at your coming. Why are you here? What do you seek? Work? A chance? A hearing? Why should you expect any of these? Who are you? No one. What are you worth? Nothing. Who wants you? Nobody.

    And so, in that one walk, between the time of closing your house door behind you and arriving at the place of business where you meant to present yourself and seek for work, you have lost all that is likely to help you in the search. Your belief in yourself has flown. The faces in the streets, the miles and miles of buildings, the great, cruel indifference of the massed city, have struck cold to your heart …

    That's where the battle comes in. Not to be crushed, not to have the purpose dissipated, is a hard struggle for an Australian in London. At home, the blue of the sky, the dazzling gold of the sunlight, the warmth and friendliness of the faces around, are all massed on the side of the fighter. In losing them here one loses so much of one's defence.[12]

Gradually Sylvia begins to win the battle. She learns the English way of making friends, and that London gives access to the Continent. She realises that 'London means everywhere to us':

To leave London and go back means to leave all Europe also. Even if we never get there, we always can—as long as we are in England. But go back to Australia and the whole world vanishes, like a dream, and becomes, after a time, only a dream again.[13]

London asserts its ascendancy over Sylvia. Although she engages in nostalgia at the scent of boronia, the cultural climate which surrounds her drives out her desire for the bush of Australia, and in words which have been echoed by countless Australians before and since she admits her addiction to the place:

London drives out the gums. London hangs pictures, and plays, and cathedrals, and operas, and intellects all over the Bush and the dazzling gold. And I say to myself, in unmistakable language, 'I don't want to go back. It's so far, far away. It's the other end of the world. I don't want to go back yet.'[14]

Sylvia finally confesses: 'I'm getting English'.[15]

Publishing in Britain

On 17 October 1900, Miles Franklin wrote to Lawson from Goulburn, New South Wales, about the success of his new book, and thanking him 'for the trouble you take with me':

I was delighted when the notices of yr last book appeared and when the 'DT' [*Daily Telegraph*, Sydney] in an article headed 'Lawson makes the billy boil', devoted a whole column to yr success in London I felt I must ... express my gratification thereat but feared it would seem presumptuous & like seeking to remind you of my remote existence. I rejoice at yr success most especially it seems a victory being won in the teeth of the great 'slump' caused by the war.

England has not our genial climate so take care of yrself during the rigour of her winter ... From the art world of London Australia must seem very crude & oh! so far away.[16]

Franklin indeed had reason to be grateful to Lawson. Later in her life she claimed that she had not been able to interest an Australian publisher in her work, and was thus forced to seek publication in Britain, but this was not necessarily so. It is far more likely that she accepted Lawson's offer to place her work in England because he was on the point of leaving for there, and publisher George Robertson of Angus and Robertson had not been able to look at it in time.[17] Whether or not Franklin would have been published in Australia after all will now never be known, but she was indeed fortunate that Lawson was able to arrange the publication of My *Brilliant Career* by Blackwoods, and took responsibility for the revision that the publisher thought necessary.[18] The reception of this novel, by a writer whom Lawson, in his preface to My *Brilliant Career*, described as 'just a little Bush girl, barely twenty-one yet',[19] was favourable for several reasons, as Franklin's biographer, Colin Roderick, tells:

> English reviewers as well as English publishers and administrators had their eyes on Australia, for the Colonies had federated, and their future relationship to Great Britain was a matter of concern. Lawson had made a good impression. His preface recommended the book. Here was another like him—and a woman to boot. Three cheers for the Colonies![20]

Miles Franklin, photographed in Chicago in 1908, several years after the publication of My Brilliant Career. *She went to London in 1915.* National Library of Australia

In the final chapter of her novel My *Career Goes Bung*, Miles Franklin's heroine Sybylla decides to go to England. Miles Franklin did not go there until 1915, after some years spent in the United States, but it is not difficult to see the common identity of Miles and Sybylla in this passage:

> And there is always England. England with her ancient historic beauty—tradition—the racial rooftree. I picture her cool green fields, her misty downs, her bare woods under the snow, her young leaves and soft flowers in spring. Her castles and cathedrals, her ivied towers, her brooks are as clear to my nostrils and closed eyes as the scents and features of 'Possum Gully'. And there is London, with its romantic fogs, its crowds and ceremonial pageants, Rotten Row and the Mall, the British Museum, the Mansion House, The Tower and Westminster. I know London much better than I do Sydney. Through

song and story it has permeated every fibre of my mind since I could first scan a pictured page, while I have spent scarcely a month in but one corner of Sydney. London—THE BIG SMOKE—London, where our dreams come true.

England acclaimed my first homespun effort. England may welcome my second and third. I will arise and go to Mother England.[21]

Miles Franklin settled in England after 1915, returning to Australia on occasions in the 1920s, then spent 1931 and 1932 back in England, where she published *Bring the Monkey* in London in 1931. This book, described by Marjorie Barnard as 'witty, gay, amusing, original, slight and unimportant' satirised the murder mystery thriller genre, and allowed Franklin to mock the English aristocracy at the same time.[22]

Other Australian writers did not find it easy to secure a publisher in Britain. Barbara Baynton in 1902, despite her social contacts reaching into the aristocracy in the person of Lord Salisbury, presentation at court and a seat in the Abbey for the coronation of King Edward VII, found trying to find a publisher for her collection of short stories, *Bush Studies*, 'dispiriting work'. She later confessed to Vance Palmer that she had contemplated 'putting it on the fire' after many refusals.[23] The Society of Authors gave her no help; she received 'rude notes' from publishers returning her manuscript, and was about to go home when she met Edward Garnett, who read for Duckworth's and who had also been of great assistance to Henry Lawson. He liked the manuscript, Duckworth's accepted it, and *Bush Studies* was published in England and Australia just before Christmas 1902, to critical acclaim in both countries.[24]

The indifference which greeted the publication in London of Victor Daley's verses, *At Dawn and Dusk*, pointed to a problem with acceptance of Australian literature in England—the ignorance of Australian writers of the tastes of the British audience.[25] A. W. Jose, who with A. G. Stephens had set up the Australasian Literary Agency in London in 1900, recalled years later his astonishment, and that of literary society in Australia, at the British rejection of Daley's poetry: 'It is hard to express to this generation our feelings about Daley the poet. We watched for his acceptance by the London critics with complete assurance, and their neglect of him staggered us ...'[26]

Victor Daley wrote an embittered poem, 'When London Calls', in the aftermath of this disappointment, depicting the imperial city as a siren who lured artistic souls to her, only to destroy them when she had taken her pleasure:

They leave us—artists, singers, all—
　　When London calls aloud,
Commanding to her Festival
　　The gifted crowd.

She sits beside the ship-choked Thames,
　　Sad, weary, cruel, grand;
Her crown imperial gleams with gems
　　From many a land.

From overseas, and far away,
　　Come crowded ships and ships—
Grim-faced she gazes on them; yea,
　　With scornful lips.

The garden of the earth is wide;
　　Its rarest blooms she picks
To deck her board, this haggard-eyed
　　Imperatrix …

The story-teller from the Isles
　　Upon the Empire's rim,
With smiles she welcomes—and her smiles
　　Are death to him …

And when the Poet's lays grown bland,
　　And urbanised, and prim—
She stretches forth a jewelled hand
　　And strangles him.

She sits beside the ship-choked Thames
　　With Sphinx-like lips apart—
Mistress of many diadems—
　　Death in her heart.[27]

Victor Daley, whose experience of publishing his poetry in London failed to meet his expectations, and those of his supporters in Australia. National Library of Australia

Australian writers of the 1890s and the early twentieth century thus found a mixed reception in London. Some thrived there; others did not, or found, like Henry Lawson, that a measure of personal success did not compensate for the disastrous effects of the visit on his family life. Publication in London, however, remained for many years the touchstone of success for Australian writers. The situation in Australia worsened, if anything, as the twentieth century progressed. Australian publishers reduced their publication of local writers in the 1920s: Hazel Rowley, the biographer of Christina Stead, has described the situation which confronted Australian writers by that time:

> Fortunate authors found an English publisher, which at least guaranteed distribution in England, for English and American publishers did not republish books published first in Australia. But Australian authors were paid lower royalties for the 'colonial edition', which was subject to heavy English income tax.[28]

So, for many years the call of London would attract aspiring Australian writers to whatever fate awaited them. To be accepted as successful writers in their native land, they had little choice but to make the journey. Some left, never to return, and swelled the ranks of Australian expatriates in Britain.

7

MONARCHY OR REPUBLIC?

In March 1963 in Canberra Australia's prime minister, newly created Knight of the Thistle Sir Robert Menzies, quoted words penned by an English poet from the time of Elizabeth I:

> I did but see her passing by
> and yet I love her till I die

to Australia's reigning monarch, Queen Elizabeth II.

The young Queen was, according to one observer, 'visibly moved'.[1] While Sir Robert's tribute to Her Majesty was regarded as appropriate by the majority of her Australian subjects, some dissident voices began to express the opinion that the 1963 royal tour had been a 'flop'.[2] In 1956, the Duke of Edinburgh, representing Queen Elizabeth, opened the Olympic Games in Melbourne.[3] Four decades later, in 1996, Australia's latest prime minister, John Howard, announced that the country's prime minister, not the Queen or her representative, will open the Olympic Games in Sydney in 2000. In the forty years since the first royal tour of Australia by a reigning British monarch—an event well within the memory of a large proportion of the Australian population—attitudes towards the retention of the constitutional link between Australia and the Queen and her heirs and successors have undergone changes which would have seemed inconceivable then, or even in 1963, when Menzies paid his poetic tribute. Australians are now debating these constitutional links, with some resolution of the dilemmas thus presented anticipated by at least the centenary of Australian federation in 2001.

An Australian republic?

Literature and its creators in Australia have, from colonial times, reflected the changing nature of attitudes to the British monarchy and its representatives, and the constitutional ties binding Britain and Australia. Charles Tompson, an Australian-born poet, celebrated Australia's continuing ties with the British monarchy in his translation of S. Smith's Latin Prize Poem, published in the *Sydney Gazette* on 13 February 1830:

And when another age shall pass away,
And fair Australia all her means survey;
When, opulent and powerful in her states,
A hundred cities she enumerates;
O, may she still, with parent Britain, share
One social Treaty, and one Prince declare![4]

Reverend Doctor John Dunmore Lang, an early advocate of an Australian republic. National Library of Australia

Two decades later this view was being questioned by some of those concerned with the formation of a constitution for the colony of New South Wales, soon to be granted self-government. The debate over this constitution brought to the forefront of public life 'two dazzling spruikers'—journalist and publisher Daniel Deniehy, and the founder of Presbyterianism in Australia, the Reverend John Dunmore Lang. Both were influenced by democratic movements in Europe which found expression in the revolutionary year of 1848: both 'saw the equities of civil life as deriving not from the Monarch but from the democratic tendencies of ordinary people'.[5] Lang, Deniehy and the then-republican (but later staunch monarchist) Henry Parkes had started the Australian League in Sydney in

1850; a couple of years later Lang was on his way to Britain to promote the separation of Moreton Bay from New South Wales, and Scots emigration to Australia. He used the voyage by ship to pen, at 'white heat', his book, *Freedom and Independence for the Golden Lands of Australia*, which was published in London when he arrived, in 1852. Reading this work nearly a century-and-a-half later, the president of the Australian Republican Movement, Australian novelist Thomas Keneally, found 'a bracing and lively experience' which led him to identify with the fiery Presbyterian divine of the 1850s:

> I began to feel a lot of fraternity with John Dunmore Lang when he complained that people would rebuff his ideas with the tedious old claim that 'the future time can be the only proper time for the consideration of so grave a question. Let us hear no more of it, therefore, for half a century to come.' This cry could justly be described as congenitally Australian, since the opponents of Federation regularly used it, and I and other Republicans are heartily sick of hearing it in this age.[6]

What did Lang think was the most appropriate—indeed the only possible—form of government for an independent British colony? His answer was unequivocal, and replete with all the oratorical devices which made him a celebrated preacher:

> … there is no other form of government either practicable or possible, in a British colony obtaining its freedom and independence, than that of a republic. Without inquiring, therefore, as to whether one form of government is better than another, we must be prepared, as British colonists, if we are ever to become free and independent, to take that particular form 'for better or worse'.
>
> And why should we be either unwilling or afraid to do so? It is now fifty years and upwards since the celebrated Charles James Fox characterized the British government as a disguised Republic; and the Reform Act has since taken away a considerable portion of the disguise. Why then should Englishmen object to a Republic without disguise for their emancipated colonies? Why should they object to a form of government which has given birth, in every department of human excellence, to a series of the greatest and noblest men that have ever trod the earth? Why should they vainly attempt to disparage those glorious republics of antiquity, from which we have inherited so much that exalts and embellishes humanity, and whose

> invaluable annals are so prolific in the most splendid achievements that the
> pen of history records.[7]

But the movement towards republicanism in Australia represented by Lang, Deniehy and the poet Charles Harpur, did not flourish among the majority of their fellow Australians in the latter half of the nineteenth century, although some kept the cause alive. Henry Lawson, for example, in the late 1880s wrote 'A Song of the Republic', which asked Australians to:

> … make choice between …
> The Land of Morn and the Land of E'en,
> The Old Dead Tree and the Young Tree Green,
> The Land that belongs to the lord and Queen,
> And the Land that belongs to you.[8]

A popular monarchy

One of the principal reasons why republicanism did not gain significant ground in these years was the long and successful reign of Queen Victoria. There were some Australians who expressed their opinions of the Queen and her family in negative terms—the *Bulletin* was always critical, and the scurrilous John Norton of *Truth* earned himself a trial for sedition for one particularly offensive outburst—but most Australians revered the Queen. Her son, the Prince of Wales, attracted more criticism, but few Australians seriously suggested abandoning the British monarchy for a republican style of government.[9]

The closing decades of the century saw Australians debating the federation of the Australian colonies. The poet W. T. Goodge mocked the hopes and aspirations of those advocating federation, and their expectations of the future of the new nation, which he saw as a bundle of contradictions:

> Let us sing of Federation
> ('Tis the theme of every cult)
> And the joyful expectation
> Of its ultimate result.
> 'T will confirm the jubilation

Of protection's expectation,
And the quick consolidation
Of freetrade with every nation;
And teetotal legislation
Will achieve its consummation
And increase our concentration
On the art of bibulation.
We shall drink to desperation,
And be quite the soberest nation
We'll be desperately loyal
Unto everything that's royal,
And be ultra-democratic
In a matter most emphatic.
We'll be prosperous and easeful,
And pre-eminently peaceful,
And we'll take our proper station
As a military nation!
We shall show the throne affection,
Also sever the connection,
And the bonds will get no fainter
And we'll also cut the painter.
We'll proclaim with lute and tabor
The millennium of labour,
And we'll bow before the gammon
Of plutocracy and Mammon.
We'll adopt all fads and fictions
And their mass of contradictions
If all hopes are consummated
When Australia's federated;
For the Federation speeches
This one solid moral teach us—
That a pile of paradoxes are expected to result![10]

The federation of the Australian colonies on the first day of the new century, 1 January 1901, created the Commonwealth of Australia as a sovereign nation under the Crown. By that time there was little opposition to the idea that the new nation would be a constitutional monarchy, and the Queen herself signed the infant Commonwealth into existence.[11] Three weeks after federation, she died, and plunged the empire into mourning.

" Westminster Gazette."]

John Bull: " It's certainly a Kangaroo, but it's uncommonly like a Lion."

W. H. Fitchett, editor of the *Review of Reviews for Australasia*, and author of a best-selling book, *Deeds that Won the Empire*, expressed the feelings of many of his fellow Australians when he wrote that:

> The death of the Queen, after an illness so brief, cast on the Empire a shadow like the blackness of an eclipse, and nowhere was that shadow darker than in Australasia. Few Australians had ever seen the Queen; the number of those who had spoken to her might almost be counted on the fingers of two hands. Yet, by some strange magic, the Queen touched the imagination of all Australians in a degree which no other human being ever approached ... Then, too, she was the symbol—the human embodiment—of the Empire. The Empire itself seemed to take visible form in her. Her personality was one of its great unifying forces. She was, in a sense, its voice; she could make its emotions and aspirations audible. And for so long had she been part of the history and life of the Empire that her subjects—in Australasia at least—had almost forgotten she was mortal. So there was a touch of astonishment in the grief which swept over these States when the news came that the Queen was dead.[12]

Lest it be thought that Fitchett's emotional response to the Queen's death, and the somewhat extravagant prose in which he expressed it, belonged exclusively to his time, similar sentiments were expressed over fifty years later by an Australian poet of the nationalist Jindyworobak movement, Rex Ingamells, on a similar theme. Ingamells gave Queen Victoria the credit for assisting in the preservation of Australia's indigenous people:

> Looking back into the past we see, during the decades of Queen Victoria's reign, the Queen's Birthday celebrated by feasts provided for the aborigines by the most philanthropic of the settlers and sometimes by official authority. The unfortunate tribes, doomed most of them to extinction, had cause to cherish the name of the Great White Queen and to note her influence for benignancy upon the masterful settlers.[13]

The Duke of York, later King George VI, reads the commission at the opening of the provisional Parliament House, Canberra, 9 May 1927. National Library of Australia

The guests attending the opening of the first parliament of the Commonwealth of Australia by the Duke of Cornwall and York (the future

King George V) were still in mourning for the Queen, giving the celebrations a more sombre aspect than those in Sydney in January. But the monochrome dress failed to extinguish the spirit of celebration, and the joy of those Australians who lined the processional routes to cheer the royal visitors. Their jubilation, however, was not shared by all Australians. Victor Daley wrote a satirical poem, 'The Procession', describing the event:

> With shriek of fifes, and bang of drums,
> Behold the Royal Circus comes ...
>
> The banners flutter in the breeze,
> From windows and from balconies;
>
> As if each house, with joyful shout,
> Had hung its gaudiest washing out ...
>
> The troops pass by—a stream of steel—
> A proud sight for the Commonweal.
>
> The people crush and crowd to see
> This Royal Circus fine—and free—
>
> That rolls along, with flags unfurled,
> And all the madness of the world.[14]

King Edward VII, successor to Queen Victoria, reigned over the era which bears his name and is synonymous with the last days of gracious living before the cataclysms which marked the twentieth century overwhelmed Europe and the world. When King George V ascended the throne to begin a reign that extended through the First World War and the Great Depression, the royal family continued the tradition established by Queen Victoria, and became exemplars of duty and of externally harmonious family life. The personality of the King was summed up in an ironical poem by Australian poet Charles W. Hayward ('T the R'):

> He did his duty both by peers and peasants
> In council chambers, gilded halls and camps;
> And in his leisure moments potted pheasants
> And perseveringly collected stamps.[15]

King George V's son, the Duke of York, as his father had before him, came to Australia to open a parliament. This time he and his wife, the former Lady Elizabeth Bowes-Lyon (now Elizabeth the Queen Mother), came to Canberra in May 1927 to open Australia's new provisional parliament house, which effectively inaugurated the occupation of the new federal capital, Canberra. Ten years later, upon the abdication of his brother, King Edward VIII, he was crowned King George VI. Mary Gilmore (later Dame Mary), for many years editor of the Women's Page in the *Australian Worker*, wrote a poem, 'Coronation Anthem', to honour his coronation:

> The ancient kingdoms of his realm declare his royal line:
> India bends down to touch his robe:
> Canada, New Zealand, and Australia obeisance make:
> Anzac and Africa before him kneel:
> For all men know that only in the King are we made one,
> Only in the King His Majesty are all these peoples one;
> In him are we crowned and he in us …[16]

Mary Gilmore, later Dame Mary, in a 1928 portrait by Adelaide Perry. National Library of Australia

Historian W. K. Hancock echoed Gilmore's sentiments several years later, in an essay on 'Monarchy' published in 1943. Hancock saw Australia as 'every bit as independent and free as the United States', having 'achieved sovereignty without the pain and loss of separation', and with the benefit of belonging 'to a family, a Commonwealth of democratic nations'. Hancock summed up his satisfaction with the prevailing constitutional arrangement between the monarchy and Australia: 'In Australia, our governments and parliaments and courts, state and federal, do their business in the King's name. That suits us well enough. We intend to keep on that way.'[17]

Affection for the Crown and for the royal family showed no signs of flagging in Australia in the immediate post-war period. The courage of the royal family in staying in London during the Blitz—part of Buckingham Palace was hit by a bomb—their visits to victims of German bombing, and the young Princess Elizabeth's service as a transport driver, all endeared them to their subjects in Britain and the Commonwealth. When King George VI died in 1952, and his daughter became Queen, her coronation in 1953 was entered into by the people of distant Australia with as much enthusiasm as in Britain. Kathy Skelton, then a young girl, describes the atmosphere in her community, the seaside town of Sorrento in Victoria, and around Australia:

> From the time Mr Menzies announced on the wireless that it was his 'very melancholy task to inform the House that the news is now officially confirmed that His Majesty the King died this morning', the prospect of a new monarch, one who was young and female, a Queen of Australia, made us obsessed with queens and crownings. There were Coronation Balls, Coronation Processions with floats, and Coronation Cookery Books. Ladies' Guilds held Coronation Tea Parties. Golf Clubs awarded Coronation Medals for Coronation holes-in-one, and there were Coronation Gifts at athletic meetings and gymkhanas. Union Jacks and sweets were handed out at Coronation bonfires. By the time Queen Elizabeth, wife of a naval officer, was crowned in 1953, the nationwide excitement had become a frenzied epidemic.
>
> Aunt Dorrie, my grandmother's sister who had no children and who worked as a cook and could save money in the bank, went to London for the Coronation ... Needless to say, we did not go to the Coronation and could not even listen to it on the wireless because it was on long past our bedtime. But we cut out pictures of the Queen and the Royal Family and pasted them on the brown paper covers of our exercise books and readers.[18]

The Queen in Australia

The excitement of the Coronation was, however, eclipsed by what Skelton called 'the Greatest Occasion of them all', the royal tour of Australia in early 1954, the first visit to Australia by a reigning monarch. A press photo of the Queen's foot poised above the Canberra airport tarmac was the first evidence for Australians that she was really here.[19] In those pre-television days an eyewitness view was necessary before the full reality of the royal presence could be felt. Vast crowds lined the roadside to see the Queen's car pass by. Kathy Skelton and her schoolmates were brought by bus from Sorrento to a place reserved for them on Melbourne's Toorak Road by their local Shire Councillor:

> We scarcely had time to get our Union Jacks aloft and in motion when a white-gloved hand and a pale face beneath a thatch of violets went by in a

In 1954 Queen Elizabeth II became the first reigning monarch to visit Australia. Accompanied by Prime Minister R. G. Menzies, she ascends the steps of Parliament House, Canberra, to deliver the Queen's speech to open the parliamentary session. National Library of Australia

big black car, and everyone was cheering. 'Was that her?' we asked and, assured that it was, reboarded the bus to come home.[20]

Not all Australians were satisfied with that fleeting glimpse of their young Queen. Poet Les Murray dates his disenchantment with Australia's constitutional links to the British monarchy, and his adherence to the republican tradition in Australia, to the 1954 royal tour when, as a fifteen-year-old youth, he and his father tried to get to Newcastle (NSW) to watch the Queen pass by. Then he realised what they were attempting to do: 'I suddenly felt we were humiliating ourselves. We were all fired up to go and stand craning uncomfortably in a crowd in order to glimpse an Englishwoman to whom we, individually, meant nothing'. For Murray this brought home to him the 'sheer unbridgability of archaic rank'.[21]

Novelist Martin Boyd, before the royal tour, wrote an essay entitled 'Their Link with Britain' for a book published in London in 1953, *The Sunburnt Country: Profile of Australia*. Boyd focused on the spiritual and emotional ties implicit in the monarchical system, and delivered a caution to those who would denigrate the connection between Australia and Britain expressed in the person of the monarch:

Vast crowds lined the royal route in the cities visited by Queen Elizabeth and Prince Philip in 1954. Here a large collection of prams indicates the post-war 'baby boom'. Australian Archives, ACT. CRS A1773, RV970.

The visit of the Queen to Australia is above all things an occasion when our continuity with that social order, and our blood relationship with Her Majesty's subjects in the old world should be made clear. Now, when the only political link between Australia and Britain is allegiance to the Crown, this visit is an opportunity to strengthen the emotional tie with newly-awakened feelings of loyalty and affection. Both our countries are monarchies, and the same Queen unites them into one family. The Queen is a living symbol of the fact that we are of one blood. The Australian whose patriotism does not extend beyond his own shores, and would minimise the influence of the Throne, is working against the wholesome strength of the British Commonwealth, and consequently against his own survival.[22]

The Queen has visited Australia on a number of occasions since 1954, for example, the opening of the Sydney Opera House in 1973, the High

Court of Australia in 1980 and the National Gallery of Australia in 1982, but none has eclipsed that first event—what historian Peter Spearritt has called 'the most popular and elaborate ritual this country has ever seen'[23] —in excitement and wonder. Perhaps the most significant of her later visits for the symbolic aspect of her role as Queen of Australia was her opening of the new Parliament House in 1988, the bicentenary year of British settlement in Australia.

Debate begins

At the time of the 1954 royal tour the loyalty of Australians to the monarchy was unquestioned. Rex Ingamells claimed:

> Loyalty has, indeed, been a constant factor in Australian life—Royalty a permanent factor in Australian thinking. The extraordinary idealisation of the Crown, in this country from which the Throne-room is so remote, has banked up within our national experience, as do the rare and mighty torrents of some inland rivers, to sweep through all barriers the distances can present, providing that phenomenal rush of loyal demonstrativeness which celebrates every Royal visit to our shores.[24]

The seemingly unchallengeable 'loyalty' was, however, being eroded by circumstances. Australia's strategic interests, which had led her prime minister John Curtin to 'look to America' at a critical point in the Second World War; and the changing nature of Australian society under the impact of non-British migration, among other factors, were prompting the reconsideration of Australia's traditional ties to Britain. By the mid-1960s some commentators were beginning to question the relevance of the British monarchy to Australia, and suggesting a republic as an alternative. Donald Horne, in his influential book, *The Lucky Country*, published in 1964, ten years after Queen Elizabeth's first triumphant tour, tackled this issue head on:

> In a sense Australia is a republic already. The traditional British forms already run much more shallow than the more elderly Australians realize. To people who are under thirty-five, who were still at school when Singapore fell or not even born, there is no basis of power or performance or reason in the monarchy ... Altogether there are more than three quarters of a million non-

British migrants. To the migrants or the under thirty-fives—and that is now a majority of the population—the Royal Family is a novelty item, charming celebrities ...

How Australia will become a republic, and when, is not predictable. However one knows that the older generations to whom such a change is unthinkable are going to die, and that in the younger generations there is likely to be little interest in preserving Australia as a monarchy. Merely to write the word is to invite derision. Hardly any Australian below a certain age would consider his country to be a monarchy yet that is its constitutional position. It will become politically practicable to make this break; all that is needed is some push from events, some dramatic reason for making it. No one can tell what that push might be, but it will be pushing against a lightly locked door.[25]

Donald Horne, author of the influential 1964 book, The Lucky Country, *and a consistent advocate of an Australian republic.*
National Library of Australia

Just over ten years later an event occurred which might have had the effect which Horne predicted, of opening that 'lightly locked door'. While it did not produce then—and still has not produced—an Australian republic, the dismissal, by the Queen's representative, of an elected Australian government was a catalyst for a renewed republican movement in Australia.

Republicanism revived

The dismissal of the Whitlam Labor government by the Governor-General, Sir John Kerr, on Remembrance Day, 11 November 1975, was arguably one of the most dramatic events in Australian history. It has iconic significance; there is a huge body of literature explaining and interpreting the course of events and the reasons why the protagonists acted as they did. This is not the place to discuss the historical background of what is always capitalised in speech and writing as 'The Dismissal'; its significance for this chapter is its role as a stimulus to Australia's writers to work towards an Australian republic.

News of the government's sacking produced outraged comments from some of Australia's leading writers, who then campaigned for Whitlam and the Labor Party in the federal election which followed. Since that time many of them have continued to promote an Australian republic. Geoffrey Dutton, who had previously written about an Australian republic in the 1960s,[26] published *Republican Australia?*, a response to the Whitlam dismissal by writers and academics, in 1977. Donald Horne, Thomas Keneally, Manning Clark, Les Murray and Patrick White all contributed to *Republican Australia?*[27]

Patrick White, Nobel Prize-winning novelist, was a committed republican until his death in 1990. White regarded the Whitlam government's dismissal as a 'cataclysm'. He urged his friends to boycott all official engagements at Government House, castigating them if he saw their names when he scanned the vice-regal column in the morning newspaper.[28]

In the 1990s two groups engage in public debate on the constitutional future of Australia: the Australian Republican Movement and Australians for a Constitutional Monarchy. The Australian Republican Movement numbers well-known Australian literary figures among its membership, including Donald Horne, Thomas Keneally, Faith Bandler, David Williamson, Bruce Petty, Blanche d'Alpuget and Richard Walsh. The late Oodgeroo of the Tribe Nununkul (Aboriginal poet Kath Walker) was also a member of the Australian Republican Movement. She said that 'European Australians must let go of England. It is time to do that'.[29] Donald Horne has claimed that 'The present Constitution needs the monarchism and the rubbish left over from the technicalities of transition to a Federation pruned out of it'.[30] Thomas Keneally, president of the Australian Republican Movement, has written an account of his involvement with Australian republicanism in *Our Republic*, published in 1993.[31] Poet Les Murray, while not a member of the Australian Republican Movement, says that his 'main objection to the monarchical system is that under it we are finally still subjects, not citizens'.[32]

The principal speakers and writers for Australians for a Constitutional Monarchy are Tony Abbott MHR, Sir Harry Gibbs, former Chief Justice of the High Court, Justice Michael Kirby, Emeritus Professor Dame Leonie Kramer, Chancellor of the University of Sydney, and the former secretary to a succession of Governors-General, Sir David Smith. They believe, in the words of Sir David Smith, that 'if there is one thing that we do not need to change it is the unifying influence of our own particular brand of constitutional monarchy'.[33] Sir Harry Gibbs has stated that debate about a republic distracts Australians from more important issues:

We are a self-governing democracy, completely independent of any exter-
nal control in all aspects of our affairs, and the Queen has no power to influence, the formation of policies or the conduct of government in Australia.
The argument that we should convert to a republic rests solely on sentiment.
The debate on the question whether we should become a republic involves
two dangers—first, that it may divide the community, in which strains are
unfortunately already becoming apparent, and secondly, that it may distract
attention from the real issues that face Australia.[34]

The debate continues, with no sign of resolution.

8
DREAMING SPIRES

A da Cambridge in her 1904 novel, *Sisters*, described a 'tall, graceful and most distinguished young fellow', 'young Dalzell' who, in the opinion of his neighbour Pennycuick, had not been improved by his overseas education:

> ... That boy has been to Cambridge, and now he loafs about the club, pretends to be a judge of wine, gets every stitch of clothes from London ... An idle, finicking chap, that'll never do an honest stroke of work as long as he lives ...[1]

The novelist's strictures on the product of a Cambridge education indicated a situation that had been common in the Australian colonies, but one which was passing even as she wrote. Australians of comfortable means had sent their children to Oxford and Cambridge for their undergraduate education; as early as the 1820s native-born Australians such as William Charles Wentworth travelled to Britain for this purpose. It is no coincidence that Wentworth chaired a select committee of the Legislative Council in 1849 to consider the establishment of the first Australian university, Sydney, in 1850, for the education of the youth of the growing colony.[2] In setting up their own first tertiary institutions Australians naturally looked to the universities of England, Scotland and Ireland for inspiration, with the system of high-class pass degrees characteristic of the

W. C. Wentworth, an early champion of tertiary education in Australia, and regarded as the founder of the University of Sydney. National Library of Australia

Scottish system adopted instead of the English emphasis on the honours degree. The influence of the ancient universities of Oxford and Cambridge was more noticeable in the colleges established by Sydney and Melbourne Universities—St Paul's and St John's at Sydney, and Trinity, Ormond and Queens at Melbourne.[3]

The academic staff of these early institutions of higher learning held firmly to three guiding principles: 'that the European tradition should be maintained in the Antipodes, that teaching should be more important than examination, and that standards comparable to those in the British Isles should be achieved'.[4] The earliest university buildings in Australia also recalled their British antecedents. To walk into the quadrangle of the main building of the University of Sydney, designed in the academic gothic style by Edmund Blacket, is to imagine oneself inside the college walls of Oxford, Cambridge, or Trinity College, Dublin. By the mid-twentieth century university buildings were no longer replicas of the old universities of the British Isles. Nevertheless, although its buildings were modern, the Australian National University, begun in the mid-1940s, owed much to the British academic tradition. The historians of the Australian National University describe the way in which the ideas of Sir Keith Hancock, of Balliol College and All Souls, Oxford, were expressed in the design of the ANU's University House:

> Hancock imagined University House with dining areas, recreation rooms, small rooms for informal discussions, quiet reading rooms, and perhaps a swimming pool and squash courts ... He hoped that older traditions would be sustained at the University, permitting 'a certain amount of gracious living'—as an inspiration to first-rate work as well as an end in itself. 'What we want is the twentieth century equivalent of that medieval institution, the

Oxford College', but 'freed from the tradition of medieval celibacy'.[5]

The Australian emphasis on undergraduate education as opposed to postgraduate meant that those seeking a scholarly profession tended to go overseas to undertake their postgraduate studies. The obvious place to do this was England—and in England Oxford and Cambridge were the draw-cards for many, particularly once the system of Rhodes Scholarships to Oxford was instituted. The twentieth century generations of Australian academics have been characterised by these and other British university connections.[6] Some of the writers featured later in this chapter—Sir Keith Hancock, Kathleen Fitzpatrick, Manning Clark—were representative of an academic tradition in Australia whose influence is still potent in Australian universities. A considerable number of Australian academics working in universities today are either graduates of or have been taught by graduates of the ancient British foundations. For example, Australian historian John La Nauze, a Rhodes Scholar from Western Australia, worked from the late 1940s to the mid-1960s in four out of the six State universities of Australia before succeeding Sir Keith Hancock in the Research School of Social Sciences in the Australian National University in 1966. At his retirement in 1976 fellow Australian historian and Oxford graduate L. F. Fitzhardinge wrote that he suspected La Nauze's first spiritual home 'was always Oxford'.[7] A similar statement could be made about a host of older or now-retired but still influential Australian academics.

Fitting in

Those whose experiences are featured in this chapter belong predominantly to the group described above: young people who had already showed considerable promise in their undergraduate years, and who believed that they would benefit from study at a British university. Only one of those examined—Patrick White—followed the older colonial tradition of beginning his undergraduate studies in England, at King's College, Cambridge. The others either embarked on a second undergraduate degree or a course of postgraduate study. They were thus older than their British fellow students who had, in most cases, just come from the school system. Ross Campbell, a Rhodes Scholar in the 1930s, related the moment when he recognised this fact:

That night I had my first dinner in the panelled hall. Looking around I noticed how young the faces were. I realised that I was beginning at Oxford with English students straight from school who were four years younger than myself. After all the time I had spent at Melbourne University trying to grow up, I would have to start over again.[8]

In later life, Sir Keith Hancock remembered the sense of awe with which he first encountered Oxford, which still remained with him after a lifetime of familiarity:

... sometimes the splendour smites me again as it did that first day when I entered the other Oxford that lies beyond Boffin's cake shop. I can still feel myself adventurous when I walk into the front quad of Balliol, and I can tell myself, and half believe it, when I read a printed placard announcing that All Souls is closed to visitors, 'This means me.' Of course, it is only a game that I play with myself, this sudden and vivid recapturing of a first experience. Almost in the same moment the later experiences are with me again and I know that All Souls has been a home to me for a generation and that I first came to Balliol thirty years ago.[9]

Historian Kathleen Fitzpatrick recorded her recollections of Oxford in the later 1920s in her autobiography, *Solid Bluestone Foundations*. She had savoured the experience of becoming part of Oxford's continuing life:

I loved to go to lectures at Christ Church, entering by Tom Tower, crossing the noble quadrangle and, never failing to look upwards, when passing under the marvellous fan vaulting of the great staircase. It was a delight to pace the perfect Gothic cloisters of New College, the meticulously tended lawns of St John's and the charming paths through the woods at Magdalen. It was a privilege to study in the dusky recesses of Duke Humphrey's Library and in the Bodleian and to feel oneself a drop in the great stream of folk which had, for so many centuries, flowed into Oxford seeking and finding knowledge there.[10]

Ross Campbell at Magdalen College noticed both the spendid architecture, and the lack of warmth of his fellow students:

To the eye Magdalen College was splendid and beautiful. It had five quadrangles, medieval cloisters, Georgian buildings, lawns, riverside walks, and

The 'dreaming spires' of Magdalen College seen from inside another of Oxford's colleges. Ross Campbell was a Rhodes Scholar at Magdalen in the 1930s.
Photograph by Michael Jones

over all its pinnacled bell-tower. I had never lived amid so much grandeur—or, for the moment, with so little company. There were no tiresome initiations here, but the camaraderie was lacking also.

After a few days a man next to me at breakfast asked: 'What do they think of the royal family in Australia?'

'There's no personal animosity against them', I said.

To my surprise he laughed. He seemed to think my reply an amusing example of colonial eccentricity.[11]

For Manning Clark, Oxford just prior to the Second World War 'was like an oasis in a desert. The dons of Balliol College were warm, eccentric and ultimately unknowable'.[12] Kathleen Fitzpatrick, despite her appreciation of the history and aesthetics of Oxford, felt lonely and isolated. She calculated that she was 'not only the sole Australian woman undergraduate in Somerville but, as far as I know, in all Oxford at that time'.[13] There were some things about the place that would forever remain repugnant to her:

What I could never reconcile myself to was the position of women at Oxford. In 1926 when I arrived there, it was only a few years since women had been admitted to the full status of members of the university, on their way to receiving degrees like the men, and since this emancipation had been won with difficulty the authorities of the women's colleges were very anxious that their

113

undergraduates should be as inconspicuous as possible and give no occasion for adverse criticism. To ensure this they subjected us to much stricter discipline than that dispensed to male undergraduates. Although I was not in the least unruly I felt the prison-like atmosphere of the college to be degrading. Outside the college, too, we were constantly reminded that we were not particularly welcome in Oxford. Some irreconcilable male dons refused to admit women to their lectures and others took the more subtle course of admitting but embarrassing them. All undergraduates were required to wear academic dress to lectures, but indoors the men took off their mortar-boards whereas women were required to wear their thick cloth caps indoors as well as out. I was at a lecture one warm spring day when a girl who was feeling the heat took her cap off. She was publicly reproved by the lecturer who told her that he would not have improperly dressed females in his lectures, as if the poor, mortified girl had stripped herself naked ... [14]

Class differences between male and female undergraduates also meant little contact between the sexes. The males of the 'smart set' belonged to 'the gentry and the prosperous upper-middle class: they were, in the main, in Oxford in pursuit of pleasure rather than of learning'. Members of the women's colleges, by contrast, were middle-class and 'hard-working and clever because, as Oxford could accept only one woman for every four men, they would enter only by a fairly rigorous entrance examination'. Socially beyond the pale through this circumstance and her colonial status generally, Fitzpatrick 'never received an invitation to anything from an Oxford man', and did not in the least appreciate her new and unfamiliar 'status as a frump'.[15]

Sport helped some young Australians at Oxford to enter the social life of the university. Historians Keith Hancock in the 1920s and Manning Clark in the 1930s had their sporting talents seized upon by their fellow-students at Balliol. Keith Hancock described his lasting first impressions of Oxford and collegiate life in his autobiography, *Country and Calling*:

I came there with a return of the old shyness that I had for a time put behind me; for I had heard much alarming talk about supercilious young men from the English public schools who kept everyone else at an unfriendly distance and conversed with each other in an accent and style deliberately assumed so as to make Australians and other colonials feel ill at ease. And indeed, no sooner was I within the porter's lodge, inquiring where my rooms might be, than a lanky, bespectacled youth emitted a falsetto flood of cacklings or twit-

Balliol College, Oxford,
cricket team, 1939.
Manning Clark is second
from left in the back row.
Photograph courtesy
of Clark family

terings which greatly entertained his companions but alarmed me. Yet it was only the elder Turton, an innocent and kindly twitterer if ever there was one, as I learnt a few days later when he came to my rooms to ask if I would write something for *The Cherwell*. He was an ingenious and irresponsible promoter of experiments and escapades—such as a mock attack on Carfax, which suddenly and hopelessly confused the policeman on traffic duty, or a prize for the man who walked into Balliol Hall wearing on his person the largest number of articles beginning with the letter Q: he himself walked in unrolling an immense ball of string, the end of which he had tied to the gate of Queen's College. I found myself at home with humour in this idiom … In my first few days at Balliol a succession of young Englishmen walked into my rooms to inquire whether I would row? whether I would play rugger? or soccer? or hockey?—and when I said that never in my life had I played this game or the other the answer always was that it made no difference. This answer astonished me, for in an Australian university skill makes a great deal of difference; the unskilled man gets no game at all. I decided to try the hockey field—it was a second eleven match against Keble and I rushed madly in the wrong direction and collided with an enemy forward who asked me if I thought I was playing rugger? I limped home muddy and happy and deeply convinced that games at Oxford were better fun than games at Melbourne.[16]

Manning Clark, at Balliol College a decade later, did not find his British fellow students as easy-going as Hancock had done. He was aware of a sense of difference expressed in a number of subtle ways. But he found, like Hancock, that sport—in his case cricket—could be a great ice-breaker, although even this held unforeseen social minefields for an unwary Australian:

> Cricket in the summer term at Oxford led to more bizarre confrontations with Englishmen. The captain of the Oxford team and his advisers liked my performances with bat and wicket-keeping gloves in the freshmen's trials. Alas, they did not like my Melbourne University cap—that being, in their eyes, too large and sloppy. So they elected me at once to the Authentics, and presented me with a cap. I did not have the money to buy the essentials. Every gentleman owned his own kit—cricketing bag, bat, batting gloves and pads, and in my case wicket-keeping pads and gloves. Humphrey Sumner was so delighted a Balliol man had a chance to play for Oxford that he paid for my equipment—all save the bag. So my Gladstone bag branded me unmistakably as an Aussie. The equipment did not come before the next trial. So I innocently wore pads lying in the dressing-room and, on returning to the pavilion for the tea adjournment, was taken by the shoulders and given a good shaking and threatened with a 'good thrashing' by a young Englishman, a wearer of the right scarf, the right tweed coat, indeed everything very much *comme il faut*, whose gear I had unwittingly used. I was a usurper: I was again an outsider …
>
> Playing cricket for Oxford worked one miracle. The English began to speak to me. The head porter of Balliol lifted his hat and smiled as I passed through the entrance gate of Balliol in the Broad … Ted Heath, then an organ scholar at the college, gave me a smile—and that, for an Englishman at the time, said quite a lot. Roy Jenkins, who will later take the other side in politics, sought me out in the Junior Common Room after Hall and asked me, if I remember rightly, why Australian batsmen danced so far down the wicket to meet the ball. It was like asking why Australians were so different to the English.[17]

The Oxford years, as well as gaining Clark a first class Master of Arts degree for his thesis, 'The Ideal of Alexis de Tocqueville', also saw his marriage to Dymphna Lodewyckx. She had been studying German on a von Humboldt scholarship in Bonn, but the alarming developments in Germany in 1939 induced Clark to bring his fiancée to England. They were married in the Anglo-Saxon church of St Michael at the North Gate in Oxford.[18] Poet Michael Thwaites, a Rhodes Scholar at New College, and Clark's contemporary at Trinity College in Melbourne and at Oxford, was also married in Oxford to Honor Mary Good, at the Church of St Peter in the East.[19] Both Dymphna Lodewyckx and Honor Good were Melbourne girls: Australian women students, had they known of Australian men students at Oxford, would probably have found them similarly committed to attachments already formed in Australia.

Patrick White entered King's College, Cambridge, on 6 November 1932, but the early part of his time there was lonely and frustrating. His autobiographical work, *Flaws in the Glass*, says very little about the Cambridge years, but his biographer, David Marr, has filled out his experience there. White, with his friend 'R', with whom he shared rooms in King's, lived a quiet and routinised existence, and observed rather than participated in the eccentricities which made the 1930s Cambridge homosexuals notorious:

> An exotic parade passed beneath their windows. King's men strolled through the courts at strange hours in fancy dress; an heir to the Cunard line went about the quadrangle in lipstick and furs. White and R remained spectators of this extraordinary existence, for the aesthetes of King's were terrifying snobs, nocturnal creatures who

Snow-covered quadrangle of King's College, Cambridge, where Patrick White, Australia's Nobel Prize winning novelist, studied in the 1930s. Photograph by Rod Muir, courtesy of Jill Waterhouse

played at night and slept all day in rooms draped with strange fabrics.[20]

Clive James entered Pembroke College on a scholarship in the 1960s, having completed a first undergraduate degree at Sydney University. His first encounter with another undergraduate, Abramovitz, gave him the key to dealing with Cambridge life. Abramovitz, who showed James 'the form'—the clubs and societies to join (James opted for the Footlights, and later became President), the laundry arrangements, how to 'sport your oak'—appeared to have been at Cambridge for years, but turned out to be a freshman who had arrived the day before. This was a revelation to James: 'It struck me on the spot that if the English had spent their lives preparing to fit into one of these places, then the only smart thing to do was to not bother about fitting in at all, and I can honestly say that from that moment on I never wasted any time trying.[21]

One of James's associates in the Cambridge of the 1960s was 'Romaine Rand'—a thin disguise for Germaine Greer—then a serious doctoral scholar in English literature, who nevertheless participated in a 'smoker' (college revue) at James's request, where she brought the house down with her rendition of 'Land of Hope and Glory':

Though Romaine did indeed turn up on the first night of the Pembroke smoker, she terrified me by announcing that she intended to do nothing except sing 'Land of Hope and Glory'. She had brought the sheet music for this, so that our piano player could accompany her. She was also carrying a dark blue straw hat with a stuffed bird on it. She put in a request to go on last, so that she would have time to practise her piece out in the corridor …

… At the end of my monologue, I was swept off the stage by a tidal wave of applause. As Romaine went past me in the dark, I tacitly challenged her to top that. For a long while nothing much happened. I peeked around the door. The preliminary cheering had died down to a provisional rhubarb. Some of the Hearties were laughing at Romaine's hat, but all the rest of the audience were refilling one another's wine glasses while she handed her sheet music to the piano player, gave him whispered instructions, stood back, folded her hands, cleared her throat, and nodded for him to begin the accompaniment.

The result was chaos. She sang 'Land of Hope and Glory' with her lips out of synchronisation with the words. When she sang the word 'hope', her mouth was pronouncing the word 'land', and so on. The effect was uncannily funny, as if the world had come loose from its pivot … [22]

Educational matters

The prime purpose of these young Australians embarking upon an Oxford or Cambridge degree was, of course, study and scholarship, however much the social, sporting or theatrical life of these places might impinge. Keith Hancock remembered with enormous gratitude the three 'grand men' who were his tutors at Balliol, for whom he would 'die for in the last ditch, the men for whom the most that I can give in loyalty and hard work seems far too little'.[23] In *Country and Calling* he described the contribution to his scholarship made by A. L. Smith, Master of Balliol, Humphrey Sumner (also Manning Clark's tutor some years later), and Kenneth Bell:

> A. L. Smith, then Master of Balliol, was my first tutor and he brought me to earth with a bump when he criticized my first essay; I had been rather pleased with the way I had grasped my theme, but he made me see that in expounding it I had spent twice as many words as I need have done. He was a great teacher of economy, that cardinal virtue of thought and style. From other tutors, particularly from two whom I was destined to know as friends in All Souls, I learnt to value some less austere virtues. Humphrey Sumner must have found me too purposeful, for he encouraged me to browse ... Meanwhile, Kenneth Bell was convincing me, by example rather than precept, that learning alone was not enough but only so many dry bones waiting for the creative imagination that would call them to life.[24]

Ross Campbell had applied to enter Magdalen College, Oxford, so that he could have C. S. Lewis as a tutor. Lewis, a 'fattish, jovial man in his mid-thirties' with a 'firm, resonant voice', seemed to Campbell to be 'like a cheerful, bookish medieval monk living at the wrong time'.[25] But Campbell was to find that the ultimate effect of Lewis's tutoring was to 'erode my self-confidence'. Lewis complained that Campbell's writing was 'jejune', which Campbell on consulting a dictionary discovered meant 'dry, unsatisfying to the soul or spirit'. Lewis elaborated his criticisms of Campbell's work in a devastating series of comments for President's Collections, particularly in relation to the latter's work in English language, Lewis's specialisation:

> ... unfortunately he has a pathetic faith that a spirit of adventure, unaided by any knowledge of grammar or vocabulary, will enable him to translate Old English. This

faith has survived many disillusionments and may prove indestructible. If it does, his prospects in the Schools will not.[26]

Clive James recalled the academic disputes of previous years when he described his supervisor of studies, Dr Stewart Frears:

> Professor Frears, as he later became, was, although the senior English don in the college, only a lecturer at that stage, but he was already an authority on the Metaphysical poets, to which his learned and common-sensical approach had already been more than enough to attract regular vilification from Dr Leavis. In life as in death—between which two states he was currently hovering—Leavis was the most contentious name in Cambridge. Like an old volcano that goes dead in its central crater but unpredictably blows hot holes through its own sides and obliterates villages which thought themselves safe, Leavis was dormant yet still bubbling. Frears caught more than his fair share of the lava and perhaps this accounted at least partly for a pronounced nervous tic ... He won't mind my recalling this trivial affliction because later on it disappeared ... While it was still happening, however, Dr Frears' flicking tic inevitably attracted some of the attention I was supposed to be directing towards the post-Elizabethans.[27]

Results

These Australians at Oxford and Cambridge were thus exposed to a variety of experiences, both scholarly and social; the results of their stays there were similarly diverse. Kathleen Fitzpatrick was devastated when she did not receive a first class honours degree from Oxford: what she perceived as failure conditioned her attitude to her scholarship for ever after. Manning Clark, in his eulogy at her funeral in 1990, described 'a wound which would not go away, with which she had to live for the rest of her life'.[28] Despite this blow, she had a very successful academic career in the History Department of the University of Melbourne. Kathleen Fitzpatrick said of her autobiography, *Solid Bluestone Foundations*, which contains the account of her Oxford years, that it was 'the only writing I ever enjoyed doing'.[29]

Keith Hancock (later Sir Keith) went on to greater academic honours which included a fellowship of All Souls, professorial appointments in Australia and Britain, and the position of Head of the Research School of

Social Sciences at the Australian National University. He was a noted Commonwealth historian, and the author of a celebrated book on his home country, *Australia*, published in 1930. He also published two autobiographical works which deal with his academic life in Oxford and Australia: *Country and Calling* and *Professing History*.

Ross Campbell, who took a BA and a BLitt at Oxford, became a journalist and a notable humourist whose columns appeared in Australian newspapers and magazines for many years.

Manning Clark returned to Australia, spent some time as a schoolmaster, became a lecturer in history at Melbourne University, then was appointed the foundation professor of history at the University College, Canberra, later the Australian National University's School of General Studies. The rest, in a word, is history—Clark is widely acknowledged as the creator of Australian history as a separate area of study rather than as a subset of British imperial history. His interpretation of that history, which began in 1962 with the publication of the first volume of *A History of Australia*, a task that continued through six volumes and lasted until 1987, has not been free of controversy to the present. Clark's life and personality, and his view of Australia's history, are still the subject of regular and often bitter debate in the Australian media. After concluding *A History of Australia*, Clark then wrote two volumes of autobiography, *The Puzzles of Childhood* and *The Quest For Grace*.

Michael Thwaites won the Newdigate poetry prize at Oxford in 1938 with his poem, 'Milton Blind', and the King's Medal for Poetry in 1940.[30] After Oxford, and war service as a Lieutenant in the Royal Volunteer Naval Reserve commanding a corvette, Thwaites took up an appointment in the Melbourne University Philosophy Department, then was recruited by the newly formed Australian Security Intelligence Organisation (ASIO). He played a role in the Petrov defection of the 1950s, ghost-writing the Soviet defectors' story, *Empire of Fear*, and also contributing his own account of the incident, *Truth Will Out*.[31] He has also published books of poetry: *Milton Blind*, *The Jervis Bay and Other Poems*, *Poems of War and Peace* and *The Honey Man*, between 1938 and 1989. He has recently participated in poetry and musical recitals in Britain with his pianist daughter Penelope, an exponent of the works of Australian composer Percy Grainger. In September 1996 Thwaites' poem 'Rain After Drought' was featured on BBC Radio's *Poetry Please* program.

Patrick White expressed his feelings about his academic studies at Cambridge in *Flaws in the Glass*: 'I knew I hadn't a scholar's mind. Such as

MILTON BLIND

THAT dreaming day it was, the bell-like air
Unclosed the naked admirable heaven,
Well made, and framing Oxford town; that day
The crocuses put out their waxen petals,
White, purple, gold, a comely darling band,
To witness God's unrivalled handiwork;
That day the droning sky let fall on China
Its bloody rain, plastering street and wall
With quivering flesh: that day the miner's wife
Strangled her starving children in their bed;
Elysian day, that day of plague and death
And horror screaming out of impersonal headlines—
That day it was I put my Milton by,
And, still with that serene immortal air
Elated, and the organ-march of sound,
Looked down into the blackened furtive street,
Looked up into the blue that boomed of death,
And in my imagination issue was joined:—

    Come down, Milton, from Olympus,
Where centuries have seated you, above common criticism,
    Cease now that stirring flight
Above the Aonian Mount, and effect a landing.

    Touch earth, Milton, and answer us.
We are the Twentieth Century, the unseated men, sceptics
    Not cynics, but questioners:
Come, stand in our midst, then, stand to our question.
    b   I

First page of Michael Thwaites's Newdigate Prize-winning poem of 1938, 'Milton Blind'. National Library of Australia

I had was more like the calico bag hanging from the sewing-room door-knob, stuffed with snippets of material of contrasting textures and clashing colours, which might at some future date be put to some practical, aesthetic, or even poetic use'.[32] White took a 'respectable' degree—second class honours, first division, and later won the Nobel Prize for literature.

Clive James regarded his Cambridge experience as a turning point in his life. It enabled him to 'develop my propensities, such as they were, to the fullest extent possible, and all at once. The result was chaos'.[33] Cambridge became his 'personal playground', where he read copiously—but not what he was supposed to be studying. He developed his theatrical talents, and writing skills, and the result was that 'In Cambridge, in the Sixties, my course was altered and fixed, for good or ill … The spires, the lawns, the spring alliance of jonquils and daffodils: I hardened my heart against these things and they all went to my head'.[34] Now a British-based critic, novelist, poet and television personality, James is probably, along with Germaine Greer and Barry Humphries, one of Australia's best known expatriates.

9

AUSTRALIANS ABROAD

The British writer Howard Jacobson, in his 1986 novel, *Redback*, has his hero Leon Forelock sailing out from England to Australia in the early 1960s. Leon has already been told that this journey is an unusual one for a Cambridge graduate such as he to be taking: it was far more common to see talented Australian writers, artists, actors and musicians travelling by sea in the reverse direction:

> I saw about fifteen other liners on the Indian Ocean alone, and they were all pointing the other way. Sometimes they would steam dangerously close to us, so that we could wave to them and they could stare in astonishment at us. On one afternoon alone I waved to Sidney Nolan, Diane Cilento, Randolph Stow, Clive James, Clifton Pugh, Germaine Greer, Barry Humphries, Thomas Keneally, Robert Helpmann, Brett Whiteley, the young Bob Hawke, Robert Hughes, Barry Tuckwell, Brian Hayes, Nigel Dempster, Carmen Callil, the future Princess Michael of Kent, and scores of minor poets and essayists all of whom would return from Oxford and Cambridge ten years later to take up Gough Whitlam creativity grants.[1]

Jacobson could also have included Barbara Hanrahan in his list of England-bound voyagers of the early 1960s.

The exodus of talented Australians to Britain at that time was by no means the beginning of Australian expatriatism, as chapter 6 has shown, although a considerable number of Australian writers who either live permanently in Britain, or who have spent a large proportion of their lives there, did leave the country then. Many of them are among those mentioned in Jacobson's tongue-in-cheek list. An expanded list would include other writers who made the change to northern climes in earlier times. They have included Henry Handel Richardson, Christina Stead, Martin Boyd and Peter Porter. An expatriate Australian, Sir Reginald Leeper, played a major role in the establishment of The British Council before the Second World War.

Why did they travel so far and stay so long? For all the reasons that their compatriots travelled to Britain around the turn of the century—to win recognition abroad as a precondition for recognition at home; to operate in a wider marketplace of ideas, inspiration and publication; to become part of the wider English-speaking milieu, some of them in the belief that they were making a pilgrimage to the source of their cultural identity.

Australians abroad have tended to divide into two groups: 'permanent' and 'temporary' expatriates. The distinction between the two is becoming blurred in the 1990s, with many who have been regarded as permanent British residents spending considerable amounts of time back in Australia, and becoming more and more involved in Australian literary life as communications between Britain and Australia have improved.[2] In the age of airline travel, easy telephone access and the Internet, no one now need feel themselves an exile. But a distinction based on permanent residence remains clear enough to describe them here under these headings; even in the electronic age there is no substitute for personal contact or for immersion in a particular place. And, after all, it is place that is the distinctive element here.

'Permanent' expatriates

Henry Handel Richardson

Henry Handel Richardson (Ethel Florence Lindesay Robertson), whose trilogy, *The Fortunes of Richard Mahony*,[3] an account of cultural alienation in colonial Victoria and in Britain, is regarded as one of the supreme literary expressions of Australia, left Australia in 1888 to study music in Leipzig and only came back for two months in 1912 to check facts for the Mahony trilogy. *The Getting of Wisdom*, another novel with an Australian setting, deals with her schooldays in Melbourne at the Presbyterian Ladies' College. Her novels were slow to gain acceptance in Australia, and it was not until the publication of the final volume of the Mahony trilogy, *Ultima Thule*, in 1929 that her work achieved success in her native land, with this novel winning the Australian Literature Society's Gold Medal that year, and boosting the reputation of all of her books from the 1930s onwards.[4]

The Mahony trilogy was based on the experiences of Ethel's father, Walter Richardson, on the Victorian goldfields and back in England. Its final sentence makes the distinction between the ability of Australia to absorb the material remains of Richard Mahony and its inability to capture his spirit, with its 'alienated European consciousness'[5]: 'The rich and kindly earth of his adopted country absorbed his perishable body, as the country itself had never contrived to make its own, his wayward, vagrant spirit'.[6]

Martin Boyd

Martin Boyd was a member of one of Australia's creative dynasties, the Boyd family, which has also included artists Merric, Penleigh, Arthur, Guy and David Boyd and architect and writer Robin Boyd. Martin Boyd served in the First World War in British units. From the 1920s he lived mostly in Britain, moving to Rome in 1957, where he died in 1972. For Martin Boyd, Britain formed the 'backcloth' to the culture in which he had been raised, and his first visit there confirmed his cultural affinity with the country of which he had heard all his life: 'For fifteen years my imagination had been historically stimulated, and when for the first time I visited the scenes of the ancient dramas, their beauty and significance struck me more forcibly than they could ever have done if I had grown up amongst them'.[7]

Boyd's work deals with the dual allegiance of Australians of his background to Australia and Britain. He complained in his autobiography, *Day of my Delight*, that 'I have suffered through being considered an Englishman in

Martin Boyd at his house at Plumstead, near Cambridge, in 1947. National Library of Australia

Australia and an Australian in England, and the target of the ill-bred of both countries'.[8] His best-known work, the Langton tetralogy of novels—*The Cardboard Crown, A Difficult Young Man, Outbreak of Love* and *Where Blackbirds Sing*—traces the eighty-year history of the Langton family and their houses, 'Waterpark' in England and 'Westhill' near Melbourne, as the characters alternate between them.

Peter Porter, Australian expatriate poet, during an oral history interview. National Library of Australia

Peter Porter

Bruce Bennett has claimed that expatriate Australian writers—Peter Porter, Barry Humphries, Clive James, Germaine Greer and Randolph Stow—have the advantage of what he has called 'bifocal vision' which 'gives them a special, if often unrecognised value to Australians'. 'London-based writers', in particular, 'have provided trenchant and memorable expatriate images of Australia'.[9] Among these Peter Porter (the subject of a full-scale study by Bennett, *Spirit in Exile: Peter Porter and his poetry*)[10] is one of the most prominent. Porter, a Queenslander, left Australia in 1951 and has lived in Britain ever since. In his poem 'Reading *MND* in Form 4B', he evokes the experience of studying Shakespeare's *A Midsummer Night's Dream* in a Queensland schoolroom:

Miss Manning rules us middle-class children
Whose fathers can't afford the better schools
With blue, small, crow-tracked, cruel eyes.
Philomel with melody—a refrain
Summoning the nightingale, the brown bird
Which bruits the Northern Hemisphere with bells—
It could not live a summer in this heat.

Queen Titania, unaware of Oberon,
Is sleeping on a bank. Her fairy watch
Sings over her a lullaby,

The warm snakes hatch out in her dream.
Miss Manning is too fat for love,
We cannot imagine her like Miss Holden
Booking for weekends at the seaside
With officers on leave. This is not Athens
Or the woods of Warwickshire,
Lordly the democratic sun
Rides the gross and southerly glass.
Miss Manning sets the homework. Thirty boys
Leave the bard to tire on his morning wing;
Out on their asphalt the team for Saturday
Wait, annunciations in purple ink,
Torments in locker rooms, nothing to hope for
But sleep, the reasonable view of magic.
We do not understand Shakespearean objects
Who must work and play: that gold stems from the sky:
It poisons 1944. To be young is to be in Hell,
Miss Manning will insulate us from this genius,
Rock the ground whereon these sleepers be.

Elsewhere there is war, here
It is early in an old morning, there is pollen
In the air, eucalyptus slipping past
The chalk and dusters—new feelings
In the oldest continent, a northern race
Living in the south. It is late indeed:
Jack shall have Jill, all shall be well,
Long past standing eternity,
Eastern Standard Time.[11]

Bruce Bennett said of 'Reading *MND* in Form 4B' that, in common with many of Porter's poems, it contains an argument 'about the power of certain artists to overcome national differences and distance'.[12] The work of Peter Porter bids fair to achieve a similar transcendence; he has been credited with creating his own literary environment, 'Porter country' (analogous to 'Greeneland'). The critic who developed this analogy, Peter Steele, has said of Porter that 'The metaphor of his own world or his own country is habitual with him'.[13] Porter himself has said that 'I think the poet's true country is his own mind, and that will receive stimuli from anywhere and everywhere … Thus it becomes honourable to be an airplant and to live wherever life will support one's imaginative labours'. His 'whole career as a poet has been conducted in England', nevertheless, he claims 'I am just as expatriated from Britain and Europe as I am from Australia'.[14] Porter draws a distinction between national identification and the creative imagination, in a statement which encapsulates one aspect of the expatriate experience: 'it has never crossed my mind to think of myself as anything other than Australian. Where I live and what I write about is another matter … I am a patriot for me. My true country is my imagination'.[15]

Germaine Greer

Germaine Greer went to Cambridge in the early 1960s and embarked on doctoral studies in English literature. Her name became synonymous with the emerging feminist movement in the early 1970s, with the publication of *The Female Eunuch*. She continued this success in feminist writing with other works dealing with the issues of women, sexuality and power. These included *The Obstacle Race*, on women artists, in 1979, *Sex and Destiny* in 1984, and *The Change: women, ageing and the menopause* in 1991. She published a collection of essays and occasional writings, *The Madwoman's Underclothes*, in 1986, and an autobiographical memoir, *Daddy, We Hardly Knew You*, in 1989, which has been described as, at one level, 'also a quest for the historical and present meaning of White Australia'.[16] Greer published a study of female poets, *Slip-Shod Sybils*, in 1995. American feminist Camille Paglia has said that in this book 'we see operating a learned, fastidious mind vastly superior to that of the pedestrian lot of women's studies professors—or to that of the woozy slatterns and twittering triflers who have provoked Greer lately in the London media'.[17] Greer's contribution to feminist thought will be examined further in chapter 12.

Clive James

Clive James, television critic and presenter, autobiographer, novelist and poet, went to Britain in 1962. His fictionalised autobiographies, *Unreliable Memoirs*, *Falling Towards England* and *May Week Was in June* trace a course from the Sydney suburb of Kogarah to Britain in the 1960s, and include memorable descriptions of other Australian expatriates, their identities flimsily disguised by pseudonyms: Bruce Jennings, 'the Green Gladiolus'

(Barry Humphries); Dave Dalziel (film maker Bruce Beresford); Romaine Rand (Germaine Greer); and Dibbs and Delish Buckley (artist Brett Whiteley and his wife Wendy). James's description of 'Bruce Jennings' captures the Barry Humphries who has revealed himself with candour and wit in his autobiography, *More Please*:

> Jennings left you in no doubt of his brilliance, though in some fear that his monologues might never end. A career drinker, he would stand balefully in the middle of a party, the only man present in a Turnbull & Asser shirt, antique Chavet tie, pin-stripe double-breasted Savile Row suit, Lobb shoes, black fedora and a monocle … When he fell to the floor he would usually take a couple of people with him. Laid to rest on a sofa, he would sleep until the party thinned out. Then, with just the right-sized audience, he would start a closed-eyed, resonant muttering which might consist of nothing but brand-names and radio jingles from the far Australian past. 'Rosella Tomato Sauce … Twice As Nice If Kept On Ice … Sydney Flour is our flour, we use it every day … I like Aeroplane Jelly, Aeroplane Jelly for me … You'll sleep tight 'cause you'll sleep right, on a Lotusland inner spring mattress …'
>
> Years later I was to realise that this was the most original side of his mind talking. He was rediscovering and reordering an Australian language which had never had any pretensions beyond the useful and had thus retained an inviolable purity … With a sure instinct reinforced by his dandyish collector's erudition, he had realised that not all the ephemeral was evanescent—that there was such a thing as a poetry of trivia, uniquely evocative for a country whose art was hag-ridden by a self-conscious striving towards autonomous respectability. Jennings was already well embarked on a salvage expedition to raise a nation's entire cultural subconscious. The obtuse among his country's intellectuals—a high proportion—thought he was lowering the tone, and belittled him accordingly.[18]

Cover of Falling Towards England, *the second volume of Clive James' autobiography,* Unreliable Memoirs. Courtesy of Pan Macmillan

James worked at an assortment of jobs in London—his tales of what he in fact contributed to the British economy make hilarious reading—then took another degree at Cambridge. James defined himself as the typical Australian expatriate, claiming that 'There are all kinds of freedoms here that I would not enjoy if I was born here. I am out of the class system, as far as I can tell every class thinks I must have come from an inferior one. The truth is the Aussies are exempt, and it gives you a wonderful mobility'.[19] He admitted at the end of his third volume of autobiography that living abroad is no longer essential for talented Australians:

> Though the Australians who have stayed abroad have made their mark, some of those who returned home have changed the history of their country … The expatriates who had repatriated themselves had realised their dreams at least as well as we had. Australia had done very well without us …[20]

James has recently expanded upon this theme in an essay for the *Times Literary Supplement* reviewing two volumes of Australian poetry: Les Murray's *Fivefathers: five Australian poets of the pre-Academic era*; and Susan Lever's *Oxford Book of Australian Women's Verse*. James' essay informs his British audience of the dimensions of Australian poetry represented by these two volumes, and concludes with a quote from a poem by Australian expatriate poet Vicki Raymond. In spite of the fact that Raymond had lived in London since 1981, said James, 'it's an Australian poem wherever it was written'. Expatriates in Britain, he concluded, 'would have to admit that the vitality grown at home in their absence has come to form the core of the total astonishment, generating the power behind what makes a small country recognizable to the world in the only way that matters—its voice, the sound of freedom'.[21]

Randolph Stow, the Western Australian novelist and poet who has been based in Britain since 1966. National Library of Australia

Randolph Stow

Randolph Stow, a Western Australian novelist and poet, has lived in England since 1966. He is equally adept at rendering the physical and cultural landscape of Western Australia, as in his most popular Australian novel, *The Merry-go-round in the Sea*, published in 1965; and the wintry November lanes and the East Anglian dialect of the denizens of his fictional 'Torn-wich' (Harwich) in his thriller novel, *The Suburbs of Hell*, published in 1984. The dedication to this book slips in the only clue to the story's origins: it reads, 'For William Grono—twenty years after "The Nedlands Monster"', an oblique reference to a serial killer in Perth, Western Australia.[22] Stow has been a consistent winner of literary prizes in both Australia and Britain:

he has won the Miles Franklin Award, the Britannica–Australia Award, the Grace Leven Poetry Prize and the Patrick White Literary Award. A prize in his name, the Randolph Stow Fiction and Poetry Award, has been established in his native Western Australia.[23]

Those who returned

Christina Stead

Some Australian expatriates have returned to Australia after long stays in Britain. They include one of the most celebrated names of Australian literature, novelist Christina Stead, who has also lived in the United States. Stead lived in Britain from 1928 to 1929, went to the United States, then returned to live in Britain from 1953 to 1974, revisiting Australia for the first time in 1969, the year after the death of her husband William Blake, and returning permanently to live in 1974 until her death in 1983. Two of her novels, *Seven Poor Men of Sydney* and *For Love Alone*, had Australian subjects, and her masterpiece, *The Man Who Loved Children*, although set in the United States, drew on her Australian childhood. None of her novels was published in Australia until 1965.[24]

Christina Stead, a celebrated Australian expatriate writer from 1928 to 1974. National Library of Australia

Stead's autobiographical novel, *For Love Alone*, tells the story of Teresa Hawkins, a Sydney girl who comes close to starving herself to achieve her ambition to travel to Britain, at one level to follow the callous and misogynistic Jonathan Crow, but at a deeper one to escape the fate of resigned matrimony or, even worse, spinsterhood, which were all that she could see ahead for her in Australia. In the character of Crow, Stead has created a powerful portrait of 'narcissistic male coldness'.[25] She uses his letters from London to Teresa, in which he alternates between encouraging and spurning her affections, to articulate his (and Stead's) views of the British class system and the life of an Australian stranded in London:

> I am longing for you to come over, he would write now, it will be company for me. I can never adapt myself to their infinite social strata, all signalized by different accents. A man with my accent is an outsider, I could not possibly get a job at the L.S.E.—all I can pick up are country lectures. That's all that goes here, pukka sahib or rank outsider—gentleman or bounder—and it's accent, accent, all the way. I have begun to see the web of their social system. It is built up on precedent and the 'by accident' or 'muddling through', which is true enough, is only the outside. Inside, they're tough; the muddle is not so muddled that an outsider can stumble inside.[26]

Rejected by Jonathan once she arrives in England, Teresa nevertheless achieves 'self-realisation': as Anthony Hassall has said, she 'does escape from what she sees as her imprisonment in Australia, and from her debilitating personal subjection to Jonathan Crow. Her "buffoon Odyssey", her quest for her personal "Cytherea", is a real, if qualified success'.[27]

Christina Stead described her return to Australia in 1969, in 'Another View of the Homestead', in terms of what she had forgotten about the country during her sojourn in 'shadowy England':

> Under the soft spotted skies of the countries round the North Sea I had forgotten the Australian splendour, the marvellous light; the 'other country' which I always had in me, to which I wrote letters and meant one day to return, it had softened, even the hills outlined in bushfire (which we used to see over Clovelly from Watsons Bay) were paler. The most exquisite thing in my recent life was a giant eucalypt on the North Shore as we turned downhill, the downward leaves so clear, the bark rags, so precise, the patched trunk, so bright. 'Look at that tree!' It was outlined in light. It was scarcely spring, but the lawn outside the house was crowded with camellias, magnolias in bloom, even falling; at both dawn and dusk the kookaburras thrilling high in the trees, the magpies—I had quite forgotten those musicians and their audacity …[28]

Christina Stead's letters to friends in Australia revealed her longing for her native land. In the year before her permanent return to Australia she confessed in a letter to Dorothy Green that a mention of 'galahs' had made her 'hungry for the time I spent on the roads in Australia … All that is so dear to me that I am surprised that I am still here'.[29]

Barbara Hanrahan

Another expatriate writer who returned to Australia to live, Barbara Hanrahan, went to London to pursue a different art form—printmaking—and began to write autobiography and fiction while she was living there. Hanrahan's fiction and autobiographical writing shuttles back and forth between the Adelaide of her childhood, and London, which saw the commencement of her writing career.

> The Adelaide of my childhood still existed inside my head. In London, while snow flew at the pane, I recalled the quince tree by the fowl-house, the geranium by the lavatory …
>
> Then, in Adelaide, my grandmother died and a flood of childhood memories surfaced. The old world seemed so real that it was unbelievable that, in a physical sense, it no longer existed. Without deliberate planning or decision I began to write of the old places, the old people … Eventually it was finished, and I found that, without meaning to, I had become a writer.[30]

Two of Hanrahan's novels, *The Albatross Muff* of 1977 and *A Chelsea Girl* of 1988, have historical London as their setting. In *The Albatross Muff* Hanrahan has her nineteenth-century Australian-born heroine, Stella, going 'home' to Britain, accompanied by a convict woman, Moak, after her grazier father had been killed in a riding accident. On the ship back to England her mother anticipates her reunion with family and friends:

> Home was a legend. So often Mamma had cried for it. Grandmamma was a fashionable dressmaker, of Hanover Square. Mama's youth had been shaded by Swiss muslin and taffeta, tarlatan, gauze. Because of Papa she'd exchanged London and fashion for a sheep station near Goulburn, New South Wales.
>
> Now she sat in the saloon with her knees covered by a kangaroo rug, and, sometimes when Baby was quiet, talked of the past the ship was taking them back to. London. Queen Victoria. Grandmamma. Mama's best friend, Miss Pensa Smith, whom time had turned into Mrs. William Hall.[31]

A Chelsea Girl traces the life of Sarah Hodge, born in 1898; from the

Barbara Hanrahan's print, Michael and Me and the Sun, *which shares this title with her autobiographical account of her first stay in London. Courtesy of Jo Steele*

deaths and coronations of monarchs and two world wars through to the 1980s and the era of Princess Di.[32] Hanrahan's evocation of the changing life of a poor Londoner, with its mass of detail about the living conditions which Sarah both endures and exploits, displays her ability to achieve a total immersion in a particular place, a talent she also put to creative use to describe her native land, capturing in both words and artworks the Adelaide suburb of her girlhood, Thebarton.

In her autobiographical work, *Michael and Me and the Sun*, Hanrahan related the story of an Adelaide girl who made the obligatory shipboard voyage to London to study at the Central School of Art in the early 1960s, the time of Carnaby Street, Pop Art and Beatles music. Hanrahan blossomed as a printmaker in this environment, and found that London had given her a new perspective: 'I'd prised myself away from all the old things I'd loved and hated and now, in London, I felt more alive and sensitive than I ever had before'.[33] But a disappointing love affair gave Hanrahan a different outlook on her London life, and she found herself organising her return to Adelaide:

> Once the great city fitted about me like a cosy overcoat—I'd had my place in it; I'd walked through its streets aware that I was walking where other artists and writers—people who were my heroes—had walked before me. And when I got home to which ever little room it was, which ever flat, I'd felt buoyed by the knowledge that London was outside, full of poetry and excitement. When I went out into it again, I just had to choose which of its countless different parts I wished to explore: London could turn into whatever sort of city I wanted it to be. But now I'd lost Michael, it was cold, an uncaring place ...
>
> One lunchtime I went to the Haymarket, where, from the Tube station underneath, the homesick could go and see on a horizontal clock what time it was in the lands they'd left behind. I only meant to make enquiries at the travel agency, but I found myself arranging for them to pick up my etching plates and folders of prints and send them back to Adelaide by sea. Then I was booking a flight home on Alitalia, and I'd never flown anywhere before.[34]

The story of an Adelaide girl artist in London is also told in Hanrahan's 1974 novel, *Sea Green*. Hanrahan had returned to London by early 1966, and for some years alternated between there and Adelaide, until she returned permanently to Australia to live until her death in 1991.[35]

Declining the expatriate option

One Australian writer has given a lucid account of her decision *not* to become an exile in Britain. Jill Ker Conway, who has pursued a distinguished academic career in the United States, has explained in her autobiography, *The Road from Coorain*, how she came to the realisation that she could never become accustomed to Britain, and did not take up the opportunity to live and study there:

> Wandering around Westminster Abbey, through some of the churches which were regular places of worship for Guards regiments, or the smaller churches which were home to a county regiment, one could not help wondering whether the Anglican Church of Elizabeth I, a compromise I admired, had become by stages more concerned with the worship of the British Empire than with matters of salvation and damnation. Plaque after plaque commemorated bloody battles—Lucknow, Omdurman, Mafeking, the first and second Opium Wars—all occasions at which some luckless colonial people had been obliged by superior force to accept the benefits of British rule. I had known in theory that the church and the army had been the pillars of traditional European society, but it took seeing the sacramentalizing of empire embodied in the walls of Anglican churches for me to comprehend what the mystical blending of church and state meant …
>
> That was the problem with my attitudes to this beautiful and perplexing country. I loved its medieval and early modern history and detested its imperial complacency. One thing was clear. I was not at home here and never could be. I could perhaps learn to speak idiomatic French and settle in Paris or Provence with no psychic difficulty, but in England these contradictions would always irritate me like a hair shirt worn under fashionable outer garments …
>
> I knew now what I was going to do. I was going home to study history. It was no use pretending I wasn't a scholar. I could certainly make myself an idle life in London being another expatriate Australian enjoying the cultural riches of the city, but that was to live perpetually by the standards of a culture I now saw as alien.[36]

The end of expatriatism?

In 1980 Australian writer Frank Moorhouse identified a watershed in Australian literary life, one that was also hinted at by Howard Jacobson in the passage from *Redback* which began this chapter. In *Days of Wine and Rage* he claimed that: 'The seventies was a ridge in our cultural history. It was the decade when writers, at least, stopped going away to live in other countries—the end of the expatriate tradition …'[37] There is no doubt that the election of the Whitlam government in late 1972, with its emphasis on encouraging the arts and creating an Australian national identity, was the signal for many Australian expatriates—writers and other creative artists to the fore—to return to Australia, where a significant number of them have remained. Nevertheless, Moorhouse has probably been premature in announcing 'the end of the expatriate tradition' as, on his own admission, writers continue to travel overseas, the difference being that they 'do not contemplate permanently living abroad'.[38] In addition, Australia's best known expatriates—Peter Porter, Clive James, Barry Humphries, Germaine Greer, Randolph Stow—show no signs of contemplating repatriation. But several at least of these writers now return to Australia at regular intervals, demonstrating that the country they left is now a worthwhile place to come back to. For the same reason, it is a country in which it is now possible to remain, and to forge a successful career as a writer. There are advantages for some writers in setting forth to conquer a wider stage, but increasingly the mechanism which produces this result is one which will be dealt with in a later chapter—the status that accrues to a writer in both Britain and Australia when he or she wins one of the literary world's 'glittering prizes'.

10

PROPHETIC INSIGHT?

I n mid-1922 English novelist D. H. Lawrence spent three months in Australia with his wife Frieda. During this short stay he generated a significant body of literary material: two novels, one, *Kangaroo*, by Lawrence himself, and another, *The Boy in the Bush*, a reworking of a novel by Western Australian writer Mollie Skinner; a poem, also entitled 'Kangaroo', and a number of letters. Lawrence's 1922 visit has also inspired Australian writers and other artists. Playwright David Allen and novelist Margaret Barbalet have drawn on Lawrence's visit in their work, and artist Garry Shead has created a series of pictures on this theme.[1]

Lawrence's novel *Kangaroo*, based on his Australian experience, has additional interest because it appeared to reveal the existence of fascist-style secret organisations in Australia a decade before the notorious New Guard of the early 1930s came to prominence in New South Wales. When the novel was published in 1923, the story of the secret army was thought to be fictional, but since then historians have accepted that the New Guard had its precursors around Australia in the 1920s.[2] Once this had been established, it was a short step to the development of the idea that Lawrence, in his brief time in Australia, may have encountered one of these military-style secret units, and used the knowledge in his novel. But for this to happen Lawrence would have needed to have been in contact with members of the secret army. It is the attempt to prove that the characters in *Kangaroo* have real-life counterparts, and that Lawrence met

S. T. Gill's painting,
Sydney from St
Leonards, *of c1865,*
shows a clustering metrop-
olis in the distance, with
rural calm in the fore-
ground. Mitchell Library,
State Library of New
South Wales

The Roll of Honour at the Australian War Memorial studded with red poppies of remembrance. This image unites the names of Australian dead—in this case those of the First World War—with the well-known symbol of the conflict on the Western Front from 1914–1918. Photograph by Roslyn Russell

The Man with the Donkey by Peter Corlett, Australian War Memorial, portrays John Simpson Kirkpatrick, English migrant and Field Ambulanceman at Gallipoli, who used a donkey to carry the wounded to the casualty clearing stations until he was himself killed. 'The Man with the Donkey' became an enduring symbol of the Gallipoli campaign. Photograph by Roslyn Russell

Camouflaged German railway gun captured by Australian forces at Amiens in 1918. It can now be seen outside the Australian War Memorial. Photograph by Roslyn Russell

The beauty of Sydney Harbour was praised constantly by British visitors to Australia. Here it is pictured by Conrad Martens in a watercolour, Sydney from Lavender Bay, c1845. National Library of Australia

Tom Roberts' sketch in oils for his 'Big Picture', The Duke of York opening the First Parliament of the Commonwealth of Australia, 9 May 1901. National Library of Australia

them while he was in Australia, that has created considerable controversy in Lawrence studies in Australia and overseas.

In 1981 Sydney journalist Robert Darroch published *D. H. Lawrence in Australia*.[3] His argument in this book—that Lawrence *did* meet people in Sydney who were the originals for the characters of Kangaroo, the leader of the secret army, Jack Callcott, his loyal lieutenant and the man who introduced Lawrence (in the person of his narrator Richard Lovatt Somers) to his chief, and Willie Struthers, the trade union leader—has been criticised by those who assert that either the novel is a work of creative imagination, a 'thought adventure', as Lawrence himself called it, or suggest other contemporary models for the principal characters. The debate has been waged for some years in the pages of scholarly journals, and in the D. H. Lawrence Society's publication, *Rananim*, and we will return to it later in this chapter. Representatives of both sides of this argument belong to the D. H. Lawrence Society, which developed in 1992 from a nucleus of interested people anxious to prevent proposed changes to the fabric of the Californian bungalow, 'Wyewurk', at Thirroul, which Lawrence and Frieda rented for those few months in 1922, and which appears in *Kangaroo* as 'Coo-ee'.[4]

English-born playwright David Allen wrote his 1979 play on D. H. Lawrence, Upside Down at the Bottom of the World, *to 'examine and experience the impact of a writer I'd grown up with in one country and in another which has become my home'. Courtesy William Heinemann Australia*

What can reading Lawrence really tell us about Australia? Leaving aside for the moment the issue of *Kangaroo*'s usefulness as an historical source, let us explore what Lawrence, a highly intelligent observer armed with his own preoccupations about the organisation of society and psychologically scarred by recent experience in his homeland,[5] made of his visit to this 'new country'.

Lawrence and the land of Australia

Focusing on whether Lawrence 'got it right' as to the existence of a secret army in Australia in the early 1920s may obscure the attention his response to the country itself deserves. On this ground even A. D. Hope—no fan of Lawrence—is prepared to admit that Lawrence had achieved a masterly evocation of Australia in some passages in *Kangaroo*.[6] Richard

Lovatt Somers, Lawrence wrote, had come with his wife Harriett to Australia for a reason: as a 'writer of poems and essays' with a small independent income, he was rejecting Europe, where 'everything was done for, played out, finished'. The solution: 'he must go to a new country. The newest country: young Australia!' So far they had been to Western Australia, Adelaide and Melbourne, and now he sat in a summer-house looking out over the 'vast town' of Sydney, which 'didn't seem to be real, it seemed to be sprinkled on the surface of a darkness into which it never penetrated'. Somers recoiled from it, and from the land itself, and recalled a terrifying experience in Western Australia:

And then one night at the time of the full moon he walked alone into the bush. A huge electric moon, huge, and the tree-trunks like naked pale aborigines among the dark-soaked foliage, in the moonlight. And not a sign of life—not a vestige.

Yet something. Something big and aware and hidden! He walked on, had walked a mile or so into the bush, and had just come to a clump of tall, nude, dead trees, shining almost phosphorescent with the moon, when the terror of the bush overcame him. He had looked so long at the vivid moon, without thinking. And now, there was something among the trees, and his hair began to stir with terror, on his head. There was a presence. He looked at the weird, white, dead trees, and into the hollow distances of the bush. Nothing! Nothing at all. He turned to go home. And then immediately the hair on his scalp stirred and went icy cold with terror. What of? He knew quite well it was nothing. He knew quite well. But with his spine cold like ice, and the roots of his hair seeming to freeze, he walked on home, walked firmly and without haste. For he told himself he refused to be afraid, though he admitted the icy sensation of terror. But then to experience terror is not the same thing as to admit fear into the conscious soul. Therefore he refused to be afraid.

But the horrid thing in the bush! He schemed as to what it would be. It must be the spirit of the place. Something fully evoked to-night, perhaps provoked, by that unnatural West-Australian moon. Provoked by the moon, the roused spirit of the bush. He felt it was watching, and waiting. Following with certainty, just behind his back. It might have reached out a long black arm and gripped him. But no, it wanted to wait. It was not tired of watching its victim. An alien people—a victim. It was biding its time with a terrible ageless watchfulness, waiting for a far-off end, watching the myriad intruding white men.[7]

The alienating bush was not the only aspect of the natural environment in Australia which inspired Lawrence to attempt to capture its mystery in words: its animals and birds stimulated in him appreciation and lyrical description. The indigenous fauna inspired a similar response to that of the first British explorers of the country in the eighteenth century—wonder, and the belief that nature had disposed things differently in the antipodes. His poem, 'Kangaroo', is reminiscent of those quoted in chapter 1 on the same subject:

In the northern hemisphere
Life seems to leap at the air, or skim under the wind
Like stags on rocky ground, or pawing horses or springy
        scut-tailed rabbits ...

Only mice, and moles, and rats, and badgers, and beavers,
        and perhaps bears
Seem belly-plumbed to the earth's mid-navel.
Or frogs that when they leap come flop, and flop to the
        centre of the earth.

But the yellow antipodal Kangaroo, when she sits up,
Who can unseat her, like a liquid drop that is heavy, and
        just touches earth.
The downward drip
The down-urge,
So much denser than cold-blooded frogs.

Delicate mother Kangaroo
Sitting up there rabbit-wise, but huge, plumb-weighted,
And lifting her beautiful slender face, oh! so much more gently
        and finely lined than a rabbit's, or than a hare's.
Lifting her face to nibble at a round white peppermint drop,
        which she loves, sensitive mother Kangaroo

Her sensitive, long pure-bred face.
Her full antipodal eyes, so dark,
So big and quiet and remote, having watched so many empty
        dawns in silent Australia ...

Still she watches with eternal, cocked wistfulness!
How full her eyes are, like the full, fathomless, shining eyes
    of an Australian black-boy
Who has been lost so many centuries on the margins of existence!

She watches with insatiable wistfulness.
Untold centuries of watching for something to come,
For a new signal from life, in that silent lost land of the South.
Where nothing bites but insects and snakes and the sun,
    small life.
Where no bull roared, no cow ever lowed, no stag cried,
    no leopard screeched, no lion coughed, no dog barked,
But all was silent save for parrots occasionally, in the
    haunted blue bush.

Wistfully watching, with wonderful liquid eyes.
And all her weight, all her blood, dripping sack-wise down
    towards the earth's centre,
And the live little-one taking in its paw at the door of her
    belly.

Leap then, and come down on the line that draws to the
    earth's deep, heavy centre.[8]

Lawrence also enjoyed his encounters with Australian birds. He described Somers as sitting in the Western Australian bush and talking to the magpies and communicating with a friendly kingfisher on the New South Wales south coast: 'It sat and cocked its head and listened. It *liked* to be talked to'.[9] A kookaburra stirred Lawrence to even greater literary heights: A. D. Hope admitted that 'The description of the kookaburra is justly famous. You feel you have never seen a kookaburra before even if you have lived in the country all your life'.[10]

A queer bird sat hunched on a bough a few yards away, just below; a bird like a bunch of old rag, with a small rag of a dark tail, and a fluffy pale top like an owl, and a sort of frill round his neck. He had a long, sharp, dangerous beak. But he too was sunk in utterable apathy. A kukooburra! Some instinct made him know that Somers was watching, so he just shuffled round on the bough and sat with his back to the man, and became utterly oblivious. Somers watched and wondered. Then he whistled. No change. Then he clapped his hands. The bird looked over its shoulder in surprise. What! it seemed to say. Is there somebody alive? Is that a live somebody? It had quite a handsome face, with the exquisite long, dagger beak. It slowly took Somers in. Then he clapped again. Making an effort the bird spread quite big wings and whirred in a queer, flickering flight to a bough a dozen yards further off. There it clotted again.[11]

In the novel Somers' wife Harriett, in a conversation with their Sydney neighbour Jack Callcott, offered her response to the land of Australia:

'Your wonderful Australia!' said Harriett to Jack. 'I can't tell you how it moves me. It feels as if no one had ever loved it. Do you know what I mean? England and Germany and Italy and Egypt and India—they've all been loved so passionately. But Australia feels as if it had never been loved, and never come out into the open. As if a man had never loved it, and made it a happy country, a bride country—or a mother country.'

'I don't suppose they ever have,' said Jack.

'But they will?' asked Harriett. 'Surely they will. I feel that if I were Australian, I should love the very earth of it—the very sand and dryness of it—more than anything.'[12]

Lawrence and the kookaburra, as pictured by artist Paul Delprat. Courtesy of Paul Delprat, Sandra Jobson and Robert Darroch

Somers and Harriett quickly moved out of Sydney to 'Mullumbimby' (Thirroul) on the New South Wales south coast, but in the novel Somers makes several visits back to the city. On one of these trips to Sydney he visited the Botanic Gardens:

Richard loved the look of Australia, that marvellous soft flower-blue of the air, and the sombre grey of the earth, the foliage, the brown of the low rocks: like the dull pelts of kangaroos. It had a wonder and a far-awayness, even here in the heart of Sydney. All the shibboleths of mankind are so trumpery. Australia is outside everything.[13]

When the time came to leave Australia, Somers had a sense of revulsion from Europe's 'vast super-incumbent buildings', while 'the frail, aloof, inconspicuous clarity' of the Australian landscape 'was like a sort of heaven—bungalows, shacks, corrugated iron and all. No wonder Australians love Australia'.[14]

Lawrence, in his incarnation as Somers, could feel this about the land itself: the people and the society they had created were a different matter.

Lawrence and Australian society

In June 1922, after he had been in the country for less than a month, Lawrence wrote to a friend in England and gave his opinion on the nature of Australians and of their society:

> If you want to know what it is to feel the 'correct' social world fizzle to nothing, you should come to Australia. It *is* a weird place. In the *established* sense, it is totally nil. Happy-go-lucky, don't-you-bother, we're in Australia. But also there seems to be no inside life of any sort; just a long lapse and drift. A rather fascinating indifference, a *physical* indifference to what we call soul or spirit … I am doing a novel here—funny sort of novel where nothing happens and such a lot of things should happen: scene Australia.[15]

He said similar things to other correspondents, for example, in a letter to his sister-in-law he penned condemnations of Australians that were echoed later in *Kangaroo*:

> They are always vaguely and meaninglessly on the go. And it all seems so empty, so *nothing*, it almost makes you sick. They are healthy, and to my thinking almost imbecile. That's what the life in a new country does to you: it makes you so material, so outward, that your real inner life and your inner self dies out, and you clatter round like so many mechanical animals … I feel as if I lived in Australia for ever I should never open my mouth once to say one word that meant anything …[16]

In *Kangaroo* Lawrence further developed his theme of Australians—a people living in a new country—as lacking a spiritual dimension, and no sense of the distinctions of class and social position:

… Somers felt blind to Australia, and blind to the uncouth Australians. To him they were barbarians. The most loutish Neapolitan loafer was nearer to him in pulse than these British Australians with their aggressive familiarity. He surveyed them from an immense distance, with a kind of horror …

… There was really no class distinction. There was a difference of money and of 'smartness.' But nobody felt *better* than anybody else, or higher, only better-off. And there is all the difference in the world between feeling *better* than your fellow man, and merely feeling *better-off* …

Somers for the first time felt himself immersed in real democracy—in spite of all disparity in wealth. The instinct of the place was absolutely and flatly democratic, *à terre* democratic. Demos was here his own master, undisputed, and therefore quite calm about it. No need to get the wind up at all over it; it was a granted condition of Australia, that Demos was his own master.[17]

One Sunday afternoon while they were still in Sydney Somers and Harriett visited the beach, and experienced the apparent 'freedom' of Australia:

Somers and Harriett lay on the sand-bank. Strange it was. And it *had* a sort of fascination. Freedom! That's what they always say. 'You feel free in Australia.' And so you do. There is a great relief in the atmosphere, a relief from

Lawrence described Jack Callcott as fascinated by a football game at Thirroul. Paul Delprat captured a similar scene in watercolour there on a visit in 1979, with an imagined Harriett and Somers watching the game in the foreground. Courtesy of Paul Delprat, Sandra Jobson and Robert Darroch.

145

tension, from pressure. An absence of control or will or form. The sky is open above you, and the air is open around you. Not the old closing-in of Europe.

But what then? The *vacancy* of this freedom is almost terrifying. In the openness and the freedom this new chaos, this litter of bungalows and tin cans scattered for miles and miles, this Englishness all crumbled out into formlessness and chaos ...

The absence of any inner meaning: and at the same time the great sense of vacant spaces. The sense of irresponsible freedom. The sense of do-as-you-please liberty. And all utterly uninteresting. What is more hopelessly uninteresting than accomplished liberty? ... Even the rush for money had no pip in it. And except for the sense of power, that had no real significance here. When all is said and done, even money is not much good where there is no genuine culture.[18]

It was passages such as these which no doubt attracted historian Manning Clark as he re-read *Kangaroo* in November 1986 while finalising the text of the final volume of *A History of Australia* Volume 6, which includes the time of Lawrence's visit. This historian, who often used the term the 'kingdom of nothingness' to describe the spiritual state of Australia, found confirmation of this in *Kangaroo*. He wrote to Kathleen Fitzpatrick:

Am re-reading *Kangaroo*. After all the work on 1919–22 I find myself now overwhelmed by the genius of the man. How did he find out so much about us in six weeks? Most of us need a life-time to find out enough for a small picture. Lawrence has written our Bayeux Tapestry—and like that work, he is often close to caricature, and the methods of the cartoonists.[19]

Somers at length turned on his Australian acquaintances, Jack Callcott and Jaz Trewhella, and gave them his explanation for the indifference of Australians to the political fate of their country:

'... The bulk of Australians don't care about Australia—that is, you say they don't. And why don't they? Because they care about nothing at all, neither in earth below or heaven above. They just blankly don't care about anything, and they live in defiance, a sort of slovenly defiance of care of any sort, human or inhuman, good or bad.'[20]

A major element of the novel's plot, in addition to reactions to the land of Australia and the political story of the secret army, is the relationship between Somers and Harriett, and their separate definitions of what marriage consists of. Their differing interpretations bring conflict. On one occasion, after a bitter row with Harriett, Somers went out for a walk at 'Mullumbimby'. He stood looking into the 'massed foliage of the cliff-slope':

> These ancient flat-topped tree-ferns, these towsled palms like mops. What was the good of trying to be an alert conscious man here? You couldn't. Drift, drift into a sort of obscurity, backwards into a nameless past, hoary as the country is hoary. Strange old feelings wake in the soul: old, non-human feelings. And an old, old indifference, like a torpor, invades the spirit. An old, saurian torpor … Would the people waken this ancient land, or would the land put them to sleep, drift them back into the torpid self-consciousness of the world of the twilight.[21]

But Somers had begun to warm to Australians, and to find them touching in their innocence, as can be seen in this description of his fellow passengers on a bus trip from Wolloona (Wollongong):

> … a lovely little boy with the bright, wide, gentle eyes of these Australians. So alert and alive and with that loveableness that almost hurts one. Absolute trust in the 'niceness' of the world. A tall, stalky, ginger man with the same bright eyes and a turned-up nose and long stalky legs. An elderly man with bright, friendly, elderly eyes and careless hair and careless clothing. He was Joe, and the other was Alf. Real careless Australians, careless of their appearance, careless of their speech, of their money, of everything—except of their happy-go-lucky, democratic friendliness …
>
> It made him feel so sad underneath, or uneasy, like an impending disaster. Such a charm. He was so tempted to commit himself to this strange continent and its strange people. It was so fascinating. It seemed so free, an absence of any form of stress whatsoever. No strain in any way, once you could accept it.[22]

That was the rub: Richard was tempted to succumb to the charms of Australia, but believed he had to resist them, as he explained to Jaz:

> '… I want Australia as a man wants a woman. I fairly tremble with wanting it.'
> 'Australia?'
> 'Yes.'
> Jaz looked at Somers with his curious, light-grey eyes.

> 'Then why not stop?' he said seductively.
>
> 'Not now. Not now. Some cussedness inside me. I don't want to give in, you see. Not yet. I don't want to give in to the place. It's too strong. It would lure me away from myself. It would be too easy. It's *too* tempting. It's too big a stride, Jaz.'[23]

Harriett's experience had been the opposite to that of Somers. While he regretted leaving Australia, she had become disenchanted and was pleased to leave:

> She had expected so much of Australia. It had been as if all her life she had been waiting to come to Australia. To a new country, to a new unspoiled country … Freed once, she wanted a new freedom, silvery and paradisical in the atmosphere. A land with a new atmosphere, untainted by authority. Silvery, untouched freedom.
>
> And in the first months she had found this in Australia … She had felt herself free, free, free for the first time in her life …
>
> Then gradually, through the silver glisten of the new freedom came a dull, sinister vibration. Sometimes from the interior came a wind that seemed to her evil. Out of the silver paradisical freedom untamed, evil winds could come, cold, like a stone hatchet murdering you. The freedom, like everything else, had two sides to it. Sometimes a heavy, reptile-hostility came off the sombre land, something gruesome and infinitely repulsive. It frightened her as a reptile would frighten her if it wound its cold folds around her. For the past month now Australia has been giving her these horrors. It was as if the silvery freedom suddenly turned, and showed the scaly back of a reptile, and the horrible paws.[24]

As Richard and Harriett left on the *Manganui*, he 'felt a deep pang in his heart, leaving Australia, that strange country that a man might love so hopelessly'.[25]

Fact or fiction?

To fill in the background to Harriett's revulsion against Australia, and elucidate the reason why the Somers left Australia so quickly, it is necessary to turn to the political story of the novel, the site of so much controversy over the last two decades.

The novel's political action begins when Somers' Sydney neighbour, Jack Callcott, introduces him to Benjamin Cooley—'Kangaroo'—the leader of a secret fascist-style returned soldiers' organisation, the 'Maggies' (in its turn a subterranean part of a wider body called the 'Diggers' Clubs) whose aim it is to provoke unrest by attacking labour organisations, then step in, restore law and order and establish a benevolent dictatorship. Cooley is anxious to recruit Somers as a spokesman to legitimate this seizing of power in the eyes of the wider world, on the basis of articles the latter has written on 'democracy'. Somers is attracted by Kangaroo, but ultimately resists his proposals. He is courted by both sides of the political struggle: he also rejects the suggestion of labour leader Willie Struthers of 'Canberra House' that he edit a labour newspaper. A riot started by the secret army at a meeting addressed by Struthers leads to a bomb explosion which causes several deaths. Kangaroo is shot and mortally wounded. Warned by Jack Callcott that he knows too much about the secret army and must leave the country, Somers and Harriett leave Australia shortly afterwards.

Australian author Margaret Barbalet's 1988 novel, Steel Beach, *is the story of an academic in the late 1980s exploring a 'mystery' surrounding D. H. Lawrence's stay on the New South Wales south coast in 1922.*
Courtesy of Penguin Books Australia

At the time of *Kangaroo*'s release in Australia in 1924 the political element of its plot was regarded as fictional. Then in the early 1930s an organisation with a strong resemblance to Lawrence's secret army in *Kangaroo* did in fact emerge in Sydney in the shape of Eric Campbell's New Guard, thus giving rise to the idea that Lawrence might have encountered a similar organisation a decade before. People began to speculate that Lawrence had in fact stumbled upon what must have been a very closely guarded secret whilst he was in Australia.[26]

In 1974 poet and academic A. D. Hope dismissed any claims to a basis in fact for the secret army element of *Kangaroo*'s plot; Lawrence's account of political life in 1920s Sydney was 'almost entirely factitious':

He has been praised for his observation of an incipient Fascist movement in Australia in the early 1920s and it is true that there are some remarkable similarities between Kangaroo's Diggers' Clubs, their aims, methods and aspirations and the New Guard which appeared a few years later. But there is a simple explanation for this. Lawrence was projecting on Australian society the image of the still unformed and largely incoherent Fascist movement which he had learned something of in Italy ... Neither the socialism of Willy Struthers as preached at Canberra Hall [*sic*] nor the fascism of Kangaroo as preached in his legal chambers, have anything to do with policies and theory of any actual party that existed anywhere, let alone in Sydney.[27]

Hope's view was to a certain extent supported by another critic and fiction writer, Michael Wilding, who in his 1980 book, *Political Fictions*, saw the major concern of the political story of *Kangaroo* as 'Lawrence's exploration of the impulse towards political commitment'. Wilding admitted that Lawrence may have been aware of the existence of quasi-military organisations in Australia, that his novel could have been 'based upon contemporary Australian realities': 'But beyond that there is no specific evidence of Lawrence's association with or knowledge of such a group: none of his published letters from Australia mention the *content* of *Kangaroo*. He writes often about its *form*; but he says nothing either way about the *source* of his materials'.[28]

Wilding made the point that Kangaroo, apart from a brief appearance on horseback at the riot, was never seen in relation to his men, only in conversation with Somers and Jack Callcott. In the novel Somers, contrary to the impression given in the 1985 film version of *Kangaroo*, never came into personal contact with the men of the secret movement apart from Kangaroo, Jack Callcott and Jaz Trewhella (who played a somewhat devious role as the person who brought Somers and Struthers together).[29]

For several years before Wilding's book was published Robert Darroch had been publishing articles arguing that Lawrence had in fact encountered members of a secret army in Sydney, 'and then committed an act of extreme treachery—he wrote a novel which dealt explicitly with its activities'.[30] In 1981 Darroch published *D. H. Lawrence in Australia*, which argued that Lawrence *had* met the leaders of the secret army depicted in

Kangaroo—whom he named as Major-General Charles Rosenthal and Major Jack Scott of the King and Empire Alliance—and had also come into contact with Jock Garden, the communist head of the Sydney Trades Hall, whom Darroch identified as the model for Willie Struthers of Canberra House.[31]

Since the publication of what has become known as the 'Darroch thesis', others have entered the fray in support of the counter-argument that Lawrence had created the political story of *Kangaroo* by an imaginative projection of what he knew was happening in Europe onto the Australian scene, in addition to information gleaned from newspapers and from conversations with people in Western Australia, Sydney and Thirroul. Anyone who wishes to examine the arguments on all sides will find themselves plunging into a Sargasso Sea of names, incidents, speculations, probabilities and improbabilities.[32] Perhaps the most apposite comment on the controversy has come from Raymond Southall:

> … it is unlikely ever to be known for certain how much of *Kangaroo* is drawn from Lawrence's own personal experience of Australia, how much from his previous experience, and how much is pure invention … The fact that an issue has been hotly debated does not make it any more relevant, however, and it is only as the result of an elementary confusion as to the kind of work it is that Lawrence's *Kangaroo* has been expected to satisfy the same criteria as his *Movements in European History*.[33]

So did D. H. Lawrence achieve a prophetic insight into Australia—the land, the national character, its subterranean political movements? We will probably never know the answer to the last question. But one thing is certain: Lawrence in *Kangaroo* certainly gave Australians plenty to think about, from the time of the novel's publication to the present.[34]

11

AUSTRALIAN BY CHOICE

Novelist and short story writer and British migrant to Australia, Elizabeth Jolley, has often explored the theme of migration in her writing, not just as a physical relocation, but as a transforming experience. In her autobiographical writing and her novels she has recalled the moment when, as the ship carrying her to Australia was waiting in the Great Bitter Lake at the entrance to the Suez Canal, she realised the enormity of what she was doing:

> ... the calm expanse of colourless water, with its lack of concern for human life, caused a sense of desolation more acute and painful than anything experienced during the first term of boarding school. Memory followed memory; the stillness of willow trees along soft green river banks and the deep grass in water meadows where sweet-breathed cows, straying close to the field paths, waited to be herded for milking ... All these images came from a time far removed from the time preceding the voyage. We had long left the Midlands and had encountered the cold hostility of Edinburgh and the apparently more affable but essentially exclusive world of Glasgow. We should have been experienced migrants. The strangest of all was the vision of my father walking alongside the ship waving farewell as he used to walk and wave alongside the train every time I left for boarding school. And ridiculous as it was, I wanted to rush back to him, to hear his voice once more. But which of us can walk on water, I mean, long distance.[1]

Migration from Britain has been a continuing theme in the history of Australia. Waves of migration from the early nineteenth century to the present have carried British people from their homeland and across the world to begin new lives. British migrants to Australia may have expected their new home to be similar to the one they had left, but with a better climate. There were obvious parallels, but there were also differences which could be disconcerting and even discouraging. Writers and potential writers have been among the vast numbers of British migrants who came to Australia in the great wave of post-war migration. Some have adjusted to the new society; others were uncomfortable and returned to Britain. Those who stayed became Australians by choice. The circumstances which led them out of their own country, their experiences of the new country, and the cultural shocks they encountered, are often vividly rendered in autobiographical or fictional works.

Australia's post-war immigration programme favoured British migrants: they were major beneficiaries of the Assisted Passage Scheme,

MV Fairsea, *one of the migrant ships which brought thousands of Britons to Australia, leaving England in 1956.* National Library of Australia

could vote in Australian elections without becoming Australian citizens, and their skills were recognised for employment, unlike those of many migrants from Europe and other parts of the world. One of the results of large-scale British migration after the Second World War has been to ensure that 'the British base is so entrenched in Australia's demographic structure that even if migration continues as it was in the late 1970s and early 1980s, the British element in the total population will still be approximately 70 per cent at the beginning of the twenty-first century'.[2] One commentator has claimed that British connections to Australia through migration can be seen clearly at times of crisis:

> Many Australians of British descent may not, these days, be especially proud of their ancestry; and the descendants of nineteenth-century migrants very rarely still have close kinsfolk in Britain. But twentieth-century family networks are considerable. During the devastating bush fires of 1983, the telephone lines from Britain to Australia were jammed by anxious Britons seeking information about their relatives.[3]

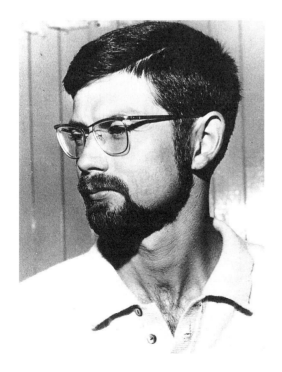

Rodney Hall as a young man. National Library of Australia

British migrants to Australia, so favoured by government policy from the 1940s to the 1970s, have been a neglected group when the issue of adjustment to cultural displacement through migration is discussed. While they can in no way be equated with those who have come to Australia without English as their primary language, and without the broad cultural values and assumptions that underlie both British society and Australian settler culture, it should not be forgotten that these migrants—often perceived by other Australians as being less 'interesting' than the more exotic new arrivals to Australia's shores—may in many cases have suffered significant cultural displacement through the migration process. They have tended to blend more easily into the Australian background; and if they have not, may not be regarded as patiently by their fellow

Australians as non-British migrants have tended to be.

Writers are now examining the real stresses that these people face as they attempt to assimilate to the new land. Rodney Hall has said that he took eight years to adjust to the shock of the reality of Australia.[4] Elizabeth Jolley, a migrant to Australia in the late 1950s, has explored the nature of migration—both physical and spiritual—in her writing: she has claimed that 'We are all migrants now. Even those who never stray far from their birth place do not have to live very long to find themselves in a strange new world'.[5] Francesca Rendle-Short, whose parents brought their children to Australia in the 1960s, in her 1996 novel *Imago* depicts the very different responses of two British migrants to Australia. Other writers such as Michael Wilding have reflected upon the experience of returning to Britain for visits after migrating to Australia.

Francesca Rendle-Short.
Photo by Jonquil
Mackey, courtesy of
Francesca Rendle-Short

Expectations of Australia

Why do people migrate to another country? The reasons why some British people made the momentous decision to uproot themselves from all that was familiar and make a new start on the other side of the world were as various as the individuals involved. Some had found jobs here; some had already visited the place and liked it or had family members in Australia; some were dissatisfied with their present life in Britain. Some had no choice: their parents brought them here as young children, and they have stayed as adults.

Their knowledge and expectations of the country they were coming to was just as diverse. Rodney Hall's mother was an Australian: during the wartime blackout she entertained her children by showing them photographs by torchlight of her family in Kangaroo Valley, New South Wales. Australia became Hall's 'secret land', and the source of good things sent from there to heavily rationed Britain—tinned pineapple, butter, melon and lemon jam, which arrived in boxes with 'beautifully fitted calico covers'. Hall, beguiled by the photographs and his mother's memories, decided 'This was my land, which one day I would claim'. He and his family made the journey in 1949, when he was thirteen.[6]

Canberra journalist Ian Warden—formerly of Cromer, Norfolk—sketched the reasons for his decision to emigrate to Australia at the age of eighteen, and his prior knowledge of the land to which he was to commit his future, in his 1980 book, *Do Polar Bears Experience Religious Ecstasy?*:

> ... I was lured here by the prospect of finding winters without frostbite, and migrant brochures which showed people basking a lot.
>
> One does not enjoy what you would call a surfeit of basking in an English winter, and it is then that the typical migrant is lured to Australia House, his chilblains throbbing, and is caught on the barbed hook of immigration.[7]
>
> I came to Australia when I was eighteen because I was bored, because it was free and because I had been told that Ken Rosewall was Australia's Prime Minister. I was misinformed but I stayed.[8]

Elizabeth Jolley, who came to Australia in 1959 with her husband Leonard and three of her children, recalled her feelings as her ship docked at Fremantle in her 1992 book, *Central Mischief: on writing, her past and herself*:

> I had no idea when I stood at the ship's rail and looked beyond the sheds, which were the customs sheds, to what seemed a flat land completely devoid of distinguishing features what it would be like to live in Australia. It occurs to me now that every person at the ship's rail, looking towards the wharf and the flat land beyond, would have had images of what their life might be, images of money, work, work-mates, colleagues—perhaps a desk of glowing wood surrounded by bookcases or a thriving business, a shop with shelves and groceries waiting to be stocked and, of course, home, the new home they were about to find or create.[9]

Francesca Rendle-Short's character, Jimmy Brown, in her 1996 novel, *Imago*, had built up an image of Australia in his mind and courted and married Molly Rose Moone in 1960 as part of achieving his dream of migration:

The day after the wedding, the newly-weds left for Australia from Waterloo Station. Everyone cried. Joyce Moone wept openly, shouting, 'Tell me how big the sky is when you get there!' Jimmy and his new wife held hands, gloved and sweaty. The station smelt of grime and smoke and the London sky hung over their heads in a stagnant grey sac.

Jimmy wooed Molly Rose Moone. All that summer he had followed her, making plans, with visions of a sun-drenched country bursting with opportunities, possibilities of a good job and a home filled with happy children. He turned his best side to her, all the while mulling over the arrangements in his mind.

She fell into his hand: a young purple fruit looking for distraction, for ripening and an escape from home.[10]

Michael Wilding in his short story 'Three Incidents for a Mercia Quartet' has hinted at the social constraints determining the actions of the story's narrator as a youth in Britain. His three encounters with 'pale and interesting and artistic' Marian are inconclusive, as uneasiness stemming from their family histories over generations renders him inarticulate and unable to respond to her. The story's final paragraph is a poignant coda which says much about why its author chose to leave Britain for Australia, where he took up an appointment as a lecturer in English at the University of Sydney in 1964:

Lonely boys belting tennis balls at walls and doors, windy grey weekends, green drainpipes with loops of old greyed string where lines had once been strung and broken, sad grey manhole covers and pale concrete, and sparrows twittering from the roof gutters. And maybe the hope of once in a while an interesting aircraft overhead.[11]

The journey out

More recent migrants to Australia have arrived by aeroplane: in the heyday of the great post-war migration they made the journey by ship, and this in itself, as Elizabeth Jolley has reminded us, focused the irrevocable nature of the decision that had been taken. The time of the voyage was also one of preparation for the new country. Jolley's character Vera, in *The Georges' Wife*, is initiated into Australian ways by a new friend, 'the rice-farm widow'. They refer to each other as 'Widow' and 'Migrant', as they

dress up, eat and drink, and tell one another about their lives. The Widow tells Vera that she will have to learn to eat more meat; and 'then she tells me that I'll know how to choose it and cook it. She says she'll teach me the cuts of beef and lamb. She says no one, but no one, can live in Australia without this simple knowledge'.[12] In reality, said Jolley, 'Almost all we were told about Australia—even the impossibility of purchasing cotton underwear—proved false. What did not prove false was the space'.[13]

Arrival in Australia meant a customs and health examination, and a rigorous search of baggage for contraband and indecent publications. Jolley experienced the zeal of Australian Customs when she and her family arrived in Fremantle (where the customs sheds were decorated with the words 'Poms Go Home'): 'It was a shock when a customs officer tore his hands on the metal strips binding our crates of books in his eagerness to pursue the immorality which must be contained within the covers of *What Katy Did* and, even worse, *What Katy Did Next*'.[14]

Jolley's first impression of Western Australia was that she had 'come to a strange and foreign land. The bright light comes from above and from below and is the chief foreign element for anyone from England'.[15]

Settling in—or not

Deciding to come to Australia and making the voyage were one thing; the next hurdle was to assimilate to the country. For some there were unexpected and disappointing things about Australia. Rodney Hall found his expectations dashed by reality:

> For my mother the journey in 1949 marked a permanent return; for us a first arrival. I can't speak on behalf of the others; but for myself, with my store of images, I knew exactly what to expect. Small wonder, then, that I have perhaps never got over my amazement at Australia as I found it to be.
>
> We disembarked at Sydney to be met by chill, blustery weather and seemingly endless bureaucratic delays through customs. The overnight train journey north to Brisbane, sitting up for the entire fifteen hours, only to stagger out into hot sunshine and steamy humidity, completed our sense of alienation. The tedium and brutality of the life I was about to live at boarding school, followed by a stiff dose of subtropical suburbia, as well as several stints drudging as a junior clerk and delivery boy in the city completed the picture. On top of all this, I was mocked and reviled for being a pommie (an accusation now grown mercifully rarer) every time I opened my mouth and let out my BBC accent.
>
> Eight years passed before I recaptured any magic at all in the word *Australia*.[16]

Francesca Rendle-Short's characters in *Imago*, Molly and Jimmy Brown, become polar opposites in their responses to Australia. Molly, the nineteen-year-old bride, with no knowledge of Australia, embraces the place without reserve from the beginning, and sees in her Canberra neighbour Marj the embodiment of all that attracts her to it. She has been able to distance herself from her mother's 'increasingly erratic letters', and stifle her conscience at having left her alone in England, by her increasing absorption in Marj and her life in Canberra:

> The letters were enjoyable to read, as good as instalments in a magazine, but Molly found it hard to feel an honest homesickness: she was too proud of her own bravery of migrating into the unknown.
>
> ... The daughter enjoyed this long-distance conversation. No more close heavy breathing in a small house, face to face with awkward silences for replies. The oceans and continents between Australia and England

fragmented their conversation, eased the tension, the sentences not meeting or making sense until way after the event. Entirely bearable, objective,
rather comic …

From her shaded perch on the front step, letter in hand, Molly gazed at
her new naked garden, the pale hardsetting beds. The thought of the English countryside made her nostalgic for its green lawns, clipped to one inch
exactly, all over, and the rows of traditional flowers in raised beds of moist
dark earth. But then she remembered the vegetable soup skies, the soft rain
watering the boggy marsh. What a contrast to where she was now. Australia
grew at the back of their house, beyond the fence and up the flank of Mount
Ainslie. It was full of powder-puff, acid yellow wattles and gums flowering in
whites and creams and pinks, the ground covered with fading purple peas
and pods. Marj knew their names: callistemon, acacia and hardenbergia.
This country had to be something you sensed. How could she ever explain
it? Of course Jimmy, if asked, would prefer the great, ordered English green,
mazes of rose beds and interloping cream statues, but she didn't ask.[17]

Jimmy, the 'adventurer' who brought Molly here to fulfil his dream, is
unable to adapt to the country and, remaining a quintessential Englishman, decides to return. Molly refuses to go back to England:

He was gone. In a way his leaving had been plain from the beginning, for he
never lost his Englishness, his foreignness. He kept his sense of separation
close like a favourite coat he couldn't do without. He'd never been *in* Australia, truly a part of the landscape, even though he'd tried. Jimmy loved
Australia as an armchair adventurer would, fairly trembling with want, from
afar, as an idea, looking into the circle from the safety of the outside rim.[18]

Elizabeth Jolley has identified a 'subtle loss of direction which can
arise from moving from one country to another'. This, she has said, may
be a result of failed expectations, to which the real-life Rodney Hall and
Francesca Rendle-Short's fictional Jimmy Brown had both fallen victim:
'The promise offered may turn out to be a deception and a disappointment
resulting from the unfulfilment of an inner vision which might have held
too many hopes, too much ambition'.[19]

For some writers, returning for a visit to Britain had the effect of
demonstrating how much they had been changed by the experience of

moving to Australia. In Michael Wilding's short story, 'American Poets in London', his English-born character Graham finds himself identifying with the Australians:

> If there were any English poets there, Graham did not recognise them. There must have been some surely. It was the Australians he knew and ended up with, however. It was a mark of how far he was expatriated, how he had become a visiting colonial. It was an improvement on being a visiting provincial proletarian. It was more lively, more seemed to be happening with the Australians. And they could respond to the Americans with an innocent openness, here were fellow forgers of new idioms. But the Americans vanished with the unrecognised English. So they presumed, the Australians. They vanished, anyway, which left the Australians gathered in ever optimistic conviviality, dragging tables together in an Indian restaurant, ordering beers and lagers as if they were a visiting football team …[20]

In 1990 a collection of Michael Wilding's short stories, entitled *Great Climate*, was published in Britain, and included the title stories from several of his other collections published earlier in Australia.[21] One story, 'Somewhere New' in one of these collections, *Aspects of the Dying Process*, contains a vivid portrait of a British literary expatriate, Gavin Mulgrave. He condemns the Britain he has left behind for having no 'cultural vitality' and denigrates Australia as a healthy, hedonistic beach society where the only people who read books are 'a few neurotic housewives and … university intellectuals who've got a vested interest in print culture to keep their jobs'.[22] For Mulgrave the newness of Australia is its chief attraction:

> 'I have to live in new places. A new flat with new furniture. I can't see any point in coming to live in Australia and living in an old building. Old buildings should be left behind in England, with the statues and geriatrics and fungus. There's not one square inch of England that hasn't been trampled over time and again. That's why Australia's so refreshing. It's untouched, it's forward looking, it's alive and vital.'[23]

Gavin Mulgrave, a perpetual migrant for whom the action is always somewhere else, finally leaves for the United States which, he claims, 'makes Australia seem like an underdeveloped country'.[24]

Coming to terms with Australia

John Douglas Pringle came from Britain, where he had worked on the *Manchester Guardian* and *The Times*, to be editor of the *Sydney Morning Herald* in 1952. He remained in this position until 1957, when he returned to England. The following year he published *Australian Accent*, which he wrote 'in the belief that it is high time that Britain should take more seriously this young and vigorous nation to which she gave indifferent birth 170 years ago; and that Australians, who, like other people, dislike criticism intensely, are now mature enough to take it'.[25] *Australian Accent* was highly critical of Australia and Australians. Author Elizabeth Jolley said that she and her husband nearly cancelled their passage to Australia after reading it: 'Perhaps we misread it. It presented to us a picture of a rigidly conformist country with not much religion but almost obligatory church going'.[26] In *Australian Accent* Pringle had set out what he considered to be the elements of the Australian character:

> ... above all Australia is Australian. It is indeed an astonishing thing how strong a character Australia has—so strong that the ever-continuing waves of British migrants have no impact on it but are ruthlessly bent to its pattern. It is a character immediately recognisable in her soldiers as in her poets, in her politicians as in her cricketers—rough rather than tough, kindly but not tolerant, a generous, sardonic, sceptical but surprisingly gullible character, quick to take offence and by no means unwilling to give it, always ready for a fight but just as ready to help a fellow-creature in distress ... it is a character formed by the peculiar conditions of Australian history and geography ...[27]

Pringle had been overly optimistic in his view that the Australian recipients of his criticism in the late 1950s could 'take it'. A dozen years after the publication of *Australian Accent*—and after its author had returned to Australia in 1964 as managing editor of the *Canberra Times* and, from 1965 to 1970, editor of the *Sydney Morning Herald*—he recalled the 'storms of abuse' which had greeted what he had considered to be 'very mild comments'. Since that time, however, other—Australian—critics had launched 'much fiercer attacks' which had been 'accepted without causing any reaction and even with approval'. Pringle even believed that this 'passion for self-denigration, so noticeable among Australian intellectuals in recent years, has now gone too far'; and that 'Judged by almost any standards, it seems to me, Australia is one of the sanest, healthiest and most democratic countries in the world, and if it cannot rival older nations in the quality of its art and literature, it is by no means the cultural desert that some critics like to imagine'.[28]

After his shattering first experience of Australia, Rodney Hall was reconciled to the country of his boyhood dreams while on a visit to Uluru (Ayers Rock) in 1957. Climbing the rock rekindled the wonder for him:

> My bushwalker companions and I stood on the top in the most absolute, cosmic silence imaginable. Indeed, the mystical power of that experience reached beyond imagining, beyond any scale the mind had previously learned. A stillness and total solitariness filled me with ecstasy.[29]

Rodney Hall has become a celebrated exponent of Australian life, in novels such as *Just Relations*, *Captivity Captive*, *The Second Bridegroom* and *The Grisly Wife*, as well as volumes of poetry.[30] His latest novel, *The Island in the Mind*, investigates the notion of the unknown South Land, *Terra Incognita*. Hall explores the theme of 'journeying from what is known to what is imagined', in what has been described as a 'book to excite and challenge the imagination'.[31]

In a book published in 1988, *Journey Through Australia*, Hall described his travels through both urban and outback Australia, and gave advice to British visitors:

> It is essential to mix with people, not to set yourself apart from them, to talk to them without quizzing them about what they do. By far the best way to elicit information is to be ready with stories of your own to tell. Nothing makes friends quicker than reminiscences about one's own failures. The instant the company laughs at what you say against yourself, their reserve will vanish and they will open up. Australians are basically generous and gregarious, but with a distinct prickliness if they feel the slightest condescension is there.[32]

Elizabeth Jolley, after many years of failing to win recognition as a writer, published her first book, *Five Acre Virgin*, in 1976, and was immediately hailed as a major new talent, a judgement that has been amply vindicated by continuing critical acclaim and numerous literary prizes for her work.[33] Jolley has said that the effect of migrating to Australia has been to transform her: 'I am not the same person who left the shores of Britain in

1959; my experience of living in Western Australia and of working there has altered my attitude and my awareness. Unless experienced, certain things cannot be imagined'.[34]

One of Jolley's most memorable creations is the lonely fantasising English spinster Miss Peabody of her novel *Miss Peabody's Inheritance*.[35] Miss Peabody is captivated by the correspondence she has initiated with an Australian novelist, Diana Hopewell, whose erotically charged novel, *Angels on Horseback*, has entranced her. Diana 'feeds' her fan extracts from her latest writing, which are interspersed with Miss Peabody's own story, creating a novel within the novel. The exploits of Miss Arabella Thorne, headmistress of Pine Hill school for girls, her friend Miss Snowdon and secretary Miss Edgely, and schoolgirls Debbie Frome and Gwendaline Manners, as they exchange Western Australia for a European tour, set in train a series of emotional encounters and unravellings. Diana Hopewell's tale of these interwoven relationships assumes a compelling reality for Miss Peabody, who is dominated by an invalid mother, and works inefficiently in an office where she is regarded with derision. Miss Peabody becomes more and more caught up in the imaginative world of the novelist, coming to believe in the reality of the characters whose story is unfolded bit by bit in letters, and stimulated by her imaginings of the life of her correspondent. A gift of coloured sheepskins from Diana Hopewell has 'become an emblem of the vibrant land where many expectations might be overturned. Australia, for Miss Peabody, is a land of enchantment'.[36] After her mother's death, Miss Peabody travels to Western Australia where, on finding that Diana Hopewell has died, she completes her 'rite of passage to Australia' and enters 'into her inheritance'.[37]

Michael Wilding is now a Professor of English and Australian Literature in the University of Sydney, and editor of a recent *Oxford Book of Australian Short Stories*, which has been described as an 'ultimately satisfying, enjoyable and, as the culture commissars would say, "distinctly Aus-

Elizabeth Jolley at the Sydney Writers' Festival in January 1994. National Library of Australia

tralian" collection'. He is well known as a literary critic and as an innovative fiction writer, and has also been involved in publishing Australian writing.[38]

Ian Warden, after taking an honours degree in political science at the University of New South Wales, came to Canberra to study for a doctorate at the Australian National University, but after two years became a full-time journalist on the *Canberra Times*, where he has remained; his acerbic style either endears him to or infuriates his fellow Canberrans.[39]

Francesca Rendle-Short, in addition to her novel *Imago*, has published poetry and short stories in literary magazines, and a novella, *Big Sister*, in 1989. She won the ANUTECH Short Story Award in 1995, and is currently editor of *Muse*, the Canberra arts magazine. She is also a contributor to *Wee Girls*, an anthology of women's writing from an Irish perspective, published in 1996.[40]

12
CAUSING A STIR

I n his 1928 novel, *Point Counter Point*, Aldous Huxley sketched a character, 'Cuthbert Arkwright', at a London party, a parodic version of the Australian expatriate publisher P. R. ('Inky') Stephensen:[1]

> Cuthbert Arkwright was the noisiest and most drunken—on principle and for the love of art as well as for that of alcohol. He had an idea that by bawling and behaving offensively, he was defending art against the Philistines ... He made his living, and in the process convinced himself that he was serving the arts, by printing limited and expensive editions of the more scabrous specimens of the native and foreign literatures. Blond, beef-red, with green and bulging eyes, his large face shining, he approached vociferating greetings.[2]

Stephensen was one of a number of Australians—many of whom have lived as expatriates in Britain—who have created a stir in the British literary world and, indeed, the wider society. They have numbered publishers, feminists and satirists in their ranks. Their targets have included respectability, gender relations, suburbia, and British and Australian society in general. Among them are some of the best-known Australian names in Britain—Germaine Greer, Barry Humphries, Richard Neville and Carmen Callil. Some of them have collaborated with British writers and publishers to promote their particular interests: 'Inky' Stephensen published the paintings of D. H. Lawrence; Barry Humphries collaborated with Nicholas Garland to produce the comic strip and later film character Barry McKenzie; Richard Neville was charged with obscenity with two Englishmen over the production of *Oz* magazine; and Carmen Callil founded Virago Press with British feminists as partners. Those who forged a lone path are just as prominent: Germaine Greer has a worldwide reputation as a pre-eminent figure in the feminist movement. Kathy Lette continues to publish books to justify her reputation as 'the Crocodile Dundee of English letters'.[3] Each of these Australians has been responsible for 'causing a stir' in Britain—and often also in Australia.

Publishers

'Inky' Stephensen spent his life 'causing a stir'; first in his youth as a communist Rhodes Scholar, where he was threatened with being sent down from Oxford if he did not curtail his revolutionary activities; then as a publisher in the Fanfrolico and Mandrake Presses in London, whose products from time to time caused the minions of the Home Office to descend upon and seize offending publications. After his return to Australia in 1932 Stephensen continued his publishing career, and fostered the work of a number of talented Australian writers, including Xavier Herbert, to forward his aim of promoting an Australian literary nationalism.[4] Stephensen became increasingly nationalistic, Anglophobe and isolationist, and during the Second World War founded the fascist-leaning Australia First movement, which opposed the war. He and other Australia Firsters were duly interned until the war ended.[5]

But Stephensen's progress from the radical left to the radical right of politics lay in the future as, in London in 1926, he met up again with his friend Jack Lindsay and his associate Jack Kirtley. They were planning to set up a London version of the Fanfrolico Press, established in Sydney in 1925 to publish fine editions of the Greek and Roman classics, and to promote the fusion of the ideas of Nietzsche and 'Dionysian precepts' that characterised the work of Jack's father, Norman Lindsay. Lindsay senior's 'vitalist' philosophy, expounded in his 1920 work *Creative Effort*, profoundly influenced Hugh McCrae, R. D. Fitzgerald, Kenneth Slessor, Kenneth McKenzie, Douglas Stewart, and his own sons, Jack and Philip. Stephensen was later to write that 'Their aim now was to re-energise

Norman Lindsay, whose
'vitalist' philosophy was
promoted in Britain by the
Fanfrolico Press.
National Library
of Australia

Britain, and the whole war-weary world, with Dionysian precepts, rather than to achieve something creditable in and for Australia'.[6]

Fanfrolico Press was duly set up in Bloomsbury and published editions of Australian and English poets as well as Jack Lindsay's translations from the Greek and Latin classics (often those of the most lubricious nature). These were lavishly illustrated and printed on hand-made paper. 'Inky' Stephensen replaced Kirtley as manager in 1927, and he and Jack Lindsay edited a literary periodical, *The London Aphrodite*, published in six issues in 1928 and 1929, and featuring British writers Richard Church and Aldous Huxley and Australian writers Kenneth Slessor, Hugh McCrae, Anna Wickham, Brian Penton and Bertram Higgins. But the Fanfrolico Press did not achieve its aim, expressed by Stephensen as 'striving … to express an idea, to try to save Britain from slithering further into the abyss of "modernistic" despair, from becoming a "Waste Land" of grey neuters' (T. S. Eliot was a particular *bête noir* for Stephensen).[7] From his isolationist perspective in the 1950s, Stephensen admitted that the Fanfrolico experiment had been a rearguard action:

> … the shrewdly-professional exploiters of current trends, and purveyors of 'escapism', were the most successful and typical British authors. Men who had the living flame in them, such as Lawrence, Douglas and Huxley, found England intolerable and went abroad into self-imposed exile …
>
> No wonder, then, that our little Fanfrolico Press attempt at a Dionysian Resurgence was doomed from the beginning! … Yet, as I now view our attempt in a retrospect, after two decades, I may claim with some modesty that it was a 'successful failure': that is, an experiment which had to be made, to test the ground.[8]

No matter: Stephensen had already found another way to cause a stir in British society. He left the Fanfrolico Press in 1929 when Brian Penton and Philip Lindsay arrived from Australia.[9] His next venture was the Mandrake Press, formed with bookseller Edward Goldston initially to publish an edition of the paintings of D. H. Lawrence, whom Stephensen had met in the south of France earlier in the year. Lawrence, it appeared, 'did not want to be associated with the Fanfrolico Press, as he disagreed with the Lindsay Aesthetic'.[10] The owners of the Mandrake Press found that attracting the attention of the authorities confirmed the adage that 'there's no such thing as bad publicity', as police swooped on the London gallery displaying the originals of the published Lawrence paintings, seizing thirteen of them and four copies of the book. The legal action for obscenity against the gallery caused deep distress to the sensitive novelist and painter, but was a 'sensational start' for the press, which also published an unexpurgated version of Lawrence's *Pansies*.[11] But Stephensen's desire to use the Mandrake Press to break down the barriers of prudery and censorship over-reached itself when he published the works of controversial poet Aleister Crowley in 1929.[12] Mandrake Press foundered, but Stephensen, as his biographer has related, 'rarely faltered long enough to look behind, just as he never troubled to look too far ahead'.[13]

Forty years after 'Inky' Stephensen joined Jack Lindsay in the Fanfrolico Press, two more young Australians went to London to test the effect of their brand of irreverence on the British public by publishing a London edition of *Oz* magazine. *Oz* was a monthly magazine published originally in Sydney between 1963 and 1969. It specialised in lampooning 'sacred cows', such as the monarchy, the church and the Returned Services League, a war veterans' organisation which has acted as a powerful force for conservatism in Australia. After a conviction for breaching the *Obscene and Indecent Publications Act*, editor Richard Neville and artist Martin Sharp began publishing *Oz* in London in 1967. There its daring graphics and irreverent satire provoked a response similar to that in Australia, earning Neville and his fellow editors Jim Anderson and Felix Dennis further charges of 'conspiracy to corrupt public morals' after the publication of *Oz 28*, which had been compiled by school children. At their trial at the Old Bailey in June 1971, John Mortimer, himself an author and creator of the quintessential eccentric barrister, Horace Rumpole, led the defence. Richard Neville was sentenced to fifteen months' imprisonment, and the others to lesser terms, but they were acquitted after an appeal. *Oz* nevertheless survived until 1973, by which time its particular style of Australian humour had gone out of vogue.

Richard Neville later reflected on the role of the magazine in the cultural life of Britain in the late 1960s and early 1970s: 'In the aftermath of Swinging London, *Oz* transmuted into a fluorescent gadfly of the establishment, providing a platform for dissident groups and strange opinions, all bubbling under the banner of "counter-culture"'.[14] Neville's reminiscences of that era were published in 1995 with the title *Hippie Hippie Shake: The dreams, the trips, the love-ins, the screw-ups … the Sixties.*[15] Lucretia Stewart, reviewing the book for the *Times Literary Supplement*, called Neville 'one of the quintessential figures of the 1960s and early 1970s in Britain', with a guaranteed place in its cultural history as 'the lynch-pin of the underground press' who 'could be said to have shaped the hearts and minds of at least two generations, his own and the one that came after it'. Her estimate of *Oz* magazine itself was less certain: she had 'only the dimmest recollection of it as a swirling mass of garish technicolor print and psychedelic images, the drugs-inspired brainchild of artist Martin Sharp … Its demise was probably no great loss'.[16]

Feminists

Jack Lindsay, of Fanfrolico Press and The London Aphrodite. *National Library of Australia*

The contribution of Australians to the feminist movement which emerged in the late 1960s in Britain was also linked very strongly to publication. British writer Jim Crace gave Australians such as Germaine Greer and Carmen Callil much of the credit for the development of feminism there: Greer by the publication in 1971 of *The Female Eunuch* and Callil for founding Virago Press, which played a vital role in restoring women's writing of the past to public notice, and promoting contemporary women's writing. Crace believes that the independence of Australian women by comparison with their British sisters is one of the reasons for their strong representation in the feminist movement.[17] Carmen Callil has commented that her 'un-English personality', and her lack of formality have both helped and hindered her in British publishing.[18]

Since *The Female Eunuch* catapulted Germaine Greer into international prominence in 1971, her name has become synonymous with the feminist movement and she is celebrated as the most significant feminist thinker of her generation. This does not necessarily mean that she has received unalloyed praise in the land of her birth: Australians are apt to reserve their most stringent criticism for those who achieve fame beyond the shores of their island continent. As Barry Humphries has commented, the Australian tendency to 'tall-poppy-lopping' really comes into play when the 'tall poppy' resides elsewhere: 'Local blooms may be trimmed, *en passant*, as a sport, but when our tall poppies escape our vigilance and come to rest in foreign vases beheading is too good for them'.[19]

And so it was with Germaine Greer, when she visited Australia in early 1972 to publicise *The Female Eunuch*. As Keith Dunstan has remarked:

> She had done what other Australian writers can only dream about. She had been acclaimed by the top literary magazines of Britain. She had reached the top eight of the best-seller lists in the United States. She was sought

Germaine Greer speaking at the National Press Club, Canberra, during her 1972 visit.
Courtesy National Press Club, Canberra and National Library of Australia

after by all the top television programmes. *Playboy* magazine interviewed her in depth over page after page after page. On the world scene she was the best-known Australian female since Dame Nellie Melba.[20]

Her book was mauled in the Australian press—by women critics. Thelma Forshaw in the *Age* called *The Female Eunuch* an 'orchestrated over-the-back-fence grizzle'.[21] Germaine Greer left Australia vowing not to return for some time, 'even at gunpoint'.[22] Since then she has published a number of works, adding to the considerable body of feminist scholarship which has followed in the train of her pioneering effort.[23] In a collection of essays published in 1986, *The Madwoman's Underclothes*, Greer restated her belief in the necessity for core female values and attributes to influence society:

> The question is often asked of me now, 'Are you still a feminist?' as if it were possible for me to be anything else. Everything I learn reinforces my conviction that the only corrective to social inequality, cruelty and callousness, is to be found in values which, if we cannot call them female, can be called sororal. They are the opposite of competitiveness, acquisitiveness and domination, and can be summed up by the word 'co-operation'. In the world of sisterhood, all deserve care and attention, including the very old, the very young, the imbecile and the outsider. The quality of daily life is what matters, the taste of the food on the table, the light in the room, the peace and wholeness of the moment ...[24]

Satirists

Barry Humphries has built a considerable reputation in Britain and Australia for his comic satires on Australian life. He has described himself in the author's note to his 1992 autobiography, *More Please*, as 'a pleasant and approachable person and a patriotic Australian'.[25] Humphries has lived on and off in Britain since the 1960s, but his stage, comic strip and film characters—Dame Edna Everage, Sandy Stone, Barry McKenzie, Sir Les Patterson and many others—have become familiar icons. Here, his most celebrated creation, Dame Edna Everage, the 'housewife megastar' from the Melbourne suburb of Moonee Ponds, celebrates a British institution, the Harrods sale, in this occasional piece of doggerel, 'Ode to Harrods'.

I'm thrilled to hear you clap and cheer,
And say what's Edna doing here?
Admittedly it's quite a coup—
I'm standing here in front of you!
By night I do my famous show,
By day I keep my profile low.
Yet though I'm frankly far from poor
I'm first in line at Harrod's door.
But, possums, please don't start to think
I'm here to buy a bargain mink,
Or snap up some cut-price diamond rings—
I've quite enough up-market things!
No, please ignore that ugly rumour,
I'm not here as a mere consumer
To stockpile satin underwear
I'm here at dawn 'because I care'!
The things that have made Britain great:
The Cashmere Scarf, the Wedgwood Plate,
Irish Linen, the Shetland Sweater
Are things no other land does better.
And all these gorgeous things and more
Are assembled in this store.
Your heart's desire you here will find
At prices that will blow your mind.
I love this land of Queens and Kings.
Frankly, I'm into English things;
Shakespeare is my favourite bard,
I adore the Trooping of the Guard!
Yet Crufts and Henley come and go,
As does the Chelsea Flower Show.
But all these institutions pale
Beside the mighty Harrods sale.[26]

Dame Edna Everage,
'housewife megastar',
Barry Humphries' most
popular comic creation.
Courtesy Megastar
Productions

A man with a finely tuned ear for social nuances and cultural distinctions extending as far as advertising slogans (as Clive James has described in another chapter) Humphries has been able to make Australians laugh at themselves—and, probably an easier task, make Britons laugh at Australians. This has created a degree of unease in Australia: one commentator has claimed that satirists such as Barry Humphries and Clive James merely perpetuate dated stereotypes of Australians:

> The British upper class and middle class still seem to feel the need, like the Webbs, to think of Australia as an uninteresting country inhabited by beer-swilling louts who talk in a comic accent. Their misconceptions are fed by some of the best-known, and highly talented, Australian expatriates ... The comedian Barry Humphries, a frequent performer on British TV who can also fill the Drury Lane Theatre for weeks with his one-man show, presents a savage picture of Australian suburbia and culture that brilliantly fuels the prejudices of his audience. Clive James wrote an account of his early years in Sydney that became a best-seller in Britain (though not in Australia) and must have given many British readers the impression that James's home country was so brash that the only course for a man of his talents was to emigrate to Cambridge.[27]

Bruce Bennett has commented that another of Humphries' satirical creations, Sir Les Patterson, the crude ex-politician 'Cultural Attaché to the Court of St James', shows 'an irrelevance to contemporary reality' which 'indicates the passing of an era when London seemed the sole base for talented Australian writers and performers to project themselves internationally'.[28]

Kathy Lette has been causing a stir in Britain since the publication of her 1993 novel *Foetal Attraction* demolishing the pretensions of the 'chattering classes' of 1990s Britain. An ability to coin 'withering one-liners about British class structure', and a will to demolish 'social sacred cows' have meant that Lette has been 'simultaneously reviled and elevated to the status of a best-selling author'.[29] *Foetal Attraction* and its 1996 sequel, *Mad Cow*, tell the story of an Australian girl, Madeline Wolfe, who follows her English television zoologist lover, Alex Drake, to Britain, and then discovers that she is pregnant. She decides to have the baby (in *Foetal Attraction*), and embarks on the life of a single mother (in *Mad Cow*). In *Foetal Attraction* Lette describes the scene at a dinner party when Maddy simultaneously discovers that her lover is married, and decodes the language of the literary set:

Maddy looked at them all blankly. What she suddenly realized was that he *had* told her. The trouble was that nobody spoke English in England. They spoke *euphemism*. She needed those little United Nations headphones. Then she could have deciphered what everybody had been saying to her since she'd lobbed into London.

'Australians,' Humphrey had said, 'so *refreshing*.' This, Maddy now realized, decoded as 'rack off, you loud-mouthed colonial'...

And Alex. Whose 'rather tricky whatnots and few loose ends to tie up' read as a mortgage, a four-wheeled drive 'breeder mobile', a 'do it yourself' deccie's kit, a *pied-à-terre* in Maida Vale and a family home in Oxford with a wife called Felicity—the syndicated columnist who wrote, as Harriet put it, a chatty, wacky little strip on wedded bliss.[30]

Mad Cow has been described as 'a comedy of heroism and paranoia', as the now single-mother Maddy copes with British society hampered by the responsibility of baby Jack. She falls foul of the law and is threatened with the loss of her child to the dreaded welfare system. Alex continues to let her down, and she finally heads back to Australia 'leaving an unjust and crumbling England behind'.[31]

The continuing popularity and productivity of 'stirrers' such as Germaine Greer, Carmen Callil, Barry Humphries, and Kathy Lette will no doubt ensure that the Australian tradition of 'causing a stir', established by 'Inky' Stephensen, Jack Lindsay and Richard Neville, is not likely to fade for some time to come.

13

KEEPING AUSTRALIA IN MIND

In 1945 Professor J. I. M. Stewart returned to England from a ten-year appointment as Jury Professor of English Language and Literature in the University of Adelaide. His period of 'exile', prolonged by the Second World War which had stranded him in Australia, had not been unmarked by controversy. Stewart had somewhat fluttered the antipodean dovecotes by saying, when invited to deliver a Commonwealth Literary Fund lecture in the early 1940s on the subject of Australian literature, that he would speak on D. H. Lawrence's 'Australian' novel, *Kangaroo*, because 'there is no Australian literature I can find to lecture about'.[1] Later Australian critics have nevertheless not indicted Stewart for cultural chauvinism on the basis of this remark. Michael Heyward has said that 'You didn't have to be English to have your doubts about this question', and cites Stewart's 'sidekick', Brian Elliott, as having given a lecture in 1944 on the subject 'Is Australian Literature Real?' His affirmative answer was noted: 'with reservations'.[2]

During his time in Australia Stewart had also become embroiled in Australia's most notorious literary scandal before the recent Demidenko affair, the 'Ern Malley' hoax. Max Harris, one of the publishers of the 'modernist' literary magazine, *Angry Penguins*, was a student of Stewart's. In 1944 he turned to his professor for an opinion when the poems of an obscure car mechanic, the late 'Ern Malley', were submitted for possible publication, supposedly by his sister Ethel, but in reality by poets James

McAuley and Harold Stewart, who were eager to discredit modernist verse by assembling a pastiche and passing it off as the work of an undiscovered poetic genius. Michael Heyward, in his definitive work on the hoax, *The Ern Malley Affair*, describes Stewart's response to the poems: he 'didn't make too much of them'. He thought they were 'the sort of highly derivative and to me, I'm afraid, rather incomprehensible verse that young men and women were writing at that time in England and America and that young poets in Australia were beginning to go after too'.[3] So it was ironic that, once 'Ern Malley' had been proved to be fictional, Stewart was among the first to be suspected as having perpetrated the hoax, on the basis of the facts that he was interested in modern poetry and was the author of the detective stories of the pseudonymous 'Michael Innes', a regular activity which over a long lifetime of prolific writing has ensured him a following among the devotees of detective fiction.[4] Aside from admitting that he had heard both of Harris and Ern Malley, Stewart did not wish to comment.[5]

Although investigative journalism had revealed that Stewart was not the mystery poet, Adelaide bookmakers offered odds of six to four that the Oxford-educated professor was the hoaxer, until Stewart issued a denial. Two days later he followed it up with a final statement that indicated his true opinion of the literary merit of the Ern Malley verses: 'I hope it is no aspersion upon a body of men,' he said, 'to suggest that some of their number are associated with the automotive industry, and I would myself rather be supposed to own a pie shop than to have written the Malley verses'.[6] James McAuley and Harold Stewart were duly revealed to be the hoaxers.

But Ern Malley had not finished with Stewart. On 1 August Max Harris was visited by a Detective Vogelesang (or Vogelsang) and questioned about the Ern Malley number of *Angry Penguins*, and on 5 September was charged with obscenity before the Adelaide Police Court.[7] Vogelesang gave evidence for the prosecution, revealing more about the preoccupations of members of the police force with goings-on after dark in parks than about his understanding of literature.[8] Stewart appeared as an expert witness for the defence. Michael Heyward has described his approach to defending his student from what was in the mid-1940s a comparatively serious charge:

> J. I. M. Stewart's testimony was heard with 'oppressive respect'. He declared that *Angry Penguins* was 'a serious

literary journal'. He took an aesthete's view that some of the writing in the issue was 'indecent in the sense of offending against delicacy' but 'would not deprave or corrupt save in point of literary style'.[9]

This evidence, with its nice distinctions between indecency and the ability of the work to deprave or corrupt, had the effect of muddying the waters rather than amounting to a clear defence. As Heyward has said, 'All the magistrate needed to be sure of was a lack of propriety'.[10] Harris was found guilty as charged. 'Ern Malley' had earned his publisher a fine of £5 in lieu of six weeks in gaol, as well as legal costs. But in 1946, after Stewart had returned to England, he dealt, in the name of Michael Innes, his own revenge on Harris's tormentors: his detective novel, *From London Far*, features a character called 'Birdsong', then 'Vogelsang'. Far from being an upholder of the law like his namesake, this Vogelsang is a criminal involved in the abduction of famous works of art from a Europe convulsed by the aftermath of war. His fate comes swiftly, within several pages of first reading the character's name; the hero, Meredith, impersonates him to hoodwink the rest of the criminal gang, then unceremoniously shoots him through the head.[11]

In the same year Stewart published another Michael Innes detective novel, *What Happened at Hazelwood*. The fruits of his recent Australian exile are manifested more directly in this novel than they are in *From London Far*, in some cases in a most repellent aspect. The arrival of Australian cousins—Hippias Simney, his son Gerard and his Australian wife from Bondi, Joyleen—at the baronial seat of Hazelwood in England, and the past dealings in Australia of those cousins and the baronet, Sir George Simney, who is murdered in the course of the novel, is the peg upon which the story is hung.

The Australians, and the Australian experience that underpins the novel's action, are depicted as being highly ambiguous. Criminality associated with the notorious trade in human beings known as 'blackbirding' is only one of several unsavoury aspects of the Simneys' Australian adventures. The sexually promiscuous Joyleen Simney—her name alone so identifiably Australian as to cause a frisson of disquiet in the reader—represents all that is crude and inimical to well-bred Britons. Her husband, Gerard Simney, by contrast, is portrayed more sympathetically. He is given some lines by the author which, for those who know of his recent sojourn in Australia, speak volumes as to what he felt about the land he had left behind: 'The old colonial days were for the most part disgusting, so far as I can make out. But Australia has her chance now. A decent sort of social-democracy can conceivably be set going there. Spiritually and culturally it will be something thoroughly inglorious. But it will be a whole heap better than most other places.'[12]

Stewart, in his Michael Innes persona, referred many times to Australian places, subjects and characters: sometimes this was merely a simple reference; at other times a more developed element of the plot. His first Michael Innes detective novel, *Death at the President's Lodging*, of 1936, was written in Australia. It used the reprehensible practice of securing Australian Aboriginal skeletal material for anthropological and other sci-

Professor J. I. M. Stewart in the cloister at Christ Church College, Oxford. Photograph by Fay Godwin

entific research to create a bizarre effect surrounding the murdered body of the President of St Anthony's College in a fictional British university.[13] He also created a mythical Australian pastoral area, 'Cobdogla', which featured in *The Daffodil Affair* (also written in Australia) and other novels.[14] But Stewart's most developed Australian character does not appear in the detective novels of Michael Innes, but in his Oxford quintet of novels, *A Staircase in Surrey*, written in the 1970s, many years after his Australian experience. The Australian Martin Fish, a fellow student who has a set of rooms on the staircase inhabited by the narrator, Duncan Pattullo, in his undergraduate days just after the Second World War, first appears in the second novel in the series, *Young Pattullo*; and re-appears in the last novel, *Full Term*, set in the 1970s. In *Young Pattullo*, Fish belies both his name and the reputation of his countrymen by being unable to swim; a circumstance used by Stewart to dramatic ends in the novel. In *Full Term*, Fish arrives back in Oxford as a cultivated person well-versed in Australian art, and a devotee of the works of Sidney Nolan—perhaps a subtle acknowledgment by his creator that Australian culture had possibilities after all.[15] A decade later, in his autobiographical memoir, *Myself and Michael Innes*, Stewart confirmed this impression with the statement that 'Indeed, if like Dr Johnson before us, we survey mankind from China to Peru, we may well conclude that Western civilization bears a rather better chance of survival in the antipodes than in either Europe or the Americas'.[16]

There have been other British writers this century whose fictional works involve characters, settings and situations in which Australians figure. Playwright and novelist J. B. Priestley visited Australia only once, in 1959, when he joined the throng of other visitors to Australia who have taken umbrage at the style of Australian newspapers which, he is reported to have said, 'with a few honourable exceptions, combine malicious editorship with downright bad reporting to an astonishing degree'.[17]

Priestley's Australian experience nevertheless produced more than an animus against the Australian press; his 1961 novel, *Saturn Over the Water*, has Australia as one of its settings.[18] In this thriller, involving an international conspiracy to foment a nuclear war in the northern hemisphere and the re-establishment of civilisation in the southern hemisphere by an elitist organisation—described first as 'the Wavy Eight' and then 'Saturn over the Water'—the narrator, painter Tim Bedford, follows a trail from England to Peru and Chile to Australia. Bedford is on a personal quest to find his dying cousin's scientist husband, who has disappeared from his job at the sinister Arnaldos Institute. After many adventures, Bedford arrives in Melbourne. Priestley is then able to use his narrator's voice to record impressions of Australia from his visit two years before:

It may seem odd that my final adventures with the Wavy Eight people should have happened in Australia. But I believe you would feel this only if you hadn't ever seen Australia. In its own way the country seemed to me just as mixed-up and contradictory, peculiar and mysterious, as the Wavy Eight setup was. Take that drive of mine from Ballarat to Charoke, across a good section of the State of Victoria. Sometimes I might have been driving through an emptier and warmer bit of Bucks or Northants, or passing central sections of Watford or Nuneaton that had been left out in the sun. Twelve coach parties from Women's Institutes might arrive at any moment. But then at the next turning the road might run straight into some lost world. If there were woods, then there were strange trees and giant ferns, good grazing for dinosaurs. But mostly, and especially late in the afternoon, I'd find myself running along a road, like a hammered rod of blue metal laid across the landscape, apparently going nowhere past a lot of nothing. That Buick might have been the Time Machine arriving at either extreme. At one place, where I stopped to use the thermos I'd bought and had filled at Ballarat, I'd had the whole visible world to myself. If anything else was alive, it kept dead quiet. Under silvery clouds the horizon all round was simply so much grey-blue haze. Between that and the road and me was desert that started as a light yellow ochre in the foreground and then deepened to a dark ochre and some patches of raw umber. And there was nothing else to be seen there except some blackened stumps of trees, which might have been slashed into a pale water-colour by somebody who was impatient and wanted to try a stick of charcoal. It was like drinking tepid strong tea and then lighting a pipe when somehow you've missed your own time by a million years. Any-body who could look at that landscape and still think in terms of votes, taxes, annual revenues and radio sets, would have to have either a lot less imagi-nation or a lot more than I have. And I might as well add here that all the time I was in Australia this sense of the huge dusty old continent, haunted not by men and their history but only by ghostly gum trees, never left me, just seeped through everything. So no matter how crazy the Wavy Eights turned out to be, they couldn't be out of place, as far as Tim Bedford's ideas of a normal life and background were concerned, here in Australia. If this was to be the last act, as I hoped it would be, then it had been given the right setting.[19]

Fay Weldon is another British writer who has used her visits to Aus-tralia to creative ends. She has found Australia to be 'a very drastic coun-try', 'a very different society', where she has had 'amazing conversations with women', one of whom uttered the throwaway line, 'My ovaries are in that building at the top of that hill', which inspired Weldon's short story, 'And Then Turn Out the Light' (1983), set in Newcastle, New South Wales.[20] An incident witnessed in Hobart became the inspiration for another short story, 'Oh Mary Don't You Cry Any More', dealing with the plight of women and children abandoned in Hobart by men who went to the mainland and never returned.[21] Weldon evokes the brooding bulk of Mount Wellington, and the black side of Tasmania's history, within her story of false optimism masking the eventual bleakness of the lives of one woman and her children.

Fay Weldon. Photograph courtesy of Fay Weldon and Penguin Books UK

The sun shone in the summertime, over Paradise: in the evenings the wall of Mount Wellington hung deep blue over the town, in the mornings, if you were up on time, stretching sleepy eyes, it was greyish pink.

'It's a wall to protect us', said Shirley, but Gracey wasn't so sure. Did the mountain protect, or threaten? Gracey had been up to the other side. It was scrubby and bare and like the moon. It was inhuman: it didn't like her or like anyone. One day it would shrug and shake all Hobart into the sea, and not think twice about it. There were ghosts in Hobart. A man climbed into a water tank to escape a bush-fire and was boiled alive. A sea captain ran his ship into the harbour bridge and a piece just fell out as if it was made of Lego and everyone who happened to be on it was killed. There was a beach where the first settlers had tied the aborigines to stakes and waited for the sea to rise and drown them.[22]

The theme of the Australian visiting Britain is explored by Iris Murdoch in her 1962 novel, *An Unofficial Rose*.[23] In the novel a young South Australian, Penn, is visiting his grandfather Hugh in Kent. Murdoch deals with great sensitivity with the cultural differences between Australia and Britain which confound the teenage boy, revealing her capacity for empathising with a homesick young Australian stranded in England among relatives who are preoccupied with personal crises. She has also captured, with remarkable accuracy for one who is not an Australian, the sense of alienation from the British landscape that some Australians, habituated to their dry land with its piercing light, often encounter in Britain.

Penn had so long and so desperately looked forward to coming to England, he had scarcely admitted to himself, let alone to his family, that when the time came to leave home he could hardly bear it. The aeroplane flight and the excitement of arriving had consoled him of course. But since then everything had been depressing and disappointing. Grandma dying had been so awful. And he found his English relatives alien to a degree which, he felt, they themselves quite failed to realise. He was perfectly aware, of course, that they all felt that his mother had married not exactly beneath her, but, well, unsuitably, regrettably. He was aware more obscurely that they were all, well, a little disappointed in him …

He had not minded, what they reproached themselves about most, their not having got him into a school. He was really rather relieved about this, since what an English school suggested to him most of all was the idea of being beaten: an experience which he had never had and the possibility of which he regarded with a mixture of fear and thrilled awe. He had not minded mooching about at Grayhallock—he was better at amusing himself than they imagined—though he would be sorry to go home without having seen a bit more of England. But he was depressed by the countryside which they all thought so pretty, and constantly exclaimed about instead of taking it for granted. He disliked its smallness, its picturesqueness, its outrageous greenness, its beastly wetness. He missed the big tawny air and the dry distances and the dust; he even missed the barbed wire and the corrugated iron and the kerosene tins: he missed, more than he would have believed possible, the absence of the outback, the absence of a totally untamed beyond.

He was not able, and this was what depressed him most of all, in any way to settle down with his English relations. Grandpa and Ann liked him of course, and he was fond of them, but it was all so awkward. He could not see into their ways. It irked him that even Ann, who was so kind, did not treat Nancy Bowshott as an equal. This instance of class-prejudice so constantly before his eyes incited him to such a degree that he had adopted an air of ostentatious affability and mateyness with Nancy: until he became aware that she thought he was flirting. After his alarmed withdrawal, coldness set in between them. This hurt him very much …

As he squatted in Steve's room in the wet green light in front of the big box of soldiers he thought with renewed longing of his own home, the lovely new-built bungalow at Marino, with its multi-coloured roof under the shadow of the great dry rustling blue gum tree: so clean and airy and modern, with its floors of precious jarrah wood and its lemony peachy garden. They had only lived there a year, since his father's promotion, and he had not got used to the wonder of it yet. Before that they had lived in Mile End, nearer to Port Adelaide, and made do with a week-end shack at Willunga. But now it was like a holiday all the time, with the sea filling half of space, and the white sand below, and the uncleared gum above, and the cries of galahs and kookaburras to wake you up in the morning. That was a real place.[24]

Nina Bawden, in her 1979 novel, *Familiar Passions*,[25] turns to a variant on the 'Prodigal Son' theme when Blodwen, an aunt of the leading character, returns after many years in Australia to visit her family. Blodwen, the family 'black sheep', had decamped to Australia with her older sister Florence's young man, leaving her to nurse their ageing cantankerous mother. Now she is returning, and Florence is the one who is having difficulty facing her. Blodwen's arrival, and the family's relapse into its old argumentative ways, are depicted with great skill by Nina Bawden, whose own brother and nieces live in Australia.[26]

Australian situations and characters also appear in works of fiction by British writers who take an international perspective, moving the focus of their work from Britain outwards to the floating world of travellers, media people and other itinerants of all races and nationalities who congregate in third world locations such as south-east Asia. Margaret Drabble in her 1991 novel, *The Gates of Ivory*, is one such writer: she has shifted her focus away from the tonier suburbs of North London to Bangkok, Hanoi and Saigon, to what she calls 'Bad Time', across the Thai–Cambodian border to the Khmer Rouge's 'killing fields'. Drabble's shift in subject and location has met with quite divergent reactions in Britain and Australia: many Australian readers have written to say how pleased they were that she had set a novel in the region closest to Australia; while some British readers have wondered why she chose to set a novel in south-east Asia and not in St John's Wood.[27]

In *The Gates of Ivory* Drabble has an 'Australian battleaxe', journalist Jacqueline Lowe, among her cast of characters adrift in south-east Asia. Lowe, hard-bitten and graceless, achieves what one of the novel's principal characters, writer and idealist Stephen Cox, has died in the attempt to do: she manages to interview senior officers of the Khmer Rouge. Another of Drabble's characters, photographer Konstantin Vassiliou, travels on board a yacht with a young Britisher who has crewed the boat from Cairns for a middle-aged British couple, a scene inspired by her son's experience of crewing a yacht from Australia to Bali.[28] As they talk, Konstantin and his crewmate eat Vegemite on toast—a situation with which many Australians can identify.[29]

By contrast with writers whose Australian scenes and characters are part of a mosaic of disparate elements which have international settings,

Margaret Drabble and her husband Michael Holroyd, 1995.
Photograph courtesy of Michael Holroyd

two recent British novelists have given their works an Australian focus, in approaches that differ widely in time, although they both explore Aboriginal themes. Young black writer Laura Fish sets her novel, *Flight of Black Swans*, in the Australian outback and among Aboriginal stockmen. The novel, according to a review of the work of the new generation of British-born black and Asian writers by Maya Jaggi in the *Guardian Weekly*, 'reflects the painful dislocations of its autobiographical "black Pom" heroine—the child of adoption by a white couple in rural England'.[30] And a new novel for adults by fantasy writer Alan Garner, *Strandloper*, examines another example of cultural dislocation—the always tantalising story of William Buckley, the 'wild white man', an escaped convict who lived for thirty-two years with Aborigines in the early nineteenth century in what is now Victoria, and never in later life revealed anything of substance about his unique experience.[31]

Jane Rogers' novel, *Promised Lands*, mentioned in a previous chapter, interweaves the early convict days in Sydney with the life of a late twentieth-century British family.[32]

Works inspired by Australia run the gamut from crime fiction to thrillers, to novels that reflect on family life and relationships, to historical novels, to comic novels and futuristic fiction. Howard Jacobson's 1986 comic satirical novel, *Redback*, uses a well-known example of Australian

William Buckley, the 'wild white man' who is the subject of Alan Garner's novel, Strandloper. *National Library of Australia*

fauna, the redback spider, to create the crisis that proves the ideological turning point for his character, Leon Forelock, a propagandist for a right-wing cultural organisation who has been recruited in Britain to advance the cause in Australia. Leon sees Australia as a magic place, as it is to there that his philandering father has fled with his mistress, Trilby, from the depressing northern English town of Partington. In spite of a strong aversion to Australian fauna of all kinds, a well-based dislike, as it turns out, Leon finds life in Australia congenial, particularly his cohabitation with synchronous swimmers Venie and Maroochie, the daughters of a leading New South Wales politician and judge respectively—until the day the redback strikes. One result of this disastrous event is to turn Leon from his allegiance to right-wing causes, and set him on a vain quest to ingratiate himself with the Sydney left.[33]

Ben Elton's novel, *Stark*, is set in the world of the near future, threatened by ecological catastrophe brought on by the careless greed of international entrepreneurs. They are ironically the first to know that the planet is doomed, and form an organisation called Stark, to organise themselves to avoid the catastrophe by colonising the moon. Stark recruits two Western Australian entrepreneurs with an uncomfortable resemblance to a number of prominent Australians now either behind bars or in exile, who are given the task of creating the 'launching pad' in the Western Australian desert for this evacuation of cowards from a disaster of their own creation. They are confronted by an odd assemblage of individuals in a loose coalition called Ecoaction—a semi-deranged Vietnam veteran, a philosophising activist, a 'pom poseur', a new convert to the environmental cause,

Australian artist Garry Shead produced a large series of paintings on the theme of D. H. Lawrence in Australia to coincide with the seventieth anniversary of the novelist's visit. Courtesy of Garry Shead

All Souls, Oxford, a college for graduates only, where Sir Keith Hancock became a Fellow. All Souls gave Hancock a model for University House in the Australian National University. Photograph by Michael Jones

P. R. ('Inky') Stephensen, by Edward Quicke, 1945. National Library of Australia

Inside the quadrangle of the main building of the University of Sydney, designed by Edmund Blacket 1854–62. Photograph by Roslyn Russell

A LITERARY PERIODICAL

THE LONDON APHRODITE

EDITED BY JACK LINDSAY & P. R. STEPHENSEN

NUMBER FOUR

Published by
THE FANFROLICO PRESS LONDON

Cover of the fourth issue of The London Aphrodite, *edited by Jack Lindsay and P. R. Stephensen, and illustrated by Norman Lindsay.* National Library of Australia

Poster for the 1972 film, The Adventures of Barry McKenzie *based on the comic strip by Barry Humphries and Nicholas Garland, published in the 1960s and 1970s in* Private Eye. *National Film and Sound Archive, Canberra*

and a middle-aged Aboriginal couple. Elton's characters, particularly the Perth entrepreneurs Silvester 'Sly' Moorcock and Ocker Tryon, are often stereotypical, but there are hints that Elton knows the territory as well. In this novel, no one wins, but the characters fighting the absconding plutocrats win the reader's respect for the pluckiness with which they face the unwinnable battle. The novel, while having its comic moments, delivers a serious message about the consequences of greed and environmental degradation, at times skilfully juxtaposing the actions of the rich with their results in the environment.[34]

All the writers whose work has been examined in this chapter have been inspired by their experiences—whether positive or negative—of Australia or Australian subjects. In their work, in one way or another, they have been keeping Australia in mind.

Howard Jacobson.
Photography courtesy
Penguin Books UK

14

PRIZEWINNERS

Western Australian writer Tim Winton spent a nervous few days in London in early November 1995. The retiring Australian had come to London because his novel, *The Riders*, had been shortlisted for the Booker Prize, and he hadn't 'had the heart or the courage to say no to his publishers'. He was confident that he was wasting his time: his money was on Pat Barker to win, with Salman Rushdie 'like the Melbourne Cup favourite whom everyone put their money on and then failed to come home'. He and his book were, to continue the racing analogy, the 'outsiders'. Despite his reluctance to engage in the 'shenanigans', Winton was 'pretty chuffed' when he was shortlisted, but he was still far from convinced that the Booker night would have much relevance for him: 'For British writers it is part of their literary culture. I'm not part of that so it is more a fun sideshow for me'. But he acknowledged that being shortlisted for the Booker was 'an affirmation that he had produced a book that was considered in the top five in the English-speaking world and gain a higher profile in the Motherland even though it was not his main gig'.[1]

Winton, for all his protestations of reluctance, knew how important the Booker shortlisting really was for his future as a writer. He admitted, 'because it is so difficult for an outsider to gain a place in the British literary mind, being nominated for the Booker prize is the best leg-up you'll ever get. It is a way of levering a way in the door ... Professionally it's great but personally I wish it was over'.[2] Once it *was* over he said, 'It was a terrific thing just to be nominated. I have a huge readership in Australia, a decent following in America and a bigger readership in Britain now because of the Booker, what have I lost?'[3]

Winton had identified one of the most effective ways in which an Australian writer—or any writer—can win acceptance in the British literary marketplace. Winning a major literary prize such as the Booker, or even being on the shortlist, is the path to a writer's acceptance within the wider context of the English-language-speaking world. Alastair Niven has acknowledged the role of literary prizes in promoting writers in Britain, and the tremendous importance of literary prizes and shortlists in winning recognition from British audiences. The fact that some Australian writers have won the Booker Prize or been shortlisted, he said, means that their names are known in Britain.[4] British

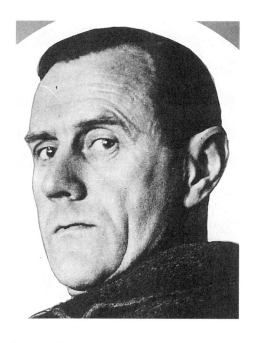

writer Jim Crace has described how British writers feel as the Booker shortlist announcement time comes around: 'You wait to see if you are on the shortlist, then when it is announced you see who is included who works in a similar style, and where you think they rank as a writer in relation to yourself.'[5]

Patrick White, the only Australian to win a Nobel Prize for Literature, in 1973, for The Eye of the Storm. *National Library of Australia*

Margaret Drabble has cited another reason for the awarding of literary prizes—they boost a writer's morale:

> Many writers lead dull, solitary, hard-working, underpaid lives, and they readily become paranoid, self-pitying, quarrelsome and litigious, convinced that they are unappreciated and unloved. Prizes and awards cheer them up. And they help to make their works more accessible and conspicuous: they pick out and display with proud labels books that might otherwise be choked by the vast indiscriminate ground cover of volumes that spreads from the publishers each year.[6]

Australian writers have won their share of British literary prizes, and two of them have won international awards which recognise their recipients as being in the forefront of practitioners of the writer's craft. Before winning the greatest prize of all, the Nobel Prize for Literature, Patrick White had won the W. H. Smith Annual Literary Award in 1958 for *Voss*. David Malouf's novel, *Remembering Babylon*, was shortlisted for the Booker Prize in 1993, and in 1996 won the Impac Dublin Literary Award, an enormously lucrative prize distinguished not only by the prize money, but also by the fact that it is open to any work of fiction regardless of the author's nationality.[7]

The Booker Prize

Thomas Keneally. His novel, Schindler's Ark, *was the first Australian novel to win the Booker Prize, in 1982. National Library of Australia*

The Booker Prize, first awarded in 1969, is the most glamorous and hotly contested—although not the most lucrative—British literary prize, and is awarded for novels first published in the United Kingdom by a British publisher. Booker, an international food and agricultural business operating in food distribution, fish and prepared foods, set up the Booker Prize, administered by Book Trust, in 1968. The intention of the prize is to reward merit, to raise the stature of the author in the eyes of the public, and to increase book sales. Competitors must be citizens of Britain, the Commonwealth, the Republic of Ireland, Bangladesh, Pakistan or South Africa. Margaret Drabble, novelist and literary historian, says that 'Winning the Booker still seems to provide a thrill, even for some of the most garlanded writers of the day'.[8]

Thomas Keneally has been a Booker Prize finalist on no less than four occasions. He entered the shortlist in 1972 with *The Chant of Jimmy Blacksmith*, was shortlisted again in 1975 for *Gossip from the Forest*, and again in 1979 for *Confederates*. In 1982 he won the Booker Prize with *Schindler's Ark*, which as motion picture *Schindler's List* won its producer, Stephen Spielberg, an Academy Award. Peter Carey became one of the select circle of novelists shortlisted for the Booker Prize in 1985 with *Illywacker*, a book which had been 'showered with awards'. Three years later in 1988 he was the winner, as *Oscar and Lucinda* became the second Australian novel to take out the Booker Prize.[9]

A review of a recent book, Richard Todd's *Consuming Fictions*,[10] a study of contemporary literary fiction in Britain, has commended the Booker Prize as 'the best thing that has happened to quality fiction since the invention of Allen Lane's Penguins in 1936', as it 'aims to encourage intelligent people to buy intelligent novels and read them intelligently, and equally but less overtly, to make good novelists write accessibly for a large reader-ship'. The choice for a Booker Prize of a book with a high degree of 'readability', Todd has emphasised, is a prime condition for the success of the award, and outstanding Booker winners have always had this quality.[11]

Carmen Callil, chair of the Booker Prize judging panel in 1996. Courtesy of Carmen Callil

The award of a Booker Prize is usually attended by controversy, and the 1996 award was no exception. This time the favourite, Graham Swift's *Last Orders*, won. Expatriate Australian publisher Carmen Callil, chairman of the Booker judging panel that year, in her speech at the awards celebrated the inclusiveness of fiction in English, which had 'benefited hugely from the richness of Commonwealth and American writing and has been in good shape for some time now'. She criticised the critics for their 'ritual moan about the dire state of the English novel'; and suggested that they were beginning to suffer from a species of 'political correctness' which led them to regard work from 'abroad' with more favour than the local product, which was permitted 'guarded praise' at most.[12] Then the criticism began: both the panel's choice and Callil's speech were attacked by fellow Booker judge A. N. Wilson.[13] The importance of winning the Booker Prize is thus highlighted by the rancour that greets the decision of almost every Booker Prize judging panel, itself an indication of just how much hinges on this particular award.

Prizes for Commonwealth writers

Australian writers have also won the Commonwealth Writers' Prize, which was instituted in 1987. They have included David Malouf for *The Great World* in 1991, and the 1993 winner, Alex Miller, for *The Ancestor Game*. In that year Australian writer Andrew McGahan was a regional winner in the Best First Book category for *Praise*.[14] Australian poets are included in an anthology, *Under Another Sky*, compiled by Alastair Niven from winners and specially commended entrants in the Commonwealth Poetry Prize, which was instituted in 1972 and is sponsored by British Airways. Australian poets whose work is represented in this anthology include Peter Kocan (commended 1976), Timoshenko Aslanides (winner 1978), Kevin Hart (commended 1978), Audrey Longbottom (commended 1980), Philip Salom (winner 1981), Peter Goldsworthy (winner 1982), Vicki Raymond (best first-time published poet 1986), and Andrew Taylor (Australia and Pacific Area winner 1986).[15]

David Malouf, whose novel, Remembering Babylon, *was shortlisted for the Booker Prize in 1993, and won the Impac Dublin Literary Award in 1996. Another of his novels,* The Great World, *won the Commonwealth Writers' Prize in 1991. National Library of Australia.*

Prizes for special categories

There are also prizes for literature in special categories. The W. H. Smith Literary Award is awarded to a British or Commonwealth citizen whose book, published in Britain in the previous year and written in English, is deemed to have made the most outstanding contribution to literature. As we have seen, Patrick White's *Voss* won in 1958.

Australian travel writer Robyn Davidson's account of her solitary journeys by camel in Central Australia, *Tracks*, won the Thomas Cook Travel Book Award in 1980. Travel books published in English from all over the world are eligible for the award, which aims to encourage and reward travel writing of high literary merit.

Barry Humphries, Australian-born satirist now living in Britain, won the Joe Ackerley Prize for Autobiography in 1993 for *More Please*. This prize has been awarded since 1982 for a literary autobiography written by a British author and published in Britain the previous year.

In January 1997 well-known Australian poet Les Murray was awarded the T. S. Eliot Prize for Poetry for his collection of poems, *Subhuman Redneck Poems*. Murray was cited by Alastair Niven as an Australian who is well known in Britain for having contributed an enormous amount to British cultural life: Niven placed Murray in the same category as another Australian poet, expatriate Peter Porter.[16] Winning the T. S. Eliot Prize confirms a reputation that Murray already enjoys in Britain. For other and lesser-known Australian writers, winning a British literary prize can be the pathway to a wider readership and recognition in the United Kingdom— and in Australia as well.

15

LITERARY VISITORS

In mid-October 1996 Australian audiences heard and saw British writer and television personality Melvyn Bragg, who was visiting the country to promote *Credo*, his novel of Dark Age Britain, and to attend the Melbourne Writers' Festival. In one twenty-four hour period Bragg could be heard on national ABC radio in the morning, talking to Margaret Throsby, on SBS television that evening with Andrea Stretton, and in person at a well-attended Literary Lunch at the Australian National University the following day. There he charmed the audience with reflections on his childhood in Cumbria, on regional identity in Britain, and the historical background of his latest novel, *Credo*. Bragg's schedule took him to the Melbourne Festival the following week, and doubtless to many other engagements before that. In Melbourne he was joined by other British and Australian expatriate literary visitors: Victoria Glendinning, Ben Okri, Peter Porter, Clive James and Steven Berkoff.[1]

In January 1997, the Sydney Writers' Festival brought Nina Bawden, Margaret Drabble, Lynda La Plante and James Kelman from Britain, and novelist Jane Gardam is scheduled to attend the Canberra Word Festival in March 1997.[2] These writers are the latest in a constant stream of British literary figures to make the trip to Australia to promote their books, meet their readers, and reinforce the links between the literary cultures of the two countries. The Melbourne Festival in October 1997 will feature a New Writers Exchange, as part of The British Council's *new*IMAGES programme to mark the fiftieth anniversary of the Council's work in Australia. Six British and six Australian writers will attend corresponding literary festivals to give readings, participate in forums and promote their work to new audiences. Writing stimulated by these visits will be incorporated in an anthology to be published in 1998.[3]

British literary visits to Australia have a history almost as long as the European history of Australia itself. As chapter 5 has shown, some British writers have come here with the specific purpose of commenting on the country. Others have come as the popular writers of the books that Australians have enjoyed reading. Before the Second World War the typical British writer's visit was a private one, or one connected with another event—or even simply a holiday. This is not to say that British writers were not recognised and fêted when they arrived in Australia before that time: they were. Robert Louis Stevenson made four visits to Sydney in the 1890s.[4] He was followed by Rudyard Kipling and Joseph Conrad, then by Sir Arthur Conan Doyle (he lectured on spiritualism) in the early 1920s.[5] John Masefield, the Poet Laureate, came to Australia in 1934 as a guest of the Victorian Centenary Celebrations,[6] and also, an appropriate task for a writer, laid one of the foundation stones for the original National Library of Australia in the raw new federal capital city, Canberra. There were many more British writers who made the journey to Australia as individuals, and were warmly welcomed.

The British Council

Nevertheless, the combination of sponsoring body and literary festival which has attracted a stream of British writers to Australia over the past few decades has reached its present state of development in the period after the Second World War. The British Council has been a vital element in creating the situation which allows the present dynamic and stimulating exchange, as writers meet other writers and readers. The growth of writers-in-residence programmes at colleges and universities has also given British writers the opportunity to live for a short time in Australia, and mix with students and staff.

The British Council was in fact the inspiration of an expatriate Australian, Sir Reginald Leeper. Founded in 1934, when Leeper was Head of the British Foreign Office News Department, the Council's task, he wrote, was to:

… examine the position of English studies in each country abroad, the teaching of English in foreign schools and universities … the provision of English books and the many other ways in which the demands for greater information about various aspects of our culture may be satisfied. It will also have to establish such contacts at home as will assist foreigners coming here to profit from their visit.[7]

Novelist Elspeth Barker came to the Sydney Writers' Festival in January 1994 to talk about her award-winning novel, O Caledonia. *Courtesy of Elspeth Barker and Penguin Books UK*

The initiative begun by Leeper has seen British Council offices established in 109 countries around the world.

In April 1945 Australia's revered wartime prime minister, John Curtin, asked John Dedman, his Minister for Post-War Reconstruction, to contact The British Council to confirm Curtin's invitation to open a Council office in Australia. Curtin, in a speech in Britain in 1944, had said:

> We are a British community in the South Seas and we regard ourselves as the trustees of the British way of life in a part of the world where it is of the utmost significance to the British Commonwealth and to the British nation and to the British Empire—call it by any name that you will—that there should be in the Antipodes a people and a territory corresponding in purpose and in outlook … to the Motherland itself.[8]

After Curtin's death, his successor Ben Chifley continued the initiative, and The British Council opened an office in Sydney in January 1947.

Over the fifty years that The British Council has operated in Australia it has, along with many other cultural programmes, sponsored visits by visiting British writers to Australia (a list of many of those who have come to Australia with British Council support can be found in the Appendix). One of these writers, Sir John Betjeman, who came to Australia in November–December 1961, wrote a report on his visit in which he said that 'I don't know whose idea it was that I should go but to whoever thought of it I would like to say that I feel ten years younger and that I have not enjoyed myself so much since I was an undergraduate at Oxford in 1925'.[9] Betjeman was amazed by the 'appreciative and sensitive' audiences, and the fact that 'people who live in a place the size, say, of Didcot (e.g. Orange) should crowd to hear an English literary gentleman of whom they had probably never heard'. He attributed his large audiences to his appearances in Australia on television and 'steam radio'. Betjeman thought that 'English people can get more out of going to Australia than they can give to it' and, in conclusion, what he 'most enjoyed about Australians was their absence of envy and pettiness'.[10]

British writers' experiences of Australia

Have the impressions of visiting British writers to Australia changed materially since Betjeman's 1961 visit? In November and December 1995 I was privileged to receive a British Council travel grant to travel to Britain to interview a number of British writers about their visits to Australia.[11] While each writer brought his or her expectations to their visits to Australia, some of the conclusions they reached after they had been there were very similar, and can be readily summarised.[12] All the writers interviewed, for example, remarked upon the excellence of Australian literary festivals, and the positive response of Australian readers. Australian bookshops were also highly commended, particularly by Richard Holmes, Jim Crace and Fay Weldon. Australia's literary community, commented many of the writers interviewed, was characterised by its 'vibrancy' and 'dynamism'. Richard Holmes, Rose Tremain, Nina Bawden and Alastair Niven mentioned friendships they had forged with Australian writers. Their visits to Australia had made some writers curious to know more about Australian writing of the past and present—Penelope Lively and Richard Holmes amassed large numbers of books by Australian writers when they were there. Professor Brian Matthews said that a visit to Australia had been a 'changing experience' for British literary visitors, and that many of these writers maintained a keen interest in Australia and Australian writing once they returned to Britain.

Here are some of their responses to my questions about Australia, Australian writers, literary festivals and literary culture, and the impact of the country and its people on a visiting British writer.

Nina Bawden always knew quite a lot about Australia—her marine engineer father went back and forth on a passenger ship, and her brother

Nina Bawden, who writes both adult and children's novels, has made several trips to Australia for literary festivals, most recently to the Sydney Writers' Festival in January 1997. Courtesy of Nina Bawden

and nieces also live in Australia. She also has many friends there, and is 'very conscious of a connection'. The first time Nina Bawden came to Australia she visited Sydney and Melbourne, and gave a lecture at the Frankston campus of Monash University. She then went to the Adelaide Festival, which she thought 'wonderful', 'absolutely lovely'; 'they hold it so attractively'.

When she first visited Australia, Nina Bawden considered that Sydney and other Australian cities were 'more English' than any other place she had been. The picture of suburban Australia in Patrick White's books, she said, conveys Australia to her. The Australian literary community is 'very nice, friendly and open'. Nina Bawden attracts a considerable response from Australian readers of her adult fiction, biography and children's books—she receives about one hundred letters a year from Australia.[13]

Jim Crace said of himself and his fellow British writers that 'we are charmed by Australians—we see the best Australians—they can be witty in a democratic way, their wit is not class-imbued'. He believes that one of the great distinctives of Australia, and Australian writing, is that there is a tradition of humour dating from the 1970s and 1980s in particular that is not class-based, as it is in Britain.

Nowadays, said Jim Crace, writers on the 'circuit' were 'desperate to go to Melbourne and Adelaide'. It is a final treat, and they come back to Britain 'enthused at what they find'. What they find is something that doesn't exist in Britain, where for a start the audiences tend to be smaller in number. There is a vibrancy about Australian literary events—'those coming from Britain see it at its best'. He loved the bookshops in Australia—'the suburban bookshop is to be cherished'. It 'provided an irresistible environment' and was 'concerned with carrying stock': British writers, he said, 'find our books in the bookshops'. Jim Crace said he would enjoy a stay as a writer-in-residence in Australia. He has launched three books in Australia—*The Gift of Stones* (1989), *Arcadia* (1992, Adelaide), and *Signals of Distress* (1994, Melbourne)—and claims that the critical response to books in Australia is very different to that in Britain. You are 'dealt with as a human being in Australia', he said. Writers are open and are not 'precious' about their art. Tom Keneally called Jim Crace 'an honorary Australian', which had pleased him immensely.[14]

Margaret Drabble and Michael Holroyd have both attended literary festivals in Australia. Margaret Drabble first came to Australia to attend the Canberra Word Festival in 1989. Michael Holroyd came for the Adelaide Festival then travelled to

Novelist Jim Crace, described by Tom Keneally as 'an honorary Australian', loves Australian bookshops. Photograph by Tim Wainwright, courtesy of Penguin Books UK

Sydney, Melbourne, Brisbane and New Zealand. He said that the Adelaide Festival was 'the best in the world—beautifully arranged, wonderful audiences of about 2000 people—people had taken the trouble to read beforehand'. Margaret Drabble agreed: 'they really read'. Michael Holroyd said it was 'very encouraging for the writers present', who 'came back feeling it had been worthwhile'.

Michael Holroyd felt that 'there was a strong sense of a literary community in Australia—very lively in Sydney'. He considers David Marr to be a 'top-rate biographer'. In his opinion Australian literature was now a world literature with international currency.

Margaret Drabble found it very interesting that there are so many non-English speaking groups and writers in Australia, an awareness she gained in Australia through watching SBS TV. She had received large numbers of letters from people in Australia about her novel, *The Gates of Ivory*. They took a different view from people in Britain, in that they were pleased that part of the novel was set in the region closest to Australia.

Are expatriate Australian writers considered Australian or British? I asked. Margaret Drabble replied that 'There is a local/global dichotomy here'. She and Michael Holroyd both agreed that expatriate writers in Britain—for example, Clive James, Peter Porter, Germaine Greer—are not thought of as Australian writers particularly, but as part of the larger literary world: as 'powerful British figures'.

Australian art is another attraction: Michael Holroyd particularly appreciates Arthur Boyd's work, and had also enjoyed meeting Sidney

Nolan. For Margaret Drabble there was only one major problem in visiting Australia: the time it takes to get there, which is still the same now as it was twenty years ago.[15]

Richard Holmes and Rose Tremain were impressed by Australian audiences, which they found were more resilient than those in Britain. If if rained the British would stay away, whereas the audience at the Adelaide Festival they attended were not daunted by heavy rain. The readings

were held in a tent, and people even stood outside under umbrellas to listen. Richard Holmes remarked that when he visited Australia he became aware of how little he knew of Australian writing, past and present. He collected a huge number of books by Australian writers with the result that his book collection cost him £50 in overweight luggage. His enthusiasm for Australia is conveyed in the essay he wrote on his return to Britain, 'Holmes Goes Waltzing Matilda':

Novelist and short story writer Rose Tremain and biographer Richard Holmes met at the Adelaide Festival in 1992. Photograph by Irmeli Jung, courtesy of Rose Tremain and Richard Holmes

I was only there for a month. First as a clean-suited, respectable guest of the Adelaide Writers' Festival; then as an increasingly crumpled itinerant lecturer heading north through Sydney, Brisbane and Mackay; and finally as an exhausted, drifting, naked snorkeller above the tropical rainbow of coral reefs (where even Sir Joseph Banks nearly foundered). But the weird enchantment lingers yet, and I have come home with a certain Ancient Mariner madness upon me, holding my friends with a glittering eye, and relating my Tales of the Antipodean Unexpected, of that 'great, good, Island in the Southern Seas' once dreamed of by navigators, botanists and ballad-writers.[16]

Richard Holmes described the Adelaide Festival as 'superb, with not a cultural cringe in sight'. For him the 'symbolic incident' which captured the mood of the festival occurred after the first night of the performance of a new opera, 'Nixon in China'. The cast went to an Adelaide restaurant to celebrate:

Here they found the new-wave British novelist Jim Crace (*Arcadia*, 1992) silently celebrating his forty-seventh birthday over a melancholy shark steak. The whole restaurant was suddenly filled with an unearthly, outback humming. The cast rose chorically to its feet, formed a vibrating circle round Jim's table, and then burst into a spontaneous, operatic 'Happy Birthday To You' that brought people running and clapping in from the street. Afterwards a breathless, blushing Crace was heard to mutter ecstatically: 'That would *never* happen in London.' Just so.[17]

Holmes, by the time he had reached Brisbane, was 'asking the big question: what is the "proper image" of Australia itself?'. He took the advice of Australian biographer David Marr, to look 'backwards and inwards: the history, the interior, the Unconsciousness of that huge land with its unknowable red heart'. Marr, said Holmes, was 'a powerful, modern voice':

David Marr's excitement, his laconic intensity, is deeply unEnglish and deeply sympathetic. It is pure Oz. The more he talked about the past, the more I felt he was really thinking about the future. Because there is, overwhelmingly, this sense of a future, a graspable construction of shared happiness, which seems to radiate from the Australian psyche. (Is that pitching it too high? I wrote in my notebook while standing in a Transit Centre waiting for a delayed inter-state coach: 'Everyone seems to feel that Australia's past has a great future. We are running late, but we'll get there. She'll be all right.')[18]

Richard Holmes concluded his essay: 'I think I've got to go back'; he and Rose Tremain said they were saving for a return trip in the year 2000.[19]

Penelope Lively 'adored Australia', and her visits there gave her a 'huge exhilaration', a 'sense of a vibrant, exciting place'. She made the point though that visiting British writers probably received a slightly distorted view of Australia from the great receptions they attracted. The Adelaide Festival, she said, was 'absolutely incredible'—'it is like an agricultural show combined with a garden party fete'. Canberra was less so. The Adelaide Festival attracted a disparate audience, which was 'not necessarily very bookish'.

Her first trip to Australia, ten years ago, was for six weeks, and the next was to Adelaide a couple of years ago. She met more Australian

Penelope Lively, Booker Prize winning novelist and short story writer, took home to England a large box of books by Australian writers of the past and present.
Courtesy of Penelope Lively

writers in Canberra, and 'got a proper sense of the difficulties under which Australian writers work'—she recognises why subsidies are necessary. Australian writers are writing in a relatively small community—competition is no bad thing. Penelope Lively said she felt that Australian writers pursue their art under the shadow of Patrick White. Elizabeth Jolley, for example, she believed was writing within the shadow of White: there is, said Penelope Lively, a 'family resemblance' to his work in hers. She also discovered earlier Australian writers, who she said are not known in England: 'people from the UK know nothing about them'. Penelope Lively said that she had asked Penguin Australia for a selection of the works of Australian writers to bring back to England. She believes that the work of these earlier writers 'informs contemporary writing in Australia', and sees a parallel here with American writing; she is 'passionate about Willa Cather and Edith Wharton'.

Before she had visited there, Penelope Lively said, she had had 'no strong perception at all' about Australia: the 'blank' about Australia had been 'filled in by literature'. She had admired Patrick White, and so had a 'literary image' of Australia, one also informed by Nolan's paintings. So she had 'a purely artistic Australia in the head—a cultural Australia in the mind'. Everything else about Australia, said Penelope, 'came as a complete revelation'. Australian birds were a great delight, and she often looks with pleasure at her book on Australian birds. After she said, during an interview on ABC Radio, that she was interested in birds, three people rang and offered to take her bird watching. She went. She was also invited to visit Government House, Adelaide, to see a stained-glass window featuring Australian birds. There she encountered an environment straight from Britain in an earlier time: little satin-covered chairs, flunkeys with silver trays, and loaf-sugar with sugar tongs. Australian museums and art galleries were an 'absolute paradise' for Penelope Lively. She enjoyed the collections of Aboriginal artefacts in Melbourne and Adelaide; and Australian painting, particularly the works of the painters of the Heidelberg School, she found 'completely mind-boggling'.

Penelope Lively says that they 'do literary festivals extraordinarily well in Australia'. Readers' letters from Australia resemble American readers' letters, and show 'very intelligent responses to the writing'.[20]

Fay Weldon was last in Australia in 1994, but made her first trip there in 1982. Her 1984 book, *Letters to Alice on first reading Jane Austen* refers to this visit, and segments of the book are set in Cairns and in Canberra.[21] She has used these as the occasion for making some comments on Australian places and society. Then she attended the Adelaide Festival, staying a further six months and teaching at Sydney Institute of Technology as a writer-in-residence. There she found the students 'extraordinarily lively', if not 'Bolshie'. They told her that her short stories did not conform to the standard description of the structure of the short story.

Fay Weldon believes that, in Australia, emotions move outwards. Audiences are very responsive. In the UK there is a great battle against reading, whereas in Australia people want to buy books. She found that at Australian dinner parties she met 'a diversity of people—very stimulating', by contrast with British dinner parties where she met mostly other writers.

Fay Weldon's remark about what she believed to be the benefit to British writers of a visit to Australia (quoted in the Introduction to this book), neatly captured the essence of the responses of the British writers I interviewed over those few weeks in late 1995: 'All British writers in search of inspiration should go to Australia. It gives one a sense of clarity. Subtexts are articulated there.'[22]

This statement, couched in the language of 1990s literary criticism, is a direct descendant of Sir John Betjeman's 1961 claim: 'I think English people can get more out of going to Australia than they can give to it'. Fay Weldon and Sir John Betjeman have both been too modest: they do not give themselves or their fellow writers enough credit for the pleasure they bring to their Australian readers when they make the long journey to Australia.

CONCLUSION

This book has traced the links between Britain and Australia as expressed in the work of British and Australian writers. These have been explored in a number of ways: from the perspectives of explorers, investigators, publishers and satirists; from the points of view of those involved in higher education, or in war, or in debate over constitutional arrangements; by examining sets of circumstances associated with transportation, expatriatism or migration in both the nineteenth and twentieth centuries; the effect of literary prizes on the reputation and marketability of Australian writers; and through the insights of one notable British writer of the 1920s, and those of a number of British writers of today.

As the introduction to this book has stated, the overall perspective on this subject is that of an historian. Historians have often referred to the saying that we can only understand the present by understanding what has happened in the past. A postmodernist and deconstructionist view of history would dispute that we can even begin to try to understand the past, with its mass of submerged histories and multiple subtexts, and the effects of power relations and class agendas on the representation and interpretation of the past. Nevertheless, some historians believe that patterns can be discerned; some talk of the 'lessons of history', and that we are doomed to blunder on forever repeating mistakes if we do not learn from them. The British historian and cultural heritage theorist David Lowenthal has, I believe, best articulated what any historian at the end of the twentieth century is attempting to do when he or she tries to identify patterns—or links—from the past to the present:

> No absolute historical truth lies waiting to be found; however assiduous and fair minded the historian, he can no more relate the past 'as it really was' than can our memories. But history is not thereby invalidated; faith endures that historical knowledge casts *some* light on the past, that elements of truth persist in it. Even if future insights show up present errors and undermine present conclusions, evidence now available proves that some things almost certainly did happen and others did not. The curtain of doubt does not cordon off historians from the past; they look through the fabric and beyond, secure in the knowledge that they approximate to the truth.[1]

This is a portentous way in which to end a book that has attempted to track the progression of a relationship from one of parent and child to another which is now more akin to that of a partnership in the same enterprise—the celebration of literature in the English language, and the striving for excellence by all its practitioners, wherever they may live, in a world brought closer by efficient communications. We can rightly celebrate the mature relationship between Australia and Britain, and the sense of partnership that has been evoked, particularly by The British Council's *new*IMAGES programme. But, as Baroness James has said, it would be foolish to take this relationship—like any other relationship—for granted. In her report on her Australian tour for The British Council in 1991, P. D. James warned that 'It is, I think, dangerously easy to assume that the ties with the old "Mother Country" are so strong that the Council's work, although valuable, is less necessary than in emerging or recently liberated countries. This, I think, would be a fatal mistake …'[2] At present, with the lively programme of literary festivals in Australia showing no sign of flagging, and the willingness of British writers to make their way to Australia to meet other writers and readers, an unclouded future for this aspect of the relationship would seem to be assured. But Baroness James's warning should be heeded nonetheless.

The situation of Australian literature in Britain is not as rosy as might appear from the celebratory note that has prevailed in general throughout the last chapters of this book. While it is true that Australian writers who have achieved prominence in Britain—whether they be expatriates who have made their name in Britain, or winners of literary prizes—are numbered among the leading figures in the literary world, the picture is not so bright when we consider the broader spectrum of the Australian literary community. Both Dr Alastair Niven and Professor Brian Matthews made the point in their interviews that it was difficult to obtain the works of many Australian writers in Britain, that the 'big three'—Nobel and Booker Prize winners White, Keneally and Carey—were the only Australian writers whose work was readily available in Britain. It would be difficult to build a course in Australian literature in many parts of Britain, Dr Niven said, as a sufficiently wide range of books was not available.[3] By contrast, a survey of the shelves of any Australian bookshop would reveal a sizeable clutch of titles by British writers, as would viewing the catalogues of most Australian public libraries.

We should not, however, be unduly cast down by the apparent lack of penetration of the British book market by Australian writing. Dr Niven has admitted that it was only in the late 1960s that Australian writing began to be taken seriously in Britain—a very short time in the long perspective of British history.[4] But the cumulative effect of Australian writers winning British literary prizes, of British writers establishing links with the Australian literary community, and of high-profile Australian expatriates such as Peter Porter and Clive James becoming involved once more in Australian literature on both sides of the world, can only be beneficial.

To close this book as it opened—in London. Jill Neville's 'London Letter' appears each week in the *Australian Weekend Review*. In October 1996 she announced the imminent return to Australia of Professor Brian Matthews, of the Sir Robert Menzies Centre for Australian Studies in London. He had, she wrote, 'presided over the last of his Literary Links evenings for 1996, which have certainly hotted up dear old Australia House'.[5] May the literary links which have been established between Australia and Britain continue to keep the relationship between the two 'hotted up'.

APPENDIX

WRITERS' VISITS TO AUSTRALIA WHICH HAVE BEEN SPONSORED BY THE BRITISH COUNCIL

Dannie Abse
Peter Ackroyd
Fleur Adcock
Diran Adebayo
John Agard
Al Alvarez
Simon Armitage
Paul Bailey
John Bayly
Iain Banks
Elspeth Barker
Julian Barnes
Jonathan Bate
Glen Baxter
Nina Bawden
Steven Berkoff
Sir John Betjeman
Michael Billington
Melvyn Bragg
Anthony Burgess
A. S. Byatt
Angela Carter

Kate Clanchy
Nancy Chambers
Jim Crace
Gillian Cross
Kevin Crossley-Holland
David Curtis
Fred D'Aguiar
David Dabydeen
Roald Dahl
Nick Dear
Berlie Doherty
Margaret Drabble
Nicholas Dromgoole
Carol Ann Duffy
Nell Dunn
Anthony Easthope
David Edgar
D. J. Enright
William Feaver
Eva Figes
Anne Fine
Penelope Fitzgerald

Michael Frayn
Peter Fuller
Jane Gardam
Victoria Glendinning
Peter Greenaway
Romesh Gunesekera
Andrew Gurr
David Hare
Jonathan Harvey
Alan Hollinghurst
Christopher Hollis
Richard Holmes
Michael Holroyd
Ted Hughes
Pat Hutchins
Kazuo Ishiguro
Ian Jack
Clive James
P. D. James
Jackie Kay
Lois Keith
James Kelman

A. L. Kennedy	Iris Murdoch	Graham Swift
Hanif Kureishi	Grace Nicholls	Robert Swindells
Linda La Plante	Anne Oakley	Emma Tennant
Lee Langley	Ben Okri	D. M. Thomas
Mike Leigh	Brian Patten	Rupert Thomson
Doris Lessing	Glen Patterson	Peter Thomson
Deborah Levy	Katherine Perera	Sue Townsend
Joan Lingard	Caryl Phillips	Barbara Trapido
Joan Littlewood	Alan Plater	Rose Tremain
Penelope Lively	Peter Porter	Joanna Trollope
David Lodge	Ian Rashid	Hugo Vickers
Christopher Logue	Peter Reading	Martin Waddell
John Lucas	Christina Reid	Marina Warner
Sara Maitland	Ruth Rendell	Fay Weldon
George Macbeth	Frank Ronan	Timberlake Wertenbaker
Patrick McCabe	Bernice Rubens	Peter Whelan
Moy McCrory	Sir Steven Runciman	Angus Wilson
Roger McGough	Salman Rushdie	Colin Wilson
John McGrath	Will Self	Jacqueline Wilson
Billy Mackinnon	Nicholas Shakespeare	Peter Wollen
James Moore	Gillian Slovo	Diana Wynne Jones
Amanda Muir	Maud Sulter	Benjamin Zephaniah

NB: This list is not complete, but is representative.
Source: The British Council, Australia.

NOTES

Introduction

1. Michele Field, 'London Toasts Our Library', 'The Reader', supplement to the *Canberra Times*, 6 December 1994.

2. Roslyn Russell, report submitted to The British Council of a visit to the United Kingdom, November–December 1995 (unpub. man.). The interview with Fay Weldon, from which this quotation is taken, was on 7 December 1995.

3. David O'Reilly, 'The Empire Strikes Back', *Canberra Times*, 16 July 1995.

4. *Bulletin*, 26 September 1995.

5. Michael Billington, 'Australian chutzpah that travels well', *Guardian Weekly*, 25 February 1996.

6. *Sydney Morning Herald*, 28 October 1995.

7. Correspondence with Fergus McClory, Hon. Australian Representative, The Brontë Society.

8. Correspondence with Rosalind Kennedy, Kipling Society of Australia Inc.

9. Jane Austen Society of Australia Inc., *Newsletter*, No. 10, June 1996.

10. Susannah Fullerton, 'What Jane Austen Would Have Thought of Our Christmas Lunch', *Sensibilities*, Number 12, June 1996, p. 63.

11. For critical works dealing with post-colonial and indigenous Australian literature, see James Tulip, 'David Malouf's *Remembering Babylon*: Issues of Race and Spiritual Transformation', pp. 69–75, and Jamie S. Scott, 'Custodians of

a British prison camp: Re-presenting the Christian Missionary in Post-Colonial Aboriginal Fiction', pp. 78–87 in Jamie S. Scott ed., *And the birds began to sing: religion and literature in post-colonial cultures*, Atlanta, Georgia, USA, 1996; Bill Ashcroft, Gareth Griffiths and Helen Tiffin, *The Empire Writes Back: Theory and Practice in Post-Colonial Literature*, Routledge, London, 1989; William McGaw ed., *Inventing Countries: Essays in Post-Colonial Literature*, SPAN No. 24, University of Wollongong, 1987; Adam Shoemaker, *Black Words, White Pages: Aboriginal Literature 1929–1988*, University of Queensland Press, St Lucia, Queensland, 1989.

Chapter 1

1. Leslie Marchant, *An Island Unto Itself: William Dampier and New Holland*, Hesperian Press, Western Australia, 1988, p. 72, has studied both Dampier's journal and the astronomical and tidal conditions of the area, and has concluded that 'the *Cygnet* was beached in the third cove on the north coast of Karrakatta Bay'. Christopher Lloyd's biography, *William Dampier*, Archon Books, Connecticut, 1966, p. 57, gives the Dampier Bay/Buccaneer Archipelago area, latitude 16°15" south as the landing place.
2. Neil Rennie, *Far-Fetched Facts: The Literature of Travel and the Idea of the South Seas*, Clarendon Press, Oxford, 1995, p. 59.
3. ibid.
4. ibid.
5. Marchant *An Island Unto Itself*, pp. 11–16, places Dampier within the intellectual context of his times, and lists his literary and scientific contemporaries.
6. Christopher Lloyd, *William Dampier*, Archon Books, Connecticut, 1966, p. 86.
7. Writers who deal with the long tradition of antipodean imaginings include Rennie, *Far-fetched Facts*, and Ross Gibson, *The Diminishing Paradise: Changing Literary Perceptions of Australia*, Sirius Books, Sydney, 1984. Rennie (preface) points out that 'The commonplaces of South Sea travel literature were present in the literature of real and imaginary travel long before the Western discovery of the South Seas, and can be traced from classical times through the early accounts of the New World of America to the accounts of the South Sea islands that lay beyond'.
8. Ross Gibson, *The Diminishing Paradise: Changing Literary Perceptions of Aus-*

tralia, Sirius Books, Sydney, 1984, pp. 1–6; John Dunmore, *Utopias and Imaginary Voyages to Australia*, National Library of Australia, Canberra, 1988.

9. Gibson, *The Diminishing Paradise*, p. 11.

10. William Dampier, *A New Voyage Round the World*, London, 1698. Literature on Dampier includes Christopher Lloyd, *William Dampier*, 1966, Alan Chester's novel, *The Cygnet Adventure*, Rigby, Adelaide, 1984, and Leslie Marchant, *An Island Unto Itself*.

11. Gibson, *The Diminishing Paradise*, pp. 11–14; Rennie, *Far-fetched Facts*, pp. 62–5.

12. Gibson, *The Diminishing Paradise*, pp. 17–18.

13. An important work in this area is Bernard Smith, *European Vision and the South Pacific* (1960, 2nd edn, 1985) which, while it deals primarily with the transformation of the consciousness of visual artists wrought by the Cook voyages also has implications for literature; his later work, *Imagining the Pacific in the Wake of the Cook Voyages* (1992) amplifies the theme of European constructions of the Pacific region.

14. Janet Browne, 'Private search for Eden', review in *Times Literary Supplement*, 30, August 1996, of Peter Raby, *Bright Paradise: Victorian Scientific Travellers*, Chatto and Windus, London, 1996.

15. Richard Drayton, 'In the savants' service', review in *Times Literary Supplement*, 30, August 1996, of David Philip Miller and Peter Hanns Reill, *Visions of Empire: Voyages, Botany, and Representations of Nature*, Cambridge University Press, Cambridge, 1996.

16. David Philip Miller and Peter Hanns Reill, *Visions of Empire: Voyages, Botany, and Representations of Nature*, Cambridge University Press, Cambridge, 1996, p. 342.

17. The entry on Captain James Cook in William H. Wilde, Joy Hooton and Barry Andrews, *The Oxford Companion to Australian Literature*, 2nd edn, Oxford University Press, Melbourne, 1994, pp. 189–190, gives an outline of literature pertaining to Cook and his voyages.

18. Paul Carter, *The Road to Botany Bay: An Essay in Spatial History*, Faber and Faber, London, 1987, p. 23. Carter takes issue with Beaglehole's interpretation of Cook's sentiments as 'nonsense', claiming rather that 'What fascinates Cook about the Australian Aborigines is, in contrast with the Tahitians, say, who swarmed over the ship, after nails, their complete detachment, their lightness of touch in dealing with the world around them'.

19. Captain James Cook, *Endeavour* Journal, August 1770, original held in the National Library of Australia, Canberra.

20. William Cowper, 'Charity', *The Poetical Works of William Cowper*, W. P. Nimmo, Hay and Mitchell, Edinburgh, 1863, p. 211.

21. Entry on Sir Joseph Banks in William H. Wilde, Joy Hooton and Barry Andrews, *The Oxford Companion to Australian Literature*, 2nd edn, Oxford University Press, Melbourne, 1994, p. 75; David Philip Miller and Peter Hanns Reill, *Visions of Empire: Voyages, Botany, and Representations of Nature*, Cambridge University Press, Cambridge, 1996.

22. Harold B. Carter, *Sir Joseph Banks 1743–1820*, British Museum (Natural History), London, 1988, p. 543.

23. John McPhee, *Australian Decorative Arts in the Australian National Gallery*, Canberra, 1982, p. 10.

24. Barron Field, 'The Kangaroo', *First Fruits of Australian Poetry*, 1819.

25. Richard Whately, 'There is a Place in Distant Seas', from Les Murray ed., *The New Oxford Book of Australian Verse*, expanded edn, 1991, Oxford University Press, Melbourne.

Chapter 2

1. This event provided the basis for a novel by Thomas Keneally, *The Playmaker* (1987), and a play inspired by the novel, Timberlake Wertenbaker's *Our Country's Good* (1988). Entry on *The Recruiting Officer* in William H. Wilde, Joy Hooton, Barry Andrews, *Oxford Companion to Australian Literature*, 2nd edn, 1994, p. 641.

2. Watkin Tench, *A Complete Account of the Settlement at Port Jackson in New South Wales*, first published London, 1793, ed. L. F. Fitzhardinge, Library of Australian History edn, Sydney, 1979, p. 152.

3. Henry Carter, 'Prologue, by a Gentleman of Leicester, on Opening the Theatre at Sydney, Botany Bay ...'

4. All chronological material in this chapter is taken from Graeme Aplin, S. G. Foster and Michael McKernan eds, *Australians: Events and Places*, Fairfax, Syme and Weldon Associates, Sydney, 1987.

5. For more information on the contract system of transportation see Charles Bateson, *The Convict Ships*, Reed, Sydney, 1974.

6. H.V. Evatt, *Rum Rebellion*, 1938; R. Fitzgerald, *Bligh, Macarthur and the rum rebellion*, 1988.

7. David Collins, *An Account of the English Colony in New South Wales*, Vol. 1, London, 1798, RAHS edn, A. H. and A. W. Reed, Sydney, 1975, pp. 99–100.

8. Michael Jones, chapter 1, 'Convicts in Paradise', *Redcliffe: First Settlement and Seaside City*, Allen & Unwin Australia, Sydney, 1988, pp. 9–27.

9. The term 'Botany Bay' to describe the penal colony in New South Wales persisted, despite the fact that the settlement was never established there.

10. *Oxford Companion*, pp. 635–6. The entry on *Quintus Servinton* gives a comprehensive account of the novel's plot, its author's background, and publication details.

11. *Oxford Companion*, p. 156; Dale Spender, *Writing a New World: Two centuries of Australian women writers*, Pandora, London, 1988, pp. 9–11.

12. Richard Cobbold, *The History of Margaret Catchpole: a Suffolk girl*, London, Ward, Lock, Bowden and Co, c. 1895.

13. Robert Hughes, *The Fatal Shore*, Collins Harvill, London, 1987, p. 451.

14. From Philip Neilsen ed., *The Sting in the Wattle: Australian Satirical Verse*, University of Queensland Press, St Lucia, Queensland, 1993, pp. 2–3.

15. Martin Cash, *The Adventures of Martin Cash: comprising a faithful account of his exploits, while a bushranger under arms in Tasmania, in company with Kavanagh and Jones in the year 1843*, ed. James Lester Burke, Hobart, 1870.

16. Robert Southey, 'Botany Bay Eclogues', *Poems*, vol. 1, Longman, Hurst, Rees and Orme, London, 1808.

17. Charles Dickens, *Great Expectations*, first published 1861, this edn Thomas Nelson and Sons, Edinburgh, n.d., p. 326.

18. Shirley Walker, '"Wild and Wilful" Women: Caroline Leakey and *The Broad Arrow*', in Debra Adelaide ed., *A Bright and Fiery Troop: Australian Women Writers of the Nineteenth Century*, Penguin, Ringwood, Vic., 1988, pp. 85–99; Spender, *Writing a New World*, pp. 112–15.

19. Marcus Clarke, *For the Term of His Natural Life*, first published 1874, this edn Chicago 18? [as per NLA catalogue], Laird and Lee, pp. 415–16.

20. 'Convict in Australian literature' in William H. Wilde, Joy Hooton, Barry Andrews, *Oxford Companion to Australian Literature*, 2nd edn, 1994, pp. 183–8. This entry gives a comprehensive list of works of literature which deal with the convict system.

21. Jane Rogers, *Promised Lands*, Faber and Faber, London, 1995, p. 271.

Chapter 3

1. Erasmus Darwin, 'Visit of Hope to Sydney Cove, Near Botany Bay', prefix [*sic*] to *The Voyage of Governor Phillip to Botany Bay*, John Stockdale, London, 1789.

2. G. Wilkes ed., W. C. Wentworth, *Australasia*, Sydney, 1982, p. 7; Coral Lansbury, *Arcady in Australia*, Melbourne University Press, Melbourne, 1970, p. 7.

3. Michael Persse, 'William Charles Wentworth', entry in Douglas Pike ed., *Australian Dictionary of Biography*, vol. 2, 1788–1850, I–Z, Melbourne University Press, Melbourne, 1967, pp. 582–9.

4. ibid., p. 584.

5. K. S. Inglis, *The Australian Colonists: an exploration of social history, 1788–1870*, Melbourne University Press, Melbourne, 1974, p. 41.

6. William Charles Wentworth, *Australasia*, London, 1823, p. 22.

7. Michael Rosenthal, 'The Penitentiary as Paradise', synopsis of a paper presented at 'Re-Imagining the Pacific: A Conference on Art History and Anthropology in Honour of Bernard Smith', National Library of Australia, 1–4 August 1996. Rosenthal claimed that artists such as Taylor tried to soften the social realities of the penal colony in a way that made it palatable back home in England, focusing on what appeared to be its social inclusiveness, with an intent to recuperate what Britain had lost with the development of agrarian capitalism. There was also a political agenda: Taylor's imagery, said Rosenthal, 'seeks to show that Sydney could develop at no cost to the environment or the inhabitants', vindicating the achievements of Governor Macquarie, the subject of severe criticism in the Bigge Reports on his administration published the previous year.

8. Bernard Smith, *European Vision and the South Pacific*, first published 1960, rev. edn, Harper and Row, Sydney, 1984, p. 235.

9. Coral Lansbury, *Arcady in Australia*, Melbourne University Press, Melbourne, 1970, pp. 60–3.

10. For an investigation of the identity of Alexander Harris, for some time a matter of conjecture, see Patricia Miles, 'In Search of Alexander Harris', in *The Push*, no. 30, 1992, pp. 46–69.

11. Margaret Kiddle, *Caroline Chisholm*, Melbourne University Press, Melbourne, 1957, p. 128.

12. ibid., pp. 130–1.

13. Robert Lowe, 'To Mrs Chisholm', in Brian Elliott and Adrian Mitchell, *Bards in the Wilderness: Australian Colonial Poetry to 1920*, Nelson Australia, Melbourne, 1970, p. 51.

14. Charles Dickens, 'Telescopic Philanthropy', chapter IV, *Bleak House*, first published London, 1853; Margaret Kiddle, *Caroline Chisholm*, Melbourne University Press, Melbourne, 1957. Kiddle's biography of Chisholm includes a section entitled 'Caroline Chisholm in Art and Literature', in ch. 6, pp. 128–34, which canvasses in detail the similarities and differences between

Mrs Chisholm and Dickens' Mrs Jellyby in *Bleak House*. In entries on Caroline Chisholm (p. 163) Charles Dickens (p. 232) in William H. Wilde, Joy Hooton and Barry Andrews, *The Oxford Companion to Australian Literature*, 2nd edn, Oxford University Press, Melbourne, 1994, the authors of the *Companion* say that Chisholm was 'possibly' the model for Mrs Jellyby. Coral Lansbury, *Arcady in Australia*, p. 103, was more definite about the identification: 'Dickens possessed the faculty of seeing people with grotesque shadows often livelier than themselves. Mrs Chisholm, admirable in herself and admired by Dickens, was manifest in Mrs Jellyby'. See also Mary Hoban, *Fifty-one pieces of wedding cake: a biography of Caroline Chisholm*, Polding Press, Melbourne, 1984, pp. 306–7 and Susanna De Vries, 'Caroline Chisholm' in *Strength of Spirit: Pioneering Women of Achievement from First Fleet to Federation*, Millennium Books, Alexandria, NSW, 1995, pp. 91–110.

15. Lansbury, *Arcady in Australia*, p. 95.
16. ibid., pp. 98–105.
17. ibid., p. 69.
18. ibid., p. 70.
19. *Melbourne Punch*, 7 July 1870.
20. Inglis, *The Australian Colonists*, p. 25.
21. Quoted in Lansbury, *Arcady in Australia*, p. 115.
22. *Illustrated London News*, 13 September 1862.
23. J. G. Knight, *The Australasian Colonies at the International Exhibition, London, 1862*, Government Printer, Melbourne, 1865, p. 6.
24. Robert Mallet ed., *The Record of the International Exhibition*, William Mackenzie, Glasgow and London, 1862, p. 92.
25. ibid.
26. Edgar Harcourt, *Taming the Tyrant: the first 100 years of Australia's international telecommunications services*, Allen & Unwin, Sydney, 1987, pp. 110–11.
27. See De Vries, *Strength of Spirit*, 'Mary McConnel (1824–1910) Founder of the Brisbane Children's Hospital', ch. 11, pp. 205–22.
28. Mary McConnel, *Memories of days long gone by*, London, 1905, pp. 6–7.
29. ibid., p. 8.
30. George Fletcher Moore, *Diary of Ten Years of an Early Settler in Western Australia*, London 1884, facsimile edn Nedlands, 1978, facing p. 64.
31. Ada Cambridge, *Thirty Years in Australia*, p. 27.
32. Graeme Davison, *The Unforgiving Minute: how Australians learned to tell the time*, Oxford University Press, Melbourne, 1993, pp. 56–7.
33. Charles Lamb, 'Distant Correspondents', *The Essays of Elia*, Macmillan, London, 1884, pp. 142–7.

34. Dale Spender, introduction to *The Letters of Rachel Henning*, Penguin Books Australia edn, 1988.

35. Mary McConnel, *Memories of days long gone by*, p. 17.

36. *The Letters of Rachel Henning*, Sydney, 1963, p. 78.

37. John Mills ed., William Thornley, *The Adventures of an Emigrant in Van Diemen's Land*, Rigby, Adelaide, 1973, pp. 80–123.

38. Henry Reynolds' works dealing with European/Aboriginal contact and its results include *The Other Side of the Frontier, The Law of the Land, With the White People, Frontier, Aboriginal Sovereignty* and *Dispossession*.

39. McConnel, *Memories of days long gone*, p. 26

40. ibid., p. 43.

41. *The Letters of Rachel Henning*, Sydney, 1963, p. 161.

42. *The Letters of Rachel Henning*, Penguin edn, 1988, p. 123.

43. ibid., p. 157.

44. G. B. Barton, *Literature in New South Wales*, Sydney, 1886, p. 1.

45. ibid., p. 7.

46. ibid., p. 3.

47. ibid., pp. 3–4.

48. Susan Sheridan, *Along the Faultlines: sex, race and nation in Australian women's writing*, Allen & Unwin, St Leonards, NSW, 1995, p. 7. Over the past few decades an enormous amount of scholarship has been devoted to bringing to light neglected works by nineteenth century Australian women writers, and establishing their place in the Australian literary canon. Scholars such as (in alphabetical order) Debra Adelaide, Patricia Barton, Patricia Clarke, Lucy Frost, Fiona Giles, Joy Hooton, Brenda Niall, Susan Sheridan, Dale Spender and Elizabeth Webby have published works showcasing and analysing the works of colonial women writers. Readers are encouraged to scan library catalogues under their names to locate these works. To list them all—and all the writers' names—would require a chapter to itself.

49. Introduction to Fiona Giles ed., *From the Verandah: Stories of Love and Landscape by Nineteenth Century Australian Women*, McPhee Gribble/Penguin Books, Melbourne, 1987, p. 3.

Chapter 4

1. J. A. Froude, *Oceana, or, England and her colonies*, Longmans, Green and Co., London, 1886, pp. 146–7.

2. ibid., p. 147.

3. ibid., p. 148.

4. ibid., pp. 149–150.

5. For a comprehensive treatment of the Sudan contingent incident see K. S. Inglis, *The Rehearsal: Australians at war in the Sudan 1885*, Rigby, Sydney, 1985. Inglis devotes a chapter to the development of the iconography of 'the little boy at Manly'.

6. Quoted in Philip Neilsen ed., *The Sting in the Wattle: Australian Satirical Verse*, University of Queensland Press, St Lucia, Queensland, 1993, p. 40.

7. Rick Hosking, 'Useful Practice—Blooding the Pups', in Ken Stewart ed., *The 1890s: Australian Literature and Literary Culture*, University of Queensland Press, St Lucia, Queensland, 1996, p. 285. This chapter is a comprehensive survey of the Australian literature of the Boer War period.

8. ibid.

9. J. D. Burns, 'For England', from In Memoriam booklet, *In the Dawning of the Day*, Melbourne, 1916.

10. Martin Boyd, *When Blackbirds Sing*, first published by Abelard-Schuman, 1962, this edn Penguin, Ringwood, Victoria, 1984; Ion L. Idriess, *The Desert Column: leaves from the diary of an Australian trooper in Gallipoli, Sinai, and Palestine*, Angus and Robertson, Sydney, 1932; Frank Dalby Davison, *The Wells of Beersheba: a light horse legend*, Angus and Robertson, Sydney, 1933; H. R. Williams, *The Gallant Company: an Australian soldier's story of 1915–18*, Angus and Robertson, Sydney, 1933.

11. Leonard Mann, *Flesh in Armour*, first published Melbourne, 1932, Allen & Unwin, Sydney, 1985.

12. Frederic Manning, *Her Privates We*, Davies, London, 1930.

13. Robert Graves, *Goodbye to All That: An Autobiography*, Jonathan Cape, London, 1958, pp. 236–7.

14. Anthony Price, *Other Paths to Glory*, first published 1974, this edn Victor Gollancz, London, 1990, pp. 186–7.

15. Mary Marlowe, *That Fragile Hour: an autobiography*, Angus and Robertson, North Ryde, NSW, 1990; Mary Edgeworth David, *Passages of Time: an Australian woman, 1890–1974*, University of Queensland Press, St Lucia, Queensland, 1975.

16. Louise Mack, *A Woman's Experiences in the Great War*, T. F. Unwin, London, 1915.

17. David Walker, 'War, women and the Bush: the novels of Mary Grant Bruce and Ethel Turner', *The Australian Legend Re-Visited*, special edn, *Historical Studies*, vol. 18, October 1978, number 71, pp. 297–315; J. T. Laird, *Other Banners: an anthology of Australian Literature of the First World War*, Australian

War Memorial and Australian Government Publishing Service, Canberra, 1971, is a comprehensive collection of literary works by Australian writers on this subject. For readers wishing to know more about the military aspects of Australia's involvement in the First World War, C. E. W. Bean's *Anzac to Amiens*, Australian War Memorial, Canberra, 1946, provides a short version of the multi-volume *Official History of Australia in the War of 1914–1918*. Other historical accounts include Alan Moorehead, *Gallipoli* (1956); Bill Gammage, *The Broken Years: Australian Soldiers in the Great War*, ANU Press, Canberra, 1974, also available in Penguin; John Robertson, *Anzac and Empire: the tragedy and glory of Gallipoli*, Hamlyn Australia, Melbourne, 1990. For an analysis of the theme of heroism—and boasting—in Australian war writing see Robin Gerster, *Big-noting: the heroic theme in Australian war writing*, Melbourne University Press, Carlton, Victoria, 1987.

18. Boyd, *When Blackbirds Sing*, p. 187.

19. Vance Palmer, 'The Farmer Remembers the Somme', *The Camp*, Sydney J. Endacott, Melbourne, 1920.

20. For the military history of Australian involvement in the Second World War, see John Roberstson, *Australia Goes to War: 1939–45*, Heinemann, Melbourne, 1981. A multi-volume *Official History*, ed. Gavin Long and published by the Australian War Memorial, gives a detailed account of Australian involvement.

21. Barney Roberts, *A Kind of Cattle*, Australian War Memorial, Collins, Sydney, 1985; Don Watt, *Stoker: the story of an Australian soldier who survived Auschwitz–Birkenau*, Simon and Shuster, East Roseville, NSW, 1995.

32. Russell Braddon, *The Naked Island*, Werner Laurie, London, 1952; entry on Russell Braddon in William H. Wilde, Joy Hooton, Barry Andrews, *The Oxford Companion to Australian Literature*, 2nd edn, Oxford University Press, Melbourne, 1994, p. 111.

23. Randolph Stow, *The Merry-Go-Round in the Sea*, Morrow, New York, 1966; David Malouf, *The Great World*, Chatto and Windus, London, 1990, Pan Macmillan edn, Sydney, 1991.

24. John McCarthy, *A last call of Empire: Australian aircrew, Britain and the Empire Air Training Scheme*, Australian War Memorial, Canberra, 1988; Don Charlwood's *No Moon Tonight*, Angus and Robertson, London, 1956, and *Journeys into Night*, Hudson Publishing, Hawthorn, Victoria, 1991, are memoirs of his wartime experiences in RAF Bomber Command.

25. Manning Clark, 'The Ideal of Alexis de Tocqueville', unpublished thesis courtesy of Dymphna Clark.

26. A. W. Martin and Patsy Hardy eds, *Dark and Hurrying Days: Menzies' 1941 Diary*, National Library of Australia, Canberra, 1993, pp. 113–14.

27. Michael Thwaites, *Poems of War and Peace*, F. W. Cheshire, Melbourne, 1968, pp. 38–40; first published 1943 in *The Jervis Bay and Other Poems*, New York and London. 'The Jervis Bay' is included in a new anthology of war poetry, *The Voice of War*, published by Penguin in 1996; Kenneth Baker ed., *The Faber Book of War Poetry*, Faber and Faber, London, 1996 also includes examples of Thwaites' poetry.

28. Dennis Haskell ed., *Kenneth Slessor: Poetry, essays, war despatches, war diaries, journalism, autobiographical material and letters*, University of Queensland Press, St Lucia, Queensland, 1991, pp. 48–49; Slessor's War Despatch, 'The La France Graves', ibid., pp. 180–1, gives part of the genesis of 'Beach Burial'; see also Geoffrey Dutton, *Kenneth Slessor: A Biography*, Viking Penguin, Melbourne, 1991, pp. 230–1 for other inspirations for the poem's imagery.

Chapter 5

1. Ellen (Mrs Charles) Clacy, *A Lady's Visit to the Gold Diggings of Australia in 1852–53*, ed. Patricia Thompson, Lansdowne Press, Melbourne, 1963, p. 19.

2. Jan Morris, *Cities*, Faber and Faber, London, 1963, p. 247.

3. A. G. Austin ed., *The Webbs' Australian Diary 1898*, Pitmans, Melbourne, 1965, pp. 13–15. Austin in his introduction says that the usually impeccable research efforts of the Webbs had not been pursued for their Australian trip. They 'approached their task', he said, in a 'disabling state of ignorance'; and this, combined with their 'forbidding' personalities meant that 'they proved themselves to be, in many ways, quite unsuitable and incompetent observers of Australian society'. Their diary, said Austin, 'is by no means a serious sociological document. It is, however, a fascinating record of the impressions Australia made on two highly intelligent and highly idiosyncratic visitors', p. 17.

4. Thomas Wood, *Cobbers*, London, 1934 , pp. 4–5.

5. Arnold L. Haskell, *Waltzing Matilda: a background to Australia*, Adam and Charles Black, London, 1940, this edn 1948, pp. xvii, xxi.

6. ibid., xvii.

7. ibid.

8. Bruce Chatwin, *The Songlines*, Viking Penguin, London, 1987, p. 161; Bruce Chatwin entry in William H. Wilde, Joy Hooton and Barry Andrews, *Oxford*

Companion to Australian Literature, 2nd edn, Oxford University Press, Melbourne, 1994, p. 159.

9. ibid., p. 166.
10. ibid, pp. 53–4, 56.
11. J. A. Froude, *Oceana, or, England and her colonies*, Longmans, Green, and Co., London, 1886, p. 88.
12. ibid., p. 103.
13. ibid., pp. 108–9.
14. ibid., pp. 155–6.
15. ibid., p. 207.
16. Keith Dunstan, *Knockers*, Cassell Australia, Melbourne, 1972, p. 34.
17. *The Webbs' Australian Diary*, p. 108.
18. ibid., p. 47.
19. ibid., p. 73.
20. ibid., p. 87.
21. Wood, *Cobbers*, pp. 178–9.
22. Morris, *Cities*, p. 89.
23. Anthony Trollope, *Australia*, first published Chapman and Hall, 1873, this edn P. D. Edwards and R. B. Joyce eds, University of Queensland Press, St Lucia, Queensland, 1967, pp. 471–2.
24. ibid.
25. Haskell, *Waltzing Matilda*, p. xviii.
26. Chatwin does not mention this fact in *The Songlines*, but until he reached Alice Springs he was accompanied on his journey into Central Australia by fellow British writer Salman Rushdie, according to Ian Hamilton, 'The First Life of Salman Rushdie', *New Yorker*, 25 December 1995 and 1 January 1996, pp. 105–6. The article states that Rushdie, after attending the 1984 Adelaide Festival Writers' Week, 'toured the outback with Bruce Chatwin, who was gathering material for his book "The Songlines"'. Rushdie and Chatwin parted company in Alice Springs, and Rushdie went to Sydney.
27. Bruce Chatwin, *The Songlines*, Jonathan Cape, London, 1987, p. 161.
28. ibid., pp. 101–2.
29. ibid., p. 13.
30. ibid., p. 14.
31. ibid., p. 57.
32. ibid., pp. 58, 98.
33. ibid., p. 60.
34. ibid., p. 286. Many tjuringa were stolen from tjuringa storehouses in earlier times; some can still be seen in museum displays and art publications, in spite

of the widely publicised caution that this is deeply offensive to Aboriginal people.

35. ibid., p. 293.
36. Trollope, *Australia*, p. 599, 530.
37. ibid., p. 530.
38. Wood, *Cobbers*, p. 160.
39. *The Webbs' Australian Diary*, p. 96.
40. Trollope, *Australia*, p. 225.
41. Webbs, *Australian Diary*, p. 22
42. Wood, *Cobbers*, p. 167.
43. Froude, *Oceana*, p. 144.
44. Wood, *Cobbers*, p. 191.
45. Jan Morris, *Cities*, p. 342.
46. Jan Morris, writing in 1992, claimed that for years she had received abusive letters about her comments on Sydney society. Jan Morris, *Sydney*, Viking, London, 1992, p. 5.
47. Jan Morris, *Cities*, p. 343.
48. Morris, *Sydney*, p. 5.
49. Arnold Haskell, *Waltzing Matilda*, London, first published 1940, this edn 1946, p. 125.
50. Jan Morris, *Cities*, London, 1963, p. 88.

Chapter 6

1. Henry Lawson, quoted in Keith Dunstan, *Knockers*, Cassell Australia, Melbourne, 1972, pp. 229–30.
2. ibid.
3. *Bulletin*, 21 January 1899; Dunstan, *Knockers*, pp. 230–1, says that Lawson's passionate description of his plight 'did not receive sympathy', with one correspondent saying that Lawson lacked the 'trait of the true poet', as 'It is very seldom that a poet abuses the land that bred him'.
4. Manning Clark, *In Search of Henry Lawson*, Macmillan, Melbourne, 1978, p. 87.
5. Colin Roderick, *Miles Franklin: Her Brilliant Career*, Rigby, Adelaide, 1982, p. 75.
6. Leonard Cronin ed., Henry Lawson, *A Fantasy of Man: Henry Lawson complete works 1901–1922*, p. 136.
7. ibid.

8. For a full account of Henry Lawson's time in London see Colin Roderick, *Henry Lawson: a life*, Angus and Robertson, North Ryde, NSW, 1991, chapter 16, 1900–1901, London, pp. 222–42.

9. Henry Lawson, 'Joe Wilson in England', *Children of the Bush*, 1902, from Cronin ed., *Henry Lawson, A Fantasy of Man*, pp. 130–1.

10. Henry Lawson, 'Jack Cornstalk', in Cronin ed., *Henry Lawson, A Fantasy of Man*.

11. Henry Lawson, 'The Sweet Uses of London', in ibid., p. 173.

12. Louise Mack, *An Australian Girl in London*, T. Fisher Unwin, London, 1902, pp. 223, 226–9.

13. ibid., p. 279.

14. ibid., p. 277.

15. ibid., p. 285.

16. Miles Franklin to Henry Lawson, 17 October 1900, Miles Franklin Papers, ML DOC 2211, Mitchell Library, Sydney.

17. Colin Roderick, *Miles Franklin: her brilliant career*, Rigby, Adelaide, 1982, pp. 75–6.

18. ibid.

19. Henry Lawson, preface to Miles Franklin, *My Brilliant Career*, William Blackwood and Sons, Edinburgh, 1903.

20. Roderick, *Miles Franklin*, p. 78. Roderick gives details of the critical responses to *My Brilliant Career* on pages 78–9.

21. Miles Franklin, *My Career Goes Bung*, Georgian House, Melbourne, 1946, pp. 232–3.

22. Marjorie Barnard, *Miles Franklin*, Twayne Publishers Inc., New York, 1967, pp. 131–2; Roderick, *Miles Franklin*, pp. 141–2.

23. Penne Hackforth-Jones, *Barbara Baynton: between two worlds*, Penguin, Ringwood, Victoria, 1989, pp. 77–80.

24. ibid., pp. 80–83; Roderick, *Henry Lawson*, p. 224.

25. Teresa Pagliaro, 'A. W. Jose and The Nineties', in Ken Stewart ed., *The 1890s: Australian Literature and Literary Culture*, University of Queensland Press, St Lucia, Queensland, 1996, pp. 316–17.

26. Arthur Jose, *The Romantic Nineties*, Angus and Robertson, Sydney, 1933, p. 13, from ibid., endnote 8, p. 358.

27. Victor Daley, 'When London Calls', in Harry Heseltine ed., *The Penguin Book of Australian Verse*, Penguin, Ringwood, Victoria, 1972, pp. 76–7.

28. Hazel Rowley, *Christina Stead: a biography*, Minerva edn, 1994, first published William Heinemann, Melbourne, 1993, p. 61.

Chapter 7

1. K. S. Inglis, 'Ceremonies in a Capital Landscape', in Stephen R. Graubard ed., *Australia: The Daedalus Symposium*, Angus and Robertson, North Ryde, NSW, p. 108; pers. comm. with Basil Atkinson, of the Sir Robert Menzies Memorial Foundation, and quoted in S. Bowman, S. Foster, and R. Russell, *Menzies In His Time*, video presentation for The Sir Robert Menzies Foundation, Melbourne, 1994.

2. Graeme Aplin, S. G. Foster, Michael McKernan eds, *Australians: Events and Places*, Fairfax, Syme and Weldon Associates, Sydney, 1987, p. 185.

3. ibid., p. 178.

4. Charles Tompson, from Appendix to the 1973 edn of his *Wild Notes, from the Lyre of a Native Minstrel* (1826), the first volume of poetry by a locally-born poet published in Australia.

5. Thomas Keneally, *Our Republic*, William Heinemann, Melbourne, 1993, p. 158.

6. ibid., p. 165.

7. John Dunmore Lang, *Freedom and Independence for the Golden Lands of Australia*, Longman, Brown, Green, and Longmans, London, 1852, pp. 64–5.

8. Henry Lawson, 'A Song of the Republic', *Bulletin*, 1 October 1887.

9. Keith Dunstan, *Knockers*, Cassell, Melbourne, 1972. His chapter on 'Royalty', pp. 178–99, relates many of the best-known criticisms of Queen Victoria and her family emanating from the *Bulletin* and other sources.

10. 'Federation', by W. T. Goodge, from Les Murray ed. *New Oxford Book of Australian Verse*, Oxford University Press, Melbourne, 1991, p. 67.

11. Mark McKenna, *The Captive Republic: A History of Republicanism in Australia*, Cambridge University Press, Melbourne, 1996, Chapter 9, pp. 188–204.

12. *Review of Reviews for Australasia*, 20 February 1901.

13. Rex Ingamells, *Royalty and Australia*, Hallcraft Publishing Company, Melbourne, 1954, p. 88.

14. Victor Daley, 'The Procession', Sydney, 1901.

15. In Les A. Murray ed., *New Oxford Book of Australian Verse*, 1991, p. 77.

16. Mary Gilmore, *Battlefields*, Angus and Robertson, Sydney, 1939, p. 7.

17. W. K. Hancock, 'Monarchy', in *Argument of Empire*, Penguin, Harmondsworth, 1943, pp. 110–12, in John Arnold, Peter Spearritt and David Walker eds, *Out of Empire: the British Dominion of Australia*, Mandarin, Port Melbourne, 1993.

18. Kathy Skelton, *Miss Gymkhana, R. G. Menzies and Me: Small Town Life in the Fifties*, McPhee Gribble, Melbourne, 1990, pp. 92–3.

19. ibid., p. 91.

20. ibid., p. 98.

21. Penelope Layland, 'Unhurried poetry of the republic: Murray's vision in the vernacular', *Canberra Times*, 8 June 1996 report of Senate Occasional Lecture Series; Les A. Murray, 'A Poet's View of the Republic', 7 June 1996.

22. Martin Boyd, 'Their Link with Britain', in Ian Bevan ed., *The Sunburnt Country: Profile of Australia*, Collins, London, 1953, p. 241.

23. Peter Spearritt, 'Royal Progress: The Queen and Her Australian Subjects', in Arnold, Spearritt and Walker eds, *Out of Empire*, p. 211.

24. Ingamells, *Royalty and Australia*, p. 88, 91.

25. Donald Horne, *The Lucky Country*, Penguin, Melbourne, 1964, p. 110.

26. Keneally, *Our Republic*, pp. 172–5.

27. Geoffrey Dutton ed., *Republican Australia?*, Sun Books, Melbourne, 1977.

28. David Marr, *Patrick White: A Life*, Random House, Sydney, 1991, p. 557: 'Even before scanning the Deaths, he turned each morning to the vice-regal column in the *Sydney Morning Herald* to see who had broken ranks to eat with Kerr and his successors at Yarralumla'; the writer recalls more than one occasion when an incident like this occurred during her employment with the late Professor Manning Clark. Clark's response to White's habitual rebuke was to shake his head and say: 'Six of the best from Mr White!'

29. Wayne Hudson and David Carter eds, *The Republicanism Debate*, University of New South Wales Press, Kensington, NSW, 1993, p. 232.

30. ibid., p. 219.

31. Keneally, *Our Republic*.

32. Murray, 1996, 'A Poet's View of the Republic'.

33. Hudson and Carter, *The Republicanism Debate*, p. 222.

34. ibid., p. 220.

Chapter 8

1. Ada Cambridge, *Sisters*, first published 1904, Penguin Australian Women's Library, Ringwood, Victoria, 1989, pp. 28–29.

2. K. S. Inglis, *The Australian Colonists; an exploration of social history 1788–1870*, Melbourne University Press, Melbourne, 1974, p. 55.

3. G. S. Harman, 'Universities', *Australian Encyclopaedia*, Vol. 8, 6th edn, Australian Geographic Society, Terrey Hills, NSW, 1996, p. 2980. The foundation dates of the oldest universities in the Australian States are as follows: Sydney, 1850; Melbourne, 1853; Adelaide, 1874; Royal Melbourne Institute

of Technology, 1887, given university status 1990; University of Tasmania, 1890; University of Queensland, 1909. ibid., p. 2981.

4. ibid.

5. S. G. Foster and Margaret M. Varghese, *The Making of the Australian National University 1946–1996*, Allen and Unwin Australia, Sydney, 1996, p. 71.

6. Harman, *Australian Encyclopaedia*, p. 2983.

7. L. F. Fitzhardinge, 'John Andrew La Nauze—Tributes on his retirement', *Historical Studies*, vol. 17, no. 67, October 1976, pp. 138–9.

8. Ross Campbell, *The Road to Oxalis Cottage*, Angus and Robertson, Sydney, 1981, p. 55.

9. W. K. Hancock, *Country and Calling*, Faber and Faber, London, 1954, p. 81.

10. Kathleen Fitzpatrick, *Solid Bluestone Foundations*, Melbourne, 1983, Penguin edn 1986, p. 200.

11. Campbell, *Oxalis Cottage*, p. 56.

12. Manning Clark, *The Quest for Grace*, Viking, Ringwood, Victoria, 1990, p. 61.

13. ibid. p. 204.

14. Fitzpatrick, *Solid Bluestone Foundations*, pp. 204–5.

15. ibid., pp. 205–6.

16. W. K. Hancock, *Country and Calling*, 1954, Faber and Faber, London, pp. 80–82.

17. Manning Clark, *The Quest for Grace*, Viking, Melbourne, 1990, pp. 91–3.

18. ibid., pp. 81–2

19. Interview with Michael Thwaites, Canberra, 28 September 1996.

20. David Marr, *Patrick White: A Life*, Random House, Sydney, 1991, p. 124. The section of Marr's biography dealing with White's Cambridge years is chapter 7, 'King's Men', pp. 115–37.

21. Clive James, *May Week was in June: Unreliable Memoirs III*, first published Jonathan Cape, 1990, this edn Pan, London, 1991, p. 19.

22. ibid., pp. 82–3.

23. Hancock, *Country and Calling*, p. 85.

24. ibid., pp. 83–4.

25. Campbell, *Oxalis Cottage*, p. 56.

26. ibid., pp. 62–3.

27. James, *May Week was in June*, p. 21.

28. Susan Davies ed., *Dear Kathleen, Dear Manning: the Correspondence of Manning Clark and Kathleen Fitzpatrick 1949–1990*, Melbourne University Press, Melbourne, 1996, pp. ix, 172.

29. Kathleen Fitzpatrick to Manning Clark, 22 September 1988, ibid., p. 135.

30. Ralph Elliott, review of Les Murray, *The New Oxford Book of Australian Verse*, new edn, Oxford University Press, Melbourne, 1996, in *Canberra Times*, 28 December 1996. While Thwaites's poems have appeared in overseas collections, his poetry has not been included in the latest edn of Les Murray's *The New Oxford Book of Australian Verse*. Elliott's review says that 'we look in vain for ... *The Jervis Bay* by Michael Thwaites, which is included in a number of overseas anthologies but strangely overlooked in Australia'.

31. Michael Thwaites, *Truth Will Out*, Collins, Sydney, 1980.

32. Patrick White, *Flaws in the Glass*, Jonathan Cape, London, 1981, p. 38.

33. James, *May Week was in June*, p. 12.

34. ibid., p. 13.

Chapter 9

1. Howard Jacobson, *Redback*, Bantam Press, London, 1986, p. 82.

2. For example, Peter Porter has recently edited *The Oxford Book of Modern Australian Verse*, Oxford University Press, Oxford, 1996, which has been described by Ralph Elliott as 'a worthwhile book, quirky at times, but clearly the product of an exceptional sensibility', *Canberra Times*, 23 November 1996. And Australian expatriates such as Porter and Clive James are frequent drawcards on the literary festival circuit in Australia.

3. *Australia Felix*, 1917, *The Way Home*, 1925, *Ultima Thule*, 1929. The trilogy was published in one volume in 1930.

4. Entry on 'Henry Handel Richardson' in William H. Wilde, Joy Hooton and Barry Andrews, *The Oxford Companion to Australian Literature*, 2nd edn, Oxford University Press, Melbourne, 1994, pp. 645–7. Other works of scholarship dealing with Richardson's fiction include Dorothy Green, *Ulysses Bound*, 1973, 1986; Karen McLeod, *Henry Handel Richardson*, 1985; and Axel Clark, *Henry Handel Richardson: Fiction in the Making*, 1990.

5. Julian Croft, 'Responses to Modernism', chapter 25 in *The Penguin New Literary History of Australia*, ed. Laurie Hergenhan, Penguin, Ringwood, Vic., 1988, p. 416.

6. Henry Handel Richardson, *The Fortunes of Richard Mahony*, first published 1930, this edn Angus and Robertson, Sydney, 1983, p. 831.

7. Martin Boyd, *Day of My Delight: an Anglo-Australian Memoir*, Lansdowne, Melbourne, 1965, p. 58.

8. ibid., p. 112.

9. Bruce Bennett, 'Perceptions of Australia, 1965–1988', chapter 26 in *The*

Penguin New Literary History of Australia, ed. L. Hergenhan, Penguin, Ring-wood, Vic., 1988, pp. 437–8.

10. Bruce Bennett, *Spirit in Exile: Peter Porter and his poetry*, Oxford University Press, Melbourne, 1991.

11. Peter Porter, *A Porter Selected*, Oxford University Press, Oxford, 1989, p. 21.

12. Bennett, *Spirit in Exile*, p. 25.

13. Peter Steele, *Peter Porter*, Oxford Australian Writers, Oxford University Press, Melbourne, 1992, pp. 12, 15.

14. Peter Porter, 'The True Country' in *Changing Places: Australian Writers in Europe 1960s–1990s*, eds Laurie Hergenhan and Irmtraud Petersson, University of Queensland Press, St Lucia, Queensland, 1994, pp. 50–1.

15. ibid. p. 53. The author received a similar response from expatriate writer and publisher Carmen Callil when she interviewed her in London in December 1995 and asked her whether she considered herself an Australian. She replied, 'Of course I'm an Australian'.

16. Entry on Germaine Greer in William H. Wilde, Joy Hooton and Barry Andrews, *The Oxford Companion to Australian Literature*, 2nd edn, Oxford University Press, Melbourne, 1994, pp. 330–1.

17. Don Woolford, 'Greer's latest boosts standing', *Canberra Times*, 16 October 1995.

18. Clive James, *Falling towards England: Unreliable Memoirs II*, Jonathan Cape, London, 1985, this edn Picador, Pan Books, London, 1986, pp. 160–1.

19. 'Helen Trinca, 'Clive's Home Truths', Weekend Review, *Australian*, 9–10 April 1994.

20. Clive James, *May Week was in June*, Jonathan Cape, London, 1990, pp. 244–5.

21. Clive James, 'The handing on of a copious view', *Times Literary Supplement*, 5, July 1996.

22. Randolph Stow, *The Suburbs of Hell*, first published 1984, this edn Fremantle Arts Centre Press, Fremantle, 1993.

23. Entry on Randolph Stow in William H. Wilde, Joy Hooton and Barry Andrews, *The Oxford Companion to Australian Literature*, 2nd edn, Oxford University Press, Melbourne, 1994, pp. 724–5.

24. Entry on Christina Stead in William H. Wilde, Joy Hooton and Barry Andrews, *The Oxford Companion to Australian Literature*, 2nd edn, Oxford University Press, Melbourne, 1994, pp. 714–15. The definitive biography of Christina Stead is Hazel Rowley, *Christina Stead: a biography*, William Heinemann, Melbourne, 1993.

25. Peter Craven, Introduction to Christina Stead, *For Love Alone*, first published

1945, this edn Collins and Angus and Robertson Australia, North Ryde, NSW, 1990, p. xiv.

26. ibid., p. 249.

27. Anthony J. Hassall, 'Quests', chapter 24 in *The Penguin New Literary History of Australia*, Laurie Hergenhan ed., Penguin, Ringwood, Vic., 1988, p. 402.

28. Christina Stead, 'Leaving 1928; Returning 1969', in *Changing Places: Australian Writers in Europe 1960s–1990s*, Laurie Hergenhan and Irmtraud Petersson eds, University of Queensland Press, St Lucia, Queensland, 1994, p. 57. Passage from 'Another View of the Homestead', in Christina Stead, *Ocean of Story: The Uncollected Stories of Christina Stead*, 1986.

29. R. G. Geering ed., *Christina Stead, Talking to the Typewriter: Selected Letters (1973–1983)*, Pymble, NSW, 1992, p. 5.

30. Barbara Hanrahan, in Stephanie Dowrick and Sybil Grundberg eds, *Why Children?*, Penguin, Ringwood, Victoria, 1980, pp. 50–52.

31. Barbara Hanrahan, *The Albatross Muff*, Chatto and Windus, London, 1977, p. 9.

32. Barbara Hanrahan, *A Chelsea Girl*, Chatto and Windus, London, 1988.

33. Barbara Hanrahan, *Michael and Me and the Sun*, University of Queensland Press, St Lucia, Queensland, 1992, p. 51.

34. ibid., pp. 157–8.

35. Entry on Barbara Hanrahan, *Oxford Companion to Australian Literature*, pp. 341–2.

36. Jill Ker Conway, *The Road from Coorain*, Alfred A. Knopf, New York, 1989, pp. 207–9.

37. Quoted in the Introduction to *Changing Places: Australian Writers in Europe 1960s–1990s*, eds Laurie Hergenhan and Irmtraud Petersson, University of Queensland Press, St Lucia, Queensland, 1994, p. xxi.

38. ibid.

Chapter 10

1. Sasha Grishin, *Garry Shead: the D. H. Lawrence Paintings*, Gordon and Breach Arts International, East Roseville, NSW, 1993. This series, says Grishin, 'is a personal, intuitive response to the novel, rather than an attempt to illustrate Lawrence's narrative'. He concludes: 'The artistic statement which Garry Shead makes in the Kangaroo paintings is one of provocative simplicity, wit and dramatic power', pp. 14, 18.

2. See Andrew Moore, *The Secret Army and the Premier: conservative paramilitary*

organisations in NSW, University of NSW Press, Kensington NSW, 1989, pp.
35–47; Keith Amos, *The New Guard*, Melbourne University Press, Melbourne, 1976, pp. 9–11; Frank Cain, *The Origins of Political Surveillance in
Australia*, Angus and Robertson, Sydney, 1983, pp. 214–22.

3. Robert Darroch, *D. H. Lawrence in Australia*, Macmillan, Melbourne, 1981.

4. The D. H. Lawrence Society of Australia was formed on 14 November 1992
    in the Thirroul Municipal Library. It now has over seventy members, pub-
    lishes a journal, *Rananim*, three times a year, conducts conferences and social
    events for members, and monitors the condition of Wyewurk, the cottage
    where Lawrence and Frieda stayed in 1922, and where he wrote *Kangaroo*.

5. 'The Nightmare' chapter of *Kangaroo* takes the reader back to wartime Corn-
    wall, where Lawrence is persecuted by the military authorities and subjected
    to a humiliating medical examination before being rejected as unfit to be
    conscripted for military service.

6. A. D. Hope, 'How It Looks to an Australian: D. H. Lawrence's Kangaroo',
    first published in *The Australian Experience*, ANU Press, ed. W. S. Ramson,
    Canberra, 1974; this version in A. D. Hope, *The Pack of Autolycus*, ANU
    Press, Canberra, 1978. Hope admitted that 'There is only one side of the
    book in which Lawrence's observation is brilliant and impressive, and that is
    his description of landscape of sea and shore, mountain and bushland and the
    raw and untidy townships. But he is best in his evocation of the strange
    brooding and secret bushland', p. 198.

7. D. H. Lawrence, *Kangaroo*, Martin Seltzer, New York, 1923, pp. 9–10.

8. D. H. Lawrence, 'Kangaroo', *Complete Poems*, eds Vivian de Sola Pinto and
    Warren Roberts, Viking, New York, 1964, pp. 392–4.

9. Lawrence, *Kangaroo*, p. 97.

10. Hope, *How it Looks to an Australian*, p. 198

11. *Kangaroo*, pp. 206–7.

12. *Kangaroo*, pp. 85–6.

13. *Kangaroo*, pp. 237–8.

14. *Kangaroo*, pp. 407–8.

15. D. H. Lawrence to Catherine Carswell, 22 June 1922. Lawrence arrived in
    Australia on 27 May 1922; this letter was written on 22 June. Harry Moore
    ed., *The Collected Letters of D. H. Lawrence*, vol. 11, Viking, New York, 1962,
    p. 711.

16. D. H. Lawrence to Else Jaffe, 13 June 1922, ibid., p. 707.

17. *Kangaroo*, pp. 17–18.

18. *Kangaroo*, pp. 25–6.

19. Manning Clark to Kathleen Fitzpatrick, 9 November, 1986, *Dear Kathleen,*

Dear Manning: The Correspondence of Manning Clark and Kathleen Fitzpatrick 1949–1990, ed. Susan Davies, Melbourne University Press, Melbourne, 1996, p. 96.

20. *Kangaroo*, p. 69.
21. *Kangaroo*, p. 206.
22. *Kangaroo*, pp. 323, 325.
23. *Kangaroo*, p. 409.
24. *Kangaroo*, p. 412.
25. *Kangaroo*, p. 420.
26. Moore, *Secret Army*, pp. 42–3, 50.
27. Hope, *How It Looks to an Australian*, pp. 196–7.
28. Michael Wilding, 'Kangaroo: "a new show"', in *Political Fictions*, Routledge and Kegan Paul, London, 1980, pp. 150–1.
29. ibid., p. 159. The 1985 film has Lawrence, left in the bush by Jack Callcott, straying away and being held up at gunpoint by members of the secret army.
30. Moore, *Secret Army*, p. 43.
31. Robert Darroch, *D. H. Lawrence in Australia*, Macmillan, Melbourne, 1981.
32. For contributions to the debate on the 'Darroch thesis' see Paul Eggert, 'D. H. Lawrence's Reception in Australia: *Kangaroo* and *The Boy in the Bush*', *Rananim*, vol. 3, no. 3, November 1995. Endnotes contain a useful list of sources for the debate. John Lowe, 'Benjamin Cooley—A Factitious Composite', *Rananim*, vol. 4, no. 2–3, December 1996; Joseph Davis, *D. H. Lawrence at Thirroul*, Imprint, Collins, Sydney, 1989, gives possibility of Thirroul connections for Lawrence's knowledge of the secret army; David Ellis, 'Lawrence in Australia: the Darroch Controversy', *D. H. Lawrence Review*, vol. 21, no. 2, summer 1989. An overseas reaction to the controversy, which concludes, on the question of whether Lawrence met members of the King and Empire Alliance in Australia, that 'the answer must be that no one has yet provided convincing evidence that he did' (p. 173). Peter Steele, 'Kangaroo: Fiction and Fact', *Meridian*, x, 1991, hints that literary critics have been shown to be better historians, in terms of their scepticism in the face of uncorroborated circumstantial evidence, than the historians who have embraced the Darroch thesis. But Steele concedes that Darroch's 'pleas for a fresh look at Lawrence in and on Australia have placed us all in his debt', p. 19.
33. Raymond Southall, introduction to Imprint edn, HarperCollins, of D. H. Lawrence, *Kangaroo*, Sydney, 1995, p. vii.

Chapter 11

1. Elizabeth Jolley and Caroline Lurie eds, *Central Mischief: on writing, her past and herself*, Penguin, Ringwood, Vic., 1992, p. 61. Jolley also touches on this theme in her 1993 novel, *The Georges' Wife*, Penguin, Ringwood, Vic., 1993, p. 120, where her character Vera, on the ship to Australia and recalling the street names of her old home town, is struck by the same desolation and wants to go back.

2. R. T. Appleyard, 'Post-war British Immigration', in *The Australian People: an encyclopedia of the nation, its people and their origins*, ed. James Jupp, Angus and Robertson, North Ryde, NSW, 1988, pp. 97–100.

3. Michael Davie, 'The Fraying of the Rope', in *Australia: The Daedalus Symposium*, ed. Stephen Graubard, Angus and Robertson, North Ryde, NSW, 1985, p. 381. This statement can be confirmed by personal experience. My father is a British migrant with family still in Britain, and an aunt made a rare telephone call from the UK at a time of severe bushfires to check on the safety of the family in Australia. British novelists Margaret Drabble and Nina Bawden both told me that they had relatives in Australia. 'Everyone', said Drabble, 'has at least two cousins in Australia'. Interviews with Margaret Drabble and Nina Bawden, November 1995.

4. Rodney Hall, *Journey Through Australia*, William Heinemann Australia, Melbourne, 1988, p. 3.

5. Jolley, *Central Mischief*, p. 60.

6. Hall, *Journey Through Australia*, pp. 1–2.

7. Ian Warden, *Do Polar Bears Experience Religious Ecstasy?*, University of Queensland Press, St Lucia, Queensland, 1980, p. 20.

8. ibid., cover note. Ken Rosewall was a famous Australian tennis player of the 1950s and 1960s, and his name, along with that of Lew Hoad, was synonymous with the great days of Australian tennis.

9. Elizabeth Jolley, *Central Mischief: on writing, her past and herself*, Penguin, Ringwood, Vic., 1992, p. 62.

10. Francesca Rendle-Short, *Imago*, Spinifex Press, Melbourne, 1996, pp. 13–14.

11. Michael Wilding, 'Three Incidents for a Mercia Quartet', from *This Is For You*, Angus and Robertson, Pymble, NSW, 1994, pp. 96–8.

12. Jolley, *The Georges' Wife*, p. 115.

13. Jolley, *Central Mischief*, p. 67.

14. ibid., pp. 62, 64.

15. ibid., p. 152.

16. Hall, *Journey Through Australia*, p. 3.

17. Rendle-Short, *Imago*, pp. 49–50.
18. ibid., p. 184.
19. Jolley, *Central Mischief*, p. 64.
20. Michael Wilding, 'American Poets in London', *Ulitarra*, 1993, no. 4., p. 24.
21. Michael Wilding, *Great Climate*, Faber and Faber, London, 1990; William H. Wilde, Joy Hooton, Barry Andrews, *Oxford Companion to Australian Literature*, 2nd edn, Oxford University Press, Melbourne, 1994, pp. 815–16, have commented on the collection's title to the effect that it derives from 'the one saving grace that Australia has for most British people'.
22. Michael Wilding, 'Somewhere New', *Aspects of the Dying Process*, University of Queensland Press, St Lucia, Queensland, 1971, pp. 4, 6.
23. ibid., p. 12.
24. ibid., p. 20.
25. J. D. Pringle, *Australian Accent*, Chatto and Windus, London, 1958, preface.
26. Jolley, *Central Mischief*, p. 67.
27. Pringle, *Australian Accent*, pp. 20–1.
28. John Douglas Pringle, *On Second Thoughts: Australian Essays*, Angus and Robertson, Sydney, 1971, preface.
29. Hall, *Journey Through Australia*, p. 3.
30. Entry on Rodney Hall, *Oxford Companion to Australian Literature*, pp. 338–9.
31. Christopher Bantick, *Canberra Times*, 10 November 1996, review of Rodney Hall, *The Island in the Mind*, Pan Macmillan, Melbourne, 1996.
32. Hall, *Journey Through Australia*, p. 55.
33. Entry on Elizabeth Jolley, *Oxford Companion to Australian Literature*, pp. 413–16.
34. Jolley, *Central Mischief*, p. 140.
35. Elizabeth Jolley, *Miss Peabody's Inheritance*, University of Queensland Press, St Lucia, Queensland, 1983.
36. Joan Kirkby, 'The nights belong to Elizabeth Jolley: Modernism and the sappho-erotic imagination of *Miss Peabody's Inheritance*', *Meanjin*, vol. 43, no. 4, 1984, pp. 484–92, in *Writing about Writing*, ed. Brian Edwards, Deakin University, Victoria, 1987, p. 103.
37. ibid., p. 101; Jolley, *Miss Peabody's Inheritance*, p. 157.
38. S. S. Kelen, 'A satisfying collection of short Australian fiction', review of *The Oxford Book of Australian Short Stories*, ed. Michael Wilding, Oxford University Press, Melbourne, 1995, in *Canberra Times*, 7 January 1995.
39. Warden, *Do Polar Bears Experience Religious Ecstasy?*, cover notes.
40. Lizz Murphy ed., *Wee Girls: Women Writing from an Irish Perspective*, Spinifex Press, Melbourne, 1996.

Chapter 12

1. Craig Munro, *Inky Stephensen: Wild Man of Letters*, first published Melbourne University Press, 1984, paperback edn University of Queensland Press, St Lucia, Queensland, 1992, p. 64.

2. Aldous Huxley, *Point Counter Point*, first published 1928, this edn Penguin, Middlesex, 1955, p. 126.

3. Michele Field, 'Australian interloper meets the British establishment', *Canberra Times*, 21 November 1993.

4. Stephensen's article 'The Foundations of Culture in Australia' in the *Australian Mercury* of July 1935, later published in expanded form in 1936, was a significant literary event, and influenced the Jindyworobak writers in particular.

5. For an excellent biography of Stephensen see Munro, *Inky Stephensen*; for a brief description of his career see entry on P. R. Stephensen in William H. Wilde, Joy Hooton and Barry Andrews, *Oxford Companion to Australian Literature*, 2nd edn, Oxford University Press, Melbourne, 1994, pp. 718–19.

6. P. R. Stephensen, *Kookaburras and Satyrs*, Talkarra Press, Sydney, 1952, p. 23.

7. ibid., p. 29.

8. ibid., p. 30.

9. The Fanfrolico Press did not survive much longer. In financial difficulties, the press moved to Hampstead, but this move was insufficient to avert bankruptcy in 1930.

10. Stephensen, *Kookaburras and Satyrs*, p. 31.

11. Munro, *Inky Stephensen*, p. 86.

12. For details of this episode see ibid., chapter 6, 'Mandrake, Magic and Depression', pp. 88–103.

13. ibid., p. 103.

14. Richard Neville, quoted in the *Sunday Age*, 23 June 1991.

15. Richard Neville, *Hippie Hippie Shake: The dreams, the trips, the love-ins, the screw-ups ... the Sixties*, Bloomsbury, London, 1995.

16. Lucretia Stewart, 'Like, where it was at, man', *Times Literary Supplement*, 19 May 1995. For those who knew the Australian version of *Oz* magazine the reviewer's description of the appearance of the British magazine is unfamiliar: the *Oz* magazine published in Sydney had characteristic line drawings and calligraphy by Martin Sharp printed on very white paper.

17. Interview with Jim Crace, 4 December 1995.

18. Interview with Carmen Callil, 30 November 1995.

19. Barry Humphries, 'Detrimental Blokes', foreword to Keith Dunstan, *Knockers*, Cassell Australia, 1972, p. xii.
20. Dunstan, ibid., p. 251.
21. ibid., p. 252. Dunstan gives several examples of the negative comments Greer's ground-breaking work attracted from the Australian press.
22. ibid., p. 253.
23. Works on feminism and women's issues by Germaine Greer include *The Obstacle Race*, on women artists (1979), *Sex and Destiny* (1984), *The Change*, on menopause (1991), *The Madwoman's Underclothes* (1986), and *Slip-Shod Sibyls*, on women poets (1995).
24. Germaine Greer, *The Madwoman's Underclothes: Essays and Occasional Writings*, London, 1989, p. xxvi.
25. Barry Humphries, *More Please*, Penguin, Ringwood, Vic., 1992, cover note.
26. Barry Humphries, 'Ode to Harrods' (1989), *Neglected Poems and Other Creatures*, Angus and Robertson, North Ryde, 1991, pp. 166–7.
27. Michael Davie, 'The Fraying of the Rope', in Stephen Graubard, *The Daedalus Symposium*, Angus and Robertson, Sydney, 1985, p. 385.
28. Bruce Bennett, 'Perceptions of Australia, 1965–1988, in *The Penguin New Literary History of Australia*, ed. Laurie Hergenhan, Penguin Books, Ringwood, Vic., 1988, p. 439. Michael Holroyd says that he went to see his friend Barry Humphries' show and confessed that he was 'shocked' by the Sir Les Patterson character. He thought that Humphries' humour was 'very cruel'. Interview with Michael Holroyd and Margaret Drabble, 27 November 1995.
29. Penelope Layland, 'Lette tilts at sacred cows to push new book', *Canberra Times*, 9 October 1996.
30. Kathy Lette, *Foetal Attraction*, Pan Macmillan, Melbourne, 1993, pp. 76–7.
31. Chris Feik, 'A Passing Phrase', review of Kathy Lette, *Mad Cow*, Pan Macmillan, Melbourne, 1996, in *Australian Book Review*, December 96, January 97, pp. 66–7.

Chapter 13

1. Quoted by Max Harris in 'Morals and Manners', in Peter Coleman ed., *Australian Civilisation*, Cheshire, Melbourne, 1962, p. 49.
2. Michael Heyward, *The Ern Malley Affair*, London, Faber and Faber, 1993, p. 66.
3. ibid.

4. Michael Innes, *What Happened at Hazelwood*, London, Victor Gollancz, 1973, first published 1946.

5. Heyward, p. 127.

6. ibid., p. 136.

7. Heyward, pp. 179–82; Peter Coleman, *Obscenity, Blasphemy, Sedition: censorship in Australia*, Brisbane, 1963, pp. 42–4. Heyward renders the arresting detective's name as 'Vogelesang'; while Coleman's version is 'Vogelsang'. Heyward also gives the English translation of his name: 'birdsong'.

8. For a discussion of Vogelesang's evidence in the *Angry Penguins* obscenity trial see Heyward, pp. 187–92 and Coleman 1963, pp. 43–4.

9. Heyward, p. 206.

10. Heyward, *The Ern Malley Affair*, p. 210; J. I. M. Stewart, *Myself and Michael Innes: a memoir*, London, Victor Gollancz, 1987, pp. 108–9.

11. Michael Innes, *From London Far*, first published Gollancz 1946, Penguin edn, 1962.

12. Michael Innes, *What Happened at Hazelwood*, Victor Gollancz, London, 1946, p. 123.

13. Michael Innes, *Death at the President's Lodging*, Penguin Crime, Ringwood, Victoria, first published Gollancz, 1936.

14. Michael Innes, *The Daffodil Affair*, Penguin Books, Ringwood, Victoria, 1968; first published Gollancz, 1942; references to Australia in other Michael Innes novels, or novels written during his time in Australia, include *Hamlet, Revenge!* (1937), *Lament for a Maker* (1938), *The Spider Strikes Back* (1939), *The Secret Vanguard* (1940), *A Comedy of Errors* (1940), *Appleby on Ararat* (1941), *The Weight of the Evidence* (1943) and *Appleby's End* (1945); 'Innes, Michael', J. I. M. Stewart, in William H. Wilde, Joy Hooton and Barry Andrews, *The Oxford Companion to Australian Literature*, 2nd edn, Oxford University Press, Melbourne, 1994, p. 401.

15. J. I. M. Stewart, *A Staircase in Surrey*, quintet of novels: *The Gaudy* (1974), *Young Pattullo* (1975), *A Memorial Service* (1976), *The Madonna of the Astrolabe* (1977) and *Full Term* (1978), all originally published by Gollancz, then in paperback by Magnum, Eyre Methuen.

16. J. I. M. Stewart, *Myself and Michael Innes: a memoir*, Gollancz, London, 1987, p. 100.

17. Quoted in *The Australian Financial Review Magazine*, 24 February 1995.

18. J. B. Priestley, *Saturn Over the Water*, London, 1961.

19. ibid., pp. 204–5. Reprinted by permission of the Peters Fraser & Dunlop Group.

20. In Fay Weldon, *Polaris and other stories*, Penguin, 1985; first published in *Cosmopolitan*, 1983, pp. 107–17.

21. Fay Weldon, *Polaris and other stories*, Penguin, 1985, pp. 182–91.

22. ibid., pp. 184–5.

23. Iris Murdoch, *An Unofficial Rose*, Chatto & Windus, London, 1962.

24. ibid., pp. 52–4.

25. Nina Bawden, *Familiar Passions*, Virago, London, 1994, first published 1979.

26. Interview with Nina Bawden, 28 November 1995.

27. Interview with Margaret Drabble, 27 November 1995.

28. Margaret Drabble, *The Gates of Ivory*, Viking, 1991, Penguin edn 1992; interview with Margaret Drabble, 27 November 1995, London.

29. Margaret Drabble, *The Gates of Ivory*, 1991, Penguin edn, 1992, pp. 390–2, 426.

30. Maya Jaggi, 'The new Brits make their mark', *Guardian Weekly*, 4 August 1996, p. 28.

31. Alan Garner, *Strandloper*, Harvill, London, UK, 1996.

32. Jane Rogers, *Promised Lands*, Faber and Faber, London, 1996.

33. Howard Jacobson, *Redback*, Bantam Press, London, 1986.

34. Ben Elton, *Stark*, Warner Books, London, 1989.

Chapter 14

1. Louise Evans, 'Outside-chance Winton terrified Riders may race off with Booker', *Canberra Times*, 6 November 1995. Winton had placed his bets correctly: Pat Barker *did* win the Booker that year with *The Ghost Road*.

2. ibid.

3. *Canberra Times*, 9 November 1996.

4. Interview with Alastair Niven, Director of Literature, Arts Council of England, 27 November 1995. Dr Niven has recently been appointed Head of Literature for The British Council, *Times Literary Supplement*, 24 January 1997.

5. Interview with Jim Crace, 4 December 1995.

6. Margaret Drabble, Introduction to *Prize-winning literature: Winners of British literary prizes since 1984*, catalogue of exhibition of books arranged by The British Council, London, 1987, p. 8.

7. *Canberra Times*, 18 August 1996.

8. Drabble, *Prize-winning Literature*, p. 6.

9. Anthony J. Hassall, *Dancing on Hot Macadam: Peter Carey's fiction*, University of Queensland Press, St Lucia, Queensland, 1994, p. 3. Hassall claims that,

contrary to expectations, Carey's writing career took a downturn with the negative reception of his next book, *The Tax Inspector*, but that 'Carey is generally acknowledged as the most exciting and prodigiously talented writer at present engaged in Australian fiction', p. 4.

10. Richard Todd, *Consuming Fictions*, Bloomsbury, London, 1996.

11. Quote from a review by John Sutherland of Richard Todd, *Consuming Fictions*, in 'Booker Prize 1997', *Literature Matters*, British Council Literature Department, no. 21, December 1996, p. 3.

12. Extract from Carmen Callil's speech at the Booker awards, reported in *Weekly Telegraph*, Issue No. 276, November 1996.

13. ibid.

14. *Literature Matters*, British Council Literature Department, no. 15, New Year, 1994.

15. Alastair Niven ed., *Under Another Sky: An anthology of Commonwealth Poetry Prize winners*, Carcanet Press, Manchester, 1987.

16. Niven interview, Arts Council of England.

Chapter 15

1. *Sydney Morning Herald*, 12 October 1996; *Weekend Australian*, 5–6, 19–20 October 1996; *Canberra Times*, 27 October 1996.

2. *Canberra Times*, 2 February 1997.

3. *The British Council Australian Newsletter*, no. 84, November 1996, p. 22.

4. John Douglas Pringle, 'R.L.S. in Sydney', *On Second Thoughts: Australian Essays*, Angus and Robertson, Sydney, 1971, pp. 59–83.

5. Conan Doyle tells the story of his Australian visit in *The Wanderings of a Spiritualist*, Brussels, 1922.

6. *Age*, 9 October 1934.

7. R. A. Leeper, 'British Culture Abroad', *The Contemporary Review*, August 1935.

8. Quoted in *British Council Australian Newsletter*, no. 84, November 1996, p. 5.

9. The full text of Betjeman's delightful report is in ibid., pp. 10, 34.

10. ibid, p. 34.

11. The writers interviewed were: Nina Bawden, novelist; Carmen Callil, publisher and writer; Jim Crace, novelist; Margaret Drabble, novelist and literary historian; Richard Holmes, biographer; Michael Holroyd, biographer; and Penelope Lively, Rose Tremain and Fay Weldon, novelists and short story writers. I also interviewed Jonathan Barker of The British Council Literature

Department, Professor Brian Matthews of the Sir Robert Menzies Centre for Australian Studies, and Dr Alastair Niven, then Director of Literature at the Arts Council of England. For a comprehensive list of British writers who have visited Australia with British Council sponsorship see Appendix.

12. The material in this section of the chapter is drawn from my unpublished report to The British Council submitted after my 1995 visit.
13. Interview with Nina Bawden, 28 November 1995.
14. Interview with Jim Crace, 4 December 1995.
15. Interview with Margaret Drabble and Michael Holroyd, 27 November 1995.
16. Richard Holmes, 'Holmes Goes Waltzing Matilda', 1992. Unpublished manuscript reproduced here with the kind permission of the author.
17. ibid.
18. ibid.
19. Interview with Richard Holmes and Rose Tremain, 7 December 1995.
20. Interview with Penelope Lively, 6 December 1995.
21. Fay Weldon, *Letters to Alice on first reading Jane Austen*, Michael Joseph, Rainbird, London, 1984.
22. Interview with Fay Weldon, 7 December 1995.

Conclusion

1. David Lowenthal, *The Past is a Foreign Country*, Cambridge University Press, Cambridge, 1985, p. 235.
2. Quoted in *The British Council Australian Newsletter*, no. 84, November 1996, p. 7.
3. Interviews with Professor Brian Matthews and Dr Alastair Niven, 23 and 27 November 1995.
4. ibid., Alastair Niven.
5. Jill Neville, 'London Letter', *Weekend Australian Review*, 5–6 October 1996.

INDEX